The Structure of Society

The Structure of Society

Julián Marías

Translated by
Harold C. Raley
Introduction by
Robert K. Merton

THE UNIVERSITY OF ALABAMA PRESS

Translated into English from *La estructura social:
teoria y metodo*. Copyright 1955 by Julian Marías.

and Addenda
English Translation and Addenda
Copyright © 1987 by
The University of Alabama Press
Tuscaloosa, Alabama 35487-2877

Library of Congress Cataloging in Publication Data
Marías, Julián, 1914-
  The structure of society.

  Translation of: Le estructura social.
  Includes bibliographical references index.
  1. Sociology—Methodology. 2. History—Philosophy.
3. Social Structure. 4. Social structure—Spain—History
—19th century. 5. Ortega y Gasset, Jose, 1883-1955.
I. Title.
HM24.M2813 1987   301'.01'8   84-185
ISBN 0-8173-0181-X

Contents

Translator's Preface

Julián Marías's writings rank very high in what he likes to call "page quality." Precise without being overly technical, clear but never superficial, at once idiomatic and exact, his style has been aptly described by one writer as being "diamond-like." Above all, he avoids the jargonistic tendency that, as Jules Romains notes, has rendered modern philosophy inaccessible not only to the masses but even to the educated. This is not to say that his work poses no problems of translation. Indeed, his acknowledged mastery of expression places on the translator the highest obligation to approximate this stylistic excellence in the other language.

Furthermore, Marías's thought is rooted in the rich legacy of modern Spanish metaphysics, particularly Ortegan and Unamunean concepts, and is therefore deeply committed to the inherent qualities and structure of the Spanish language. Decades ago rigorous distinctions were drawn in Spanish thought between such areas as life and existence, beliefs and ideas, and being and essence. In attempting to render Marías's work in English one must bear in mind that Anglo-American thought exhibits no such sophistication of concepts and that in the main it has dealt rather shabbily (if at all) with the metaphysical principles on which Marías's thought--including the present work--ultimately comes to rest.

All of which means that whereas the Spanish tongue has been molded into a supple instrument for expressing this way of thinking, English is hampered by its customary vagueness in the very areas wherein exactness is essential for understanding. For these reasons the English-speaking reader may find the following comments regarding Marías's terminology to be helpful, keeping in mind, of course, that any final deficiencies of expression are shortcomings of the translator and not the responsibility of the author.

(A) Coexistir, coexistencia: In Marías's view men do not "coexist" but rather "co-live," i.e., they live together (convivir). Thus, whereas societies may be said to "coexist,"

individuals within a given society "co-live" (convivir). In
another sense, inanimate and abstract realities "coexist," but
living involves an entirely different kind of being. Hence the
careful distinction that Marías makes between "coexistence" and
"co-living" (convivencia). Unfortunately, English does not allow
one to maintain these subtle shadings. In the present translation
we have at times been obliged to translate both coexistencia and
convivencia as "coexistence." In other cases, we have tried to
approximate the meaning of convivencia with other expressions
(See B below).

(B) Convivir, convivencia: Convivir means literally and
etymologically "to live with," and convivencia, "living with"
or "life with." It refers to the social nature of individual
life; men live together societally, sharing experiences and
reacting to similar pressures and realities. In the absence of
precise English cognates and after considering and rejecting
such terms as the etymologically redundant "co-living with" and
the unacceptable "cohabit" and "cohabitation," the translator
has attempted to render these expressions, according to contex-
tual exigencies, as "coexist" and "coexistence" (see A above),
"collective life," "social life," "living together," and occasionally as "collective existence."

(C) Pretensión, pretender: In the context of the present
work Marías defines one's pretensión as ". . . the preconceived
plan of life toward which we launch ourselves . . ." (Ch. V).
We have translated it as "aspiration," though it is well to bear
in mind that pretender and pretensión suggest striving for as
well as aspiring to something.

(D) Solencia: Because this term is a neologism in Spanish,
we have taken the liberty of introducing its equivalent in English: "solence."

(E) Vigencia: In view of its rigorous meaning and prior
introduction into the English language (Generations: A Historical Method, The University of Alabama Press, 1970), we have decided to retain this term in the English translation.

(F) Vital: In many cases this term has been translated into
its English cognate. (Occasionally and where confusion might
otherwise result, it has been rendered as "life.") However, it
should be remembered that Marías uses the term in its etymological and primary sense as that which pertains to life (Latin,
vita) and not in its common English meaning of "extremely important" or "essential."

Houston, Texas   Harold C. Raley

Introduction

This introduction is largely redundant. Little in it cannot be found in the book it introduces. Were it being written at an earlier time, before the advent of information theory and the much-advertised space travel, recognition that the introduction was redundant would have led me to scrap it. I should have simply confided the manifest secret of its superfluity to my admired friend, Julián Marías, and reminded him that when he did me the honor of asking me to do the introduction, I had replied that books written as clearly as his needed no introduction from me— or, for that matter, from anyone else. But the concept of re-dundancy has changed. It now appears more evident than ever before that, though boring, redundancy, like other safety pre-cautions, can be useful. Before they arranged for expeditions to the moon, engineers had long worked from the axiom that safety resides in redundancy of material strength and backup systems just as information theorists more recently have adopted the theorem that as redundancy increases, failures in the transfer of information decrease, exponentially. All this must stand as a possibly redundant explanation for retaining a redundant intro-duction.

What most distinguishes this book for me is the author's firm control of the intellectual bases and contexts needed to deal with its vast subject matter. Throughout, Julián Marías knows what he is up to. This inevitably puts me in mind of a maxim dear to the distinguished American physiologist and self-taught sociologist of science, L. J. Henderson, who happened to be one of my teachers. Henderson was fond of telling his atten-tive students, and at least one of them is now fond of repeating, "It's a good thing to know what you are doing."

This is precisely the case with Marías in this multilayered and multidisciplinary book. He draws with practiced ease upon philosophical, historical, and sociological perspectives to help us understand the structure, workings, and changes of human soci-ety. As we know from his many other books, Marías has a deep knowledge of major (though not necessarily popular) currents of philosophical thought, past and contemporary. This knowledge provides, to adapt one of his own expressions, the philosophical "subsoil" for his historical and sociological interpretations. Marías makes his readers the beneficiaries of his own acute awareness of epistemological problems inherent in these interpretations. Thus equipped, he does not run the risk, elucidated by A. N. Whitehead, of committing the "fallacy of misplaced concreteness." He does not confuse, as many of us do, a concept with the reality the concept is about. He is quick to remind us, for example, that "historical consciousness is not the same thing as historicism, since the former is a real situation and the latter, a theory." Marías also exhibits a thoroughgoing awareness of the reflexivity of thought. He develops and puts to use that kind of knowledge about knowledge which Plato in his way and Aristotle in a more ample way began to explore. As a result of Marías's self-knowledge, his book remains sound in its hidden parts.

Marías himself notes that this is not a work of theoretical sociology. But it is pervaded by sociological sensibilities. And for Marías, as for his master Ortega, sociology and history are inseparable. He therefore pronounces a plague on both the houses of an ahistorical (or, at times, even an achronic) sociology and an atheoretical historiography, both alike in making for unintelligibility. For Marías, "history [is] the way in which society exists."

Although Marías himself does not conduct monographic sociological investigations in this book, he is abidingly aware of the need for them. When examining the institutions of marriage and family from the standpoint of social structure, for example, he writes in the "of course mood": "the study of social structure requires that a series of samplings be taken, for societies are not homogeneous, and the conditions of marriage are hardly ever the same in all social classes or groups, in the big cities and the small communities." He then turns to the historical framework of cohort analysis, going on to note that "indeed they may differ at the same time for couples belonging to different generations."

The distinctive style of Marías's intellectual work allows him to move freely and easily between different levels of abstraction and concreteness, of ideas and evidence, of problems and puzzles. He no sooner introduces an abstract concept than he quickly deploys and develops it into a variety of historical and sociological specifications. This style of work is bound to be congenial to all of us who find the sociological understanding most fully at hand in theories of the middle range.

Like all of Marías's writings, this book is peppered with aperçus worth remembering. More often than not, they are multiphased. There is first the sudden insight provided by the original remark and then the progressively enlarged insight as the

remark becomes embedded in a systematic analytical apparatus.
It is not easy to convey this hallmark of Marías's style in short
compass, if only because the particular instances require elabo-
rate contexts for understanding. But consider this observation
on oral communication: "In societies where freedom is shaky,
the spoken word assumes incomparably greater importance. But
since the spoken word tends to disappear after a time, this makes
it extraordinarily hard to do a later study of a society in such
a condition." The observation links up at once with the implications of the advent of printing for thought and society of the
kind drawn by Elizabeth Eisenstein in basic monographs on the
subject.

Or consider what Marías calls "the liturgical temper." He
begins with the broad claim that "primal beliefs" appear to be
inexhaustible. When someone expresses a deep-seated belief, he
always conveys less than its entirety. It is this, Marías suggests in his often paradoxical way, that

> explains the surprising fact, though no one is surprised
> by it, that one may sing the Creed, whereas it would be
> absurd to do the same with the Pythagorean Theorem,
> Maxwell's Laws, the Kantian categories, or the twenty-
> four Thomas theses. Singing the Creed is quite differ-
> ent from merely reciting or reading it, for something
> important is added to it, not in the way of meaning,
> but as belief. It is a matter of the general meaning
> of the liturgy and worship, of the way in which reli-
> gious beliefs live--and correlatively are endowed with
> life. By means of such recourse, compensation is made
> for the distortion and mutilation of the full belief
> by formulation.

Georg Simmel would have taken pleasure in this observation on
form and content.

Along with the substantive perspectives, methodological com-
mitments, and style of work exhibited in this book its tone reveals the distinctive quality of mind and character of its author.
Among other things this finds varied expression in the humility
of the authentic scholar. It is not the kind of ostentatious
humility that finds its ultimate caricature in those celebrated
words by Charles Richet's celebrated scientist: "I possess every
good quality, but the one that distinguishes me above all is
modesty." Marías's unannounced humility is rather the kind expressing a sense that, however strongly persuaded he might be of
the truth of this interpretation or that one, he just might be
mistaken. His is also the humility, especially apt for practi-
tioners in the social sciences and humanities, that comes from
recognizing the vastness of our collective ignorance about the
subjects we explore. Comparisons may be odious, or odorous,
but they can also be instructive. We need not exaggerate the

Introduction

accomplishments of the physical and life sciences nor adopt the
vulgar positivism of sedulously aping their special procedures
to discover in their collective experience that long, hard, interlocking work is required to achieve serious gains in knowledge.
Writing of the problems involved in the empirical investigation
of generations in society, Marías observes:

> . . . it would be surprising if the first attempts were
> rigorously successful. Imagine the work that has been
> required for the most modest advances in our knowledge
> of the laws of genetics, the thousands of experiments
> and observations of Drosophila melanogaster or of peas,
> the years of patient research that the slightest increase
> of biological or physical knowledge requires, research
> that may absorb the energies of whole teams of experts,
> and then consider how incongruous it is to expect that
> in human affairs, which are much more complex, a few
> hours of improvised thought would be sufficient to
> clarify them. Only by means of a rigorous method of
> inquiry and after a series of very strict theoretical
> considerations made in the presence of ample empirical
> material that has been subjected to precise analysis,
> could one determine the real succession of generations
> with any degree of certainty.

This is no narrowly positivistic manifesto; it is merely the case
for intellectual candor and the case against oracular sociology.
    Marías's unobtrusive humility finds expression also in
homage paid to scholars who have prepared the way for his own
work, above all others, his master, friend, and collaborator
over the years, José Ortega y Gasset. Now it is true, as Marías
repeatedly insists as though he were forever engaged in trying
to repay an inexpungible debt, that he draws upon a great variety of ideas in the Ortegan sociology and philosophy. In this
book, to take a few cases in point, he makes use of Ortega's
ideas about the articulation of a mass with a minority, generations, cumulative times and eliminative (or polemic) times, and,
most comprehensively, the Ortegan concept of social vigencias.
And it also is true that as a young associate in that intellectual constellation known as the "School of Madrid" and as co-
founder with him of the independent Instituto de Humanidades,
Marías has inherited and proundly wears the mantle of Ortega.
But these are truths that threaten to become misleading as they
become obsolescent. Plainly, as Marías advances in his work,
Ortega recedes. Although much in the great and growing oeuvre
of Julián Marías—or, more aptly, his Obras—originates in the
thought of his master, much more is to be found there than was
dreamed of in the Ortegan philosophy, as this most recently
translated book of his bears witness.
    I will not provide a synopsis of the book. I will not

because I cannot. The rich content of this book is itself a syner-
gistic distillate of several of Marías's books. But I can and
will draw attention to some of the ideas in it that resonated
for one practicing sociologist.

Throughout the book, social structures are treated as dynamic
and functional, as "vectoral systems" of directed tensions and
movements. In this connection, Marías develops a conception of
dissent in society that strikes me as especially significant in
these days of mock battles between advocates of so-called consensus and conflict orientations in academic sociology. It is
good to see Marías taking it as a matter of course "that society
is far from meaning unanimity. . . . It is also based on dissent
and therefore is always problematic and uncertain. . . . Its
existence consists of creating and defending itself." He then
goes on to develop the idea of the normality of dissent in certain kinds of society. An extract from that discussion may serve
as an aperitif:

> The existence of dissident groups in society is in
> itself a vigencia the complex of law, custom, be-
> lief, and prevailing modes actually in effect . In
> other words, their ideas are not predominant--whether
> such groups have a certain way of painting or of under-
> standing poetry, whether they wear a beard or frown on
> makeup, whether they believe that everything in exist-
> ence is superfluous, etc., none of this prevails in
> society at large--but what is socially accepted is
> the fact that they affirm their views polemically
> over against the general system of prevalent vigencias.
> This is tantamount to saying that one of the latter
> holds that they must be challenged, violated, and
> denied by means of certain rites and formulas, for
> instance, with publicity, novelty, and subjection to
> a particular style (a vigencia) and to certain esthetic
> norms (which are also predominant). When society is
> very firm and stable, that is, when the vigencias
> are solid and fully vigorous, polemic dissent of this
> type not only is tolerated but even required, imposed
> by that particular vigencia that seeks its own infrac-
> tion. In contrast, weak societies that are dissociated
> and in discord neither demand nor accept these dissent-
> ing elements. A good barometer for judging the stabil-
> ity of a society is the normality of this kind of
> phenomena (Italics added).

Marías takes up and greatly develops Ortega's distinction
between beliefs and ideas. Beliefs are tacit assumptions of
varying psychic and cognitive depth, known only through their
effects; ideas are explicit formulations that derive from a
total situation that includes basic beliefs. The conceptual

pairing of beliefs and ideas bears a family resemblance to
Pareto's conceptual pairing of residues and derivations. But
as we would expect, in the actual course of using their respective distinctions, Pareto and Marías move down different paths
(which we need not travel here). In Marías's hands, the distinction between beliefs and ideas helps clarify theoretical problems
in various domains: in the sociology of knowledge, the existen-
tial bases of ideas; more generally, the relations between culture and social structure; and not least, differences in patterns
of social change. In the last domain, I found particularly instructive Marías's idea that deep-seated beliefs that are "solid
and authentic" allow for rapid social change to be coupled with
social stability. The idea provides a powerful reminder that
social change is not the same as social instability and that
both social and cultural structures vary greatly in their receptivity to distinct kinds of change.

Another of Marías's congenial ideas treats systems of valuation as central to social structure. As much as anything else,
it is the changes in evaluations of aspects and parts of given
social structures that constitute specifiable historical change.
The general idea opens up a question that has been only touched
upon in sociology: how do different systems of evaluation develop
in the various institutional spheres so that the very processes,
not merely the criteria, of evaluation come to differ in, say,
science from those found in politics or religion? In connection
with the process of perception and evaluation, Marías's concept
of "intellectual image of the world" is akin to the concept of
"images of knowledge" developed by the historian of science,
Yehuda Elkana. Diagnostically enough, both Marías and Elkana
are led to consider the implications of such images for scientific
education.

In studying this book, it seemed for a time that I might
manage to sound a note of sharp disagreement in this otherwise
unavoidably admiring Introduction. The point at issue is what
I have described elsewhere as the "Doctrine of the Insider":
"the claim as a matter of epistemological principle that particular individuals or groups in each moment of history have monopo-
listic access to particular kinds of knowledge." This I take to
be an untenable epistemological position, conspicuously so for
historians and social scientists. To adopt the doctrine that
only members of a given society or group can acquire an understanding of that society or group is to abandon the possibility
of doing most historical inquiry and much social science. If
understanding of social formations can be achieved only by their
members, then the historian who elects to write the history of
a time and place other than his or her own is embarked on a fool's
errand just as social scientists of whatever kind, aiming to acquire an understanding of other sex, age, racial, ethnic, political or religious groups, and strata in their own time, are
condemned to ignorance and error.

Introduction

Because all this seems abundantly clear to me, it came as
something of a shock to find Marías apparently adopting a version of the Insider Doctrine in the statement ". . . life can
be understood only from within. If we are situated outside of
a social structure, its vigencias are unintelligible." The
more I reflected on this passage, the more nearly I became non-
plussed. After all, in his capacity as historical sociologist,
Julián Marías is the very exemplar of a scholar who has elected
to study, presumably with an aim to understanding, societies of
the past (which are, in his expressed sense, alien to him) as
well as various societies of the present which are alien to him
in the structural sense that he is not continuously located within
them. Marías's practice evidently belies Marías's doctrines.
He regularly demonstrates in practicing the art of historical
sociology that, although an Outsider in structural terms, he can
provide understanding that both overlaps and complements under-
standings provided by Insiders. And yet, he seems to deny that
this sort of thing is possible. While still fixated on this
passage, I decided to remind my admired friend one day that, his
adoption of the Insider Doctrine notwithstanding, whatever is,
is possible.

That I need not do. For as I read on, it soon became evident that the puzzling clash of opinion between Julián Marías
and myself was only apparent. The sentences I have quoted from
him turn out to be preliminary ones and, when isolated from their
further context, thoroughly misleading. Marías deploys them only
as an expository device for getting to the thesis that he actually
wants to develop. He is concerned only to reject an extreme objec-
tivistic viewpoint—one might say, a vulgar and now largely vanished positivism—in which reliance upon external numbers and
other kinds of indicator information is regarded as enough to
achieve understanding of a society. So it is that Marías goes
on from the sentences I have quoted to write:

> This is the same as saying that in the case of an alien
> society, foreign or past, the most exhaustive accumula-
> tion of materials, the most complete statistics, the
> most extensive information, will not allow us to under-
> stand social reality. The first thing needed—under-
> stand well, the first—is imagination. It is paradox-
> ical and unfortunate that the father of sociology,
> Auguste Comte, tried to substitute observation for
> imagination and to base his own method on the constant
> predominance of the former. The only way that data,
> information, and statistics serve a purpose is by
> "going to live" imaginatively in the society under
> study and in this way receiving the impact of vigencias.
> Thus, one can reconstruct the alien or past world with
> its tone of life by imaginarily—novelistically—
> placing oneself in that world. . . . In other words,

one may achieve a hermeneutical transmigration to the
situation in question.

With this formulation, Marías remains within the domain of
self-consistent scholarship. He does not adopt the Insider
Doctrine. He is only engaged in attacking a naïve form of positivism. After all, the case for imagination in making vicarious
observations of a society through the use of all manner of indi-
cators and indexes, qualitative and quantitative, had been made
by such founding fathers of sociology as Emile Durkheim and
Max Weber long before Herbert Butterfield called for the exercise
of the "historical imagination" a generation ago or, more recently,
C. Wright Mills called for the exercise of the "sociological imagination." But, of course, as Marías is quick to observe, if a
"mere" piling up of data is not enough to achieve understanding,
neither is the "mere" exercise of unrestrained imagination. When
arguing that sociology "must be joined to the novel and its many
shortcomings," Marías immediately adds "but naturally without
surrendering the many possibilities of knowledge it holds." In
short, the productive imagination needs to be rooted in dependable
observation just as productive observation needs to be informed
by imaginative conjectures. Either, to the exclusion of the other,
is dead--a conclusion, once stated, that will be rejected only by
those who find obvious truths peculiarly offensive.
Beyond its broad theoretical and methodological concerns,
this book examines just about every corner of the social structure
and, in doing so, provides insight for sociological specialists
of just about every stripe.
Students of public opinion will profit from the penetrating
distinction between 'opinion' and the paired concepts of 'beliefs'
and 'ideas' as they also will from the operative distinction between 'private opinion' and 'public opinion' (the latter being
qualitatively different from the mere aggregation of opinions
privately held).
Students of the sociology of literature will find value in
the Ortegan and here much-elaborated conception of the use of
stories ('novels') for the investigation of historical societies.
Students of mass culture will find perceptive observations
on the social implications of the "popular entertainments of a
society" (provided by what Ortega liked to call the "felicitary
occupations").
Students of social stratification will find interesting
problems for investigation in the analysis of class, particularly
of that form of identification with social class which Marías
calls "installation," the "feeling at home" in a particular
class (which does not preclude deep discontent with the condition
of that class and action designed to change that condition).
Students of power structures will find an extension of the
longstanding question of the relations between State and civil
society. Of particular analytical interest is the difference

drawn between the power of the State, involving its degree of command and authority, and its "potentiality," its efficacy in carrying out particular functions. There is reason to explore further the seeming paradox that it is the State which is internally weak and uncertain that will assert itself most strongly, forbidding or countering alternative sources of power within the society.

Students of the sociology of gender will find stimulus for thematic investigations in Marías's conceptions of sex models and exemplarity. In the Marías scheme of things, "sex is not a mere 'difference,' but also a relation, more precisely a polarity; each of the sexes co-implicates or 'complicates' the other."

Students of interpersonal relations will find a provocative analysis of social distance and, specifically, of the conditions required to institute and maintain friendship, an analysis quite Simmelian in character and tone.

Students of social ethics will find a conception of the curvilinear social bases of freedom, in which the constraints deriving from social isolation (the "Robinson Crusoe" pattern) begin to have moral consequences for the individual resembling those resulting from the constraints of an overpopulated and structurally complicated society.

Beyond these specifics, there is a surplus of value in having this book added to the many others of Julián Marías's books now appearing in English. It should help erase the national parochialism that still limits portions of contemporary scholarship. To judge from the public record of discussion, Ortegan sociology and, more in point, its substantial development by Marías, are largely unknown to American sociology. Correlatively, we note that concepts and ideas evolved in Spain are of a kind that also have been evolved in the United States. As the translator Harold Raley observes, the concept of <u>vigencias,</u> which we have seen to be central to the Ortega-Marías sociology, does not readily translate into an English equivalent. Still, vigencia, as the <u>operative</u> complex of law, custom, usage, and belief that is 'in force,' has more than a passing resemblance to the concepts of 'culture' and 'subculture.' So, too, the Ortega-Marías concept of 'usages' as both facility and limitation resembles William Graham Sumner's concept of folkways and mores with both formulations having an important formal similarity to Talcott Persons's notion that the same units of society can operate as both 'facility' and 'reward,' with all three conceptions in turn being related to the Hobbesian notion of power as a "present means to any future good." Plainly, similarities of sociological ideas transcend national boundaries.

As I noted at the outset and have, in the interim, fully demonstrated, this introduction is altogether redundant. It would have been quite enough to say that, being vintage Marías, this is one of those rare books "worthy to be read more than once."

Columbia University   Robert K. Merton

The Structure of Society

I
The Theme of the Inquiry:
The Social Structure

This book is problematic to the third power. This is normal enough today for all books that try to blend the fullness of reality with theoretical rigor. I refer to books that are not simple inertial writings conceived according to patterns arising from earlier and different situations, nor mere arbitrary gropings springing from caprice or improvisation. The first level of problematicalness, the content itself, is inseparable from all other doctrines, whereas the other two levels, which lie deeper, are found only in certain intellectual situations. And to call them "intellectual" is to call them "historical" situations, since intellectual life is possible and meaningful only within and as a function of the totality of real life. One of these levels is the very outline of the theme, the area or zone of reality that presents itself as such to the investigator and calls for an inquiry. The other is the method by which such an inquiry is conducted, and this involves therefore (it is important to emphasize this word) its literary genre, its ultimate form and reality as a book.

The theme of the inquiry that has led to the writing of this volume could not be more precise: the social structure of Spain during the Romantic period. This involves geography, historical and temporal considerations, and as the title indicates, a social factor. Nevertheless, the direction of this inquiry is by no means obvious, and it cannot be channeled into traditional patterns. It might appear that we are to deal with a study of the history of Spain in the first half of the nineteenth century. If the statement is made that neither the War of Independence nor the uprising of Riego nor the first Carlist War is to be told in this book, then one might suppose that we are dealing with what history books usually refer to as "internal history," as opposed to the majority of the chapters that make up such works and that obviously amount to "external history." Of course the "within" and "without" implied by such terms are in themselves highly problematical, for they are the inside and outside of something that is not at all clear. Furthermore, a glance at the table of contents of this book will show that it is not an internal history. Indeed, from the very outset it must be stated that this is not a work of history at all. Possibly it could be called a "pre-history": what I mean is that just as the reality prior to what we know as history is called prehistory, so it would be possible by preserving the nonfortuitous ambiguity of the term to apply it, not to the science of that prehistorical reality, but rather to that form of knowledge that must antedate historical science.

Were there only one form of knowledge prior to history, the matter would be relatively simple; but there are several, and their internal connection alone poses a delicate problem. First of all, we have of course the matter of historiography; but if we take it in the strict sense of analysis of res gesta or historical reality, then it is a general analytical theory of the dimension of human life that we call historical "life." This is not what we are after. Because we are speaking of the social structure, we have a certain right to suppose that this study is an aspect of sociology, yet this supposition would be hasty and incorrect. For the present study is not a theory of social structures, but an investigation of a particular structure, that of Spain in the Romantic period. From the outset, then, it displays an empirical, concrete, and historical dimension that we cannot ignore. Yet at the same time we must bear in mind that we are still far from the actual substance of history itself. Our task is to deal with a specific social structure, placing structural and specific elements on an equal footing, as we do.

The meaning and precise scope of these difficulties can come to light only as we come to grips with them. Yet even this brief preview is enough to reveal the triple problem to which I refer, and rather than enter directly into the study of the reality of nineteenth-century Spain, I believe it justifies the need to preface this work with an introduction dealing with my method so as to situate and make possible the inquiry I propose. Even so, I deem it necessary to point out that this is by no means a detached and independent introduction; that is, it is not a portion of some sociological, historiographical, or gnoseological doctrine arrived at by various means and then "applied" to this specific study, but rather has an intrinsic relation to it. Its origin lies in the analysis of the structure in question, though in turn only this methodological introduction will allow it to be completed. Once again we are dealing with the circular motion, the coming and going, characteristic of all knowledge of reality, especially the reality that we know under the name of human life.

As for this introduction, it presents a method of investigating social structures that has application beyond the society from which it arose. In other words, this method can be discovered and formulated only through the analysis of one or several specific and real structures. Yet once it has been discovered and formulated, it becomes an instrument by means of which the structure of other societies may be investigated. For this reason I have given free rein to the method contained in this introduction rather than restricting myself to its main requisites within the body of the following empirical inquiry. In this way the reader has at his disposal the means necessary for extending his interest beyond the theme of this book, which thus becomes the first illustration of a class of studies of collective life.

1. Society and History

Let us imagine a given society and attempt to study it at a certain moment of time in order to determine its structure. To begin with, we find a certain place wherein a number of persons collectively live. Diverse relationships exist between and among those persons. A great many of those relationships are interindividual and therefore do not properly belong to the society in question.[1] Others are strictly social in nature; that is, they affect the collectivity and are neither created by nor reducible to the personal life of individuals. These are relationships that transcend each person and the simple summation of personal lives. As for the latter, they are inserted in collective modes and formed from social substance; their individual reality is conditioned by these social modes which occur in the life of everyone. In other words, these modes are rooted in individual life, which is inexorably social in nature. Stated in yet another way, the only effective reality in a society is that of individual lives, but society is something that happens necessarily to each of them. Individual life is, therefore, constitutively and intrinsically social. One's interpretations of things, their articulation in certain images of the world, and the language, usages, beliefs, and ideas that sustain one in personal reality are social ingredients of one's life, and their reason for being is to be found only in collective life.

But let me attempt the study of a society, so understood, at a given moment of time. Is such a study possible? Using this approach, the only things given me are data: I may know, for instance, that such a society has a certain number of inhabitants, that these make up so many families, that the total wealth of the society amounts to so much and is divided in a certain way, that it boasts of a certain volume and distribution of resources, that its population is grouped in a specific way, into classes, estates, etc., and carries on a given number of professional activities, and, finally, that its predominant opinions and preferences are such and such. Now all this may be the subject of statistics and may afford me information about a series of facts, but facts alone are meaningless and devoid of

3

structure. One could say that the relation between facts is not a matter of fact and cannot be reduced to data. The reason why this is so is that each fact or datum is a result, or better, a resultant, of forces in action that come from a past and aim for a future. For example, the economic condition of a society is not a pure fact but a condition that has been created; it exists by virtue of a series of vicissitudes through which the society has passed, or, to state it another way, the present condition arises from an earlier one, and it is only in view of that prior condition that the present situation becomes meaningful. The same is true with regard to the division of social classes, to the family structure, or to prevailing opinions. Only the variation that the society has experienced constantly can explain why its different ingredients are what they are, and it is this change that links and binds them into a real structure. In other words, our attempt to understand a society makes it necessary for us to turn from its present condition and consider its earlier stages, that is, the prior societies from which it came; in a word, we must return to history.

The expression I have just used needs correcting. The previous societies that spawned the present social structure are, in principle at least, the same society. The present society is made up of the past; it is essentially old; its reality proceeds from what happened before. What we find in it today is there because previously other things happened to make it so. The roots of its usages, customs, beliefs, opinions, values, and forms of coexistence are all found in the past. These in turn function as the models, patterns, norms, possibilities, and pressures that condition what will be tomorrow, that is, what the future society will be. To put it in more rigorous terms, the same society that was past, and is present, will also be in the future. Thus at any given moment we find the intrinsic complication of temporality. We cannot understand a society solely within a given moment of time because its reality (and therefore our understanding of it) is constituted by the presence of the past and the future, in a word, by history.

When Auguste Comte spoke of a static and dynamic social state he glimpsed the fluid condition of collective life, but he also fell into a serious error: in effect he would have us think that society is a static reality whose dynamic element is history. But this is not the case. Society itself is dynamic; it consists entirely of dynamism and it exists as a system of operating forces, that is, it is intrinsically historical by nature. Society is inseparable from history; it exists historically, not only by being in history but also in the sense of creating and constituting itself in the very movement of history. For this reason, it is idle to attempt to study a society in a single moment of time. A serious study of this type will include a series of moments in historical distension. We shall see later just how necessary and profound this is and how it affects all

4

the formative ingredients of any society. But this means that
although a social structure can only be studied historically,
history may not be the product of the study itself. In no case,
then, is the elemental "unity" utilized by theory a single moment
of time, but rather, the temporal articulation of several time
zones within a given period, although the nature of the articulation is another matter. We shall see, too, that the period chosen
cannot be selected arbitrarily. The chronological boundaries of
the inquiry are imposed by the very structure of the reality in
question.

Of course, the connection between society and history seems
clear enough: they are inseparable, and history is the way in
which society exists. But if we invert the terms of the question
a new problem emerges. In effect what we have done heretofore
is to presuppose a society and then discover history within it,
or, what amounts to the same thing, we have discovered the intrinsic historical nature of society. Yet if we take history as our
point of departure, if we begin with the happening of historical
events in time, then we must ask ourselves to whom these things
happen and what the reality we call historical is in the strict
sense. To pose the question more clearly, we must ascertain who
the subject of history is.

2. The Subject of History

In Chapter 10 of my Introducción a la Filosofía (translated
as Reason and Life [1956]), which is devoted to an inquiry into
historical life and to which I shall presently refer, I took the
time to point out two errors that becloud the understanding of
the topic. Both have to do with the relationship of individual
life to history, or if you like, with the form of historicity
assumed by human life. One of these errors goes beyond what is
correct and the other, as a reaction, falls short of it. One
might think, in effect, that for history to exist there need be
only human life. Yet if this were so, then the mere temporality
of individual life, its successive and fluid nature alone, would
be a sufficient reason for man, even if there were only one man
in the world, to possess history. But this is not the case, for
historical life implies an adherence to a specific variety of
humanity that exists among other varieties. Thus, historical
being means to live in a time zone that is qualified, a time
that is determined by a certain level, in contrast to cosmic or
mere biological time. And I say "mere" because real biographical
time is in fact historical, because human life is rooted in history at a certain concrete level. There can be no history unless
there are many men who live successively rather than simultaneously. But they are not absolutely successive; for instead of
forming disjunctive groupings, their lives partially overlap and
coexist. Thus, the old man of "another day" may coexist with

5

the man of "today," so that two or more qualified times are
found in the same present moment. As I have written elsewhere,
"History affects men insofar as they form a plurality that is at
once coexistent and successive; historical life is therefore historical coexistence."[2]

The other possible error, of a different sign altogether,
stems from the view that inasmuch as human life alone is insufficient for history to come into being, then it may be inferred
that individual life is not historical at all but simply within
history, which is something that is added to the primary and essential reality of man. Consequently, history is thought to be
supervenient and consecutive. This view could not be more erroneous. The ingredients with which we forge our individual life,
interpretations of things, an image of the world, beliefs, language, usages, etc., are all historical, and so is life itself,
for it is always realized in a historical situation. There can
be no history without successive coexistence, but it is no less
certain that there can be no individual life except in successive
coexistence. Thus, history is something that befalls me in the
radical and irreducible reality of my own life, and in turn it
essentially transcends my life.

This clarifies the primary question of who or what the subject of history is. Naturally it is not the individual but rather
the reality that we have called "successive coexistence." Yet
we must keep in mind that the latter is formed of individuals
without whom there would be nothing. Thus to pose the question
of the subject of history is to inquire into the structure and
limits of successive coexistence, and more specifically, into
the different units of coexistence, that is, into societies.
Now the question arises as to which societies are meant, and
what began as given point of departure itself becomes the focus
of the problem.

A society is defined by a system of common prevailing modes,
or vigencias--usages, beliefs, ideas, values, and aims.[3] Therefore it is not enough simply to group men in a certain way in
order to form a society; if different systems of vigencias operate within a certain grouping, then more than one society is
present. Likewise, if the same set of vigencias applies beyond
the putative society, then the real society defined by those
vigencias extends beyond the group in question. But the notion
of vigencia (one of the most fertile ideas of Ortegan sociology)
is not so simple as it might first appear. Later we shall be
obliged to study it more closely, and then we shall see how its
complexity corresponds to the manifest and obvious fact of the
complication of societal or coexistential units and their superimposition on several planes. Correlatively, we shall encounter
the difficulty of making an absolute determination of their respective boundaries. To begin with, we must reject abstract
societies, that is, those that reflect only isolated attention
to a single dimension, facet, or activity of men. Thus, such

groupings as Semites, painters, Moslems, the young, the married, proletarians, women, the rich, the black, lyric poets, socialists, polygamists, aristocrats, and priests do not form complete societies, real societies, regardless of the importance of the principles by which they are so grouped. Think, for instance, of such groupings as "men" or "women." We must also exlude units that do indeed constitute "units of coexistence" but are at once surpassed by larger units, as is the case of the family. For quite different reasons, we must do the same with humanity in its entirety, in which unity is not exactly a matter of coexistence and in which there is no operable system of vigencias—for the present at least.

Beyond these rather elementary difficulties there arises another of greater importance. If we define rigorously the units of coexistence or societies in terms of the predominance within them of a system of basic vigencias, we find that in the majority of historical situations there is a kind of secondary coexistence: the coexistence of these several societies with one another. Take the case of the simple societies of the Greek cities within the larger society we call Hellas, or the latter in conjunction with Persia, Egypt, or Rome. To what degree does this new kind of "coexistence" imply common vigencias and thus form a new "society"? Do all such contacts or relationships among societies require a community of vigencias? Is the relationship of the various existing social units the same as their coexistence within a greater unit? The answers to these questions will occupy us throughout this study.

This brings us to a final question. We have seen, for such was our point of departure, that any society is historical, that each society arises from past societies. Within certain limits we may state that this series of chronologically successive societies is really the same society, or in other words, that the societies in the series are diverse historical situations of a single society. Yet if we take a sufficiently long period of time, or if historical change is particularly energetic and rapid, then we shall come to a moment when we can no longer speak of the "same" society but must instead consider different societies created in various ways from their earlier counterparts. This creation may come about by union through conquest, annexation, incorporation, etc., by division, by alterations in the internal structure, or by migrations. Thus the problem of the persistence of these societies presents itself, for the replacement of a given society does not necessarily mean its disappearance. And this in turn leads to the question of the modes of coexistence between levels that nevertheless coincide in the same historical period. And without a clear understanding of this dynamic interplay one cannot determine the subject of history. But all this is too abstract to be fully understandable. Let us consider the situation within the European background.

7

The Structure of Society

3. Regions, Nations, Europe

The basis of the European nations is the incorporation of smaller units of different contextures that were the real societies of the Middle Ages. In modern times the units of coexistence, i.e., societies _sensu stricto_, are nations; and insofar as certain European zones are not strictly national they adopt historical pseudomorphoses that are national in appearance and brought about by an unexpressed _vigencia_ of nationality and by an express will to become a nation, almost always arising from diplomatic motives, which in the end contributes more or less slowly to a process of real nationalization. But if it is true that from the sixteenth to the twentieth centuries Europe was composed of nations, it would be incorrect to state that during that time Europe contained nothing but nations. The previous units, those elements incorporated into nations, persist not as political units, or at most as residual political units, but as a very new and peculiar form of "society": regions.

A region is something quite different from the medieval state, though their boundaries may coincide. A region is an incomplete society; by that I mean that it is defined by a repertory of _vigencias_ that are common but also partial and weak. In other words, they leave out important areas and exert comparatively light pressure. We might say that regional "usages" tend to become mere "customs." Man does not feel that his life is regulated by regional _vigencias_ alone. He must seek guidelines for his behavior beyond his region in the general society (which in this case is a national society)—and at the same time it is from the latter that the strongest pressures and stimuli come willy nilly into his life. This is so true that we can identify three very revealing features of regionalistic attitudes: (1) They are voluntary attitudes, that is, one is not simply regionalistic but rather one wishes to be so; whereas frequently a man may feel that he is Spanish or German without appeal, perhaps despite his personal wishes and detachment, regionalism always implies attachment; it is voluntary adherence to and even cultivation of regional belonging. (2) To a certain degree regional attitudes are archaic; they refer to old, bygone portions of life and feed on the past that is present and "preserved." For this reason the regionalisms of all countries are "traditionalistic" and at bottom "reactionary," even in cases where for tactical reasons they assume the forms of political extremism. (3) Regional attitudes arise from a withdrawal movement, that is, they spring from the society in general and then withdraw from it; no regional attitude is primarily or naturally regionalistic, but rather, bases itself on the nation as a whole and then directs itself toward the region. This accounts for the interesting phenomenon of pseudomorphic nationalism displayed by regionalisms. They disguise themselves as "nationalisms," and this is proof of their essentially derivative character.

But we must not confuse regionalism with regional condition.

8

The latter clearly exists as a kind of secondary society. Let us refrain from referring to it as an abstract society, for it is anything but abstract. One is not Catalonian, Navarrese, Burgundian, or Swabian in the same way that one may be a doctor, a radical socialist, or an Anglican. A region involves what we might call an "insertive" society: it functions as a component or partial ingredient, but it is not detached from the national society and thus cannot be considered as abstract. And this occurs in a very precise way: the insertion of individuals into it. In other words, the individual, at least in many countries and throughout long periods of modern history, is not directly national. Instead his way of belonging to the nation is regional. To be Andalusian, Basque, or Galician is, depending on the case, a way of being Spanish; and in the same way to be Bavarian or Westphalian, Breton or Provençal, is the concrete way of being German or French.

For this reason, both regionalism and antiregionalism are abstractions. The first emphasizes the region, pretends that it is a full and sufficient society, detaches it from the collective totality of which it is an ingredient and in which it has its being, and thus reduces it to lifelessness. The second abolishes the intermediate zone between the individual and the nation; it removes the regional placenta in which the qualified and organic integration of the individual into the national whole takes place. This imposes a violent schematic uniformity that impoverishes reality and at the same time, though antiregionalism does not suspect it, weakens the individual ties to the nation, because it cuts the natural ways (meaning, of course, the historical ways) in which an individual is rooted and inserted into the general society. Both of them are forms of uprooting. Regionalism cuts the regionalistic roots of national society and converts the region into a potted, artificial plant devoid of vital juices and almost always delicate. The antiregional attitude—as opposed to the antiregionalistic—uproots individuals from the immediate terrain of their region and by doing so weakens and destroys the inner structure of the nation, its basic construction, or vital organization.[4]

From another point of view, the nation is articulated with the larger "society" of Europe. I write "society" in quotation marks because during the whole of modern history, from 1500 to 1900 in round figures, and even today despite our wishes, the fully real society is not Europe but the various European nations, although at the time I am writing the latter are becoming less and less self-sufficient and today no national society is a full and complete unit, though neither is Europe itself for that matter. But the interesting point is that ever since the different nations came into being, they have existed within Europe, that is to say, Europe existed as an ambit prior to the formations of the various nationalities. Europe is not the sum of the European nations, not a secondary aggregate of their realities; rather it precedes

and underlies them, albeit without being a society sensu stricto
(at least not until now). How is this possible? And if the nations themselves are insufficient, if their effective reality
derives from, and is grounded in, Europe, then how can one say
that they are real units of collective life, that is, societies
in a real and rigorous sense?

Just as I spoke earlier of "insertive" societies (regions)
and of the function of the regional insertion of individuals in
a nation, so we may speak now of a relationship of "implantation"
of the nations of Europe. The various nations are "made of"
Europe; they have originated within its ambit as plants sprout
in the earth and are nourished by it, although the earth is not
itself an organism. When one speaks of "European" nations, the
adjective is not an extraneous addition of a mere geographical
determination. Rather it means that the nations are essentially
linked to the European ambit, or "world," wherein they are located
and within which they were engendered and now coexist. What I
wish to express in this way is a fundamental condition of their
structure: the national societies share a common area of coexistence and thus constitute a type of society, though not in all dimensions of life. It is not a question of actual social units
but of a form of coexistence within a common ambit that is previous
to those units.

With this in mind two things can be clarified at once: first,
the reason why Europe is not equal to the sum of the European nations, since it is the subsoil, as it were, in which the latter
have originated, just as other societies of a different nature
arose during the Middle Ages; and second, the difference between
the mutual relationship of two European nations and that which
exists between any one of them and, say, an Asian country. For
whereas in the latter relationship there is no society in common,
properly speaking, and thus no common vigencias are required (except for the most abstract and elementary modes that regulate all
human contact), in the former a partial "society" exists that is
more tenuous than the national societies but defined nonetheless
by a repertory of vigencias. The relationship of one nation to
the other is defined in terms of "foreignness," unlike what occurs,
for example, between two Spanish American countries, but such
"foreignness" is not absolute. We have seen the polemic and
competitive relationship that exists among European nations,
which takes the form of "models" or "examples" that aspire to
predominance. But the essential point is that the relationship
is com-petitive, that is, competition with others. Europe is
a community in which each nation tries to be the best. The movement of this complex and dynamic structure of national and European vigencias constitutes the real history of Europe and its
members (for the nations are members and not mere parts of the
structure).

This also explains a phenomenon that otherwise would appear
paradoxical: the parallel between the process of nationalization

10

and that of the unification of Europe. If the several nations
and Europe were "opposite" realities, as nationalism may be
contrasted to internationalism, then the fulfillment of one of
them could happen only at the expense of the other. In other
words, as the nations became more real, Europe would disappear,
and vice versa, European unity could come about only through the
demise of the nations. (Bear in mind the disturbing influence
of this idea on the actual history of our continent, as well as
its effect on efforts at unification.) But this is not the case.
The development of Europe toward a real society has been possible
only through a process of "maturity" on the part of the nations,
that is, through the actual nationalization of the European
members. We have observed that a society is always in motion,
that its reality is intrinsically historical, and that it pro-
gresses from one situation to another and, taking the long view,
from a parent society to another born of it. Thus, just as the
past is preserved and remains active, so the future acts under
the guise of anticipation. Societies exist in the form of the
coexistence of different historical levels. The regions persist
in the heart of the nation that incorporated them as partial and
"insertive" units, which articulate the ways in which individuals
belong to the national body. In this way they qualify that belonging, making it organic, just as they chronologically systema-
tize vigencias and represent the persistence of the old and even
archaic strata of any society. On the other hand, Europe represents the horizon of the several nations; it is their terminus
ad quem, a future that exists already as an element of their
makeup. The "Europeaneity" of the nations is the condition of
their future. For this reason unification affects the areas of
life that we could call prospective or projective. While the
archaic substratum of the nation lives on in its regional structures, and the importance of the latter cannot be overemphasized,
their projective dimension rests in their European condition.
The life "plot" of all the nations is found in Europe, and this
is why European politics has always amounted to foreign policy,
as it has commonly been called without full awareness of what was
meant by the term "foreign." A more accurate description would
be European politics; and insofar as a nation turns its back on
Europe and retreats into itself, it finds itself bereft of a
future. (Today, after a dual process of nationalization in
Europe and unification of Europe, the whole of Europe, as well
as each of the countries, faces a new horizon, a new future,
an undertaking or program called the Western World, and turning
away from this greater reality today amounts to the same kind
of desertion of Europe mentioned above. Just as isolationism
of individual nations not only cut them off from Europe but also
deprived them of any national future, so today any form of European withdrawal, of exaggerated Europeanism, represents the
obstruction of the European future. To put it another way, it
amounts to disEuropeanization.)

11

The Structure of Society

These specific references to our world are made for no
other purpose than to render understandable what I was trying
to demonstrate theoretically: the simultaneous coexistence and
the internal dynamic nature of different levels and strata of
societies, that is, of units of coexistence that correspond to
different historical "levels." Such is the nature of all human
reality, from the family to world history. Incredible as it may
seem, in its treatment of the reality of the family, sociology
obstinately persists in skipping over its historical component.
It concentrates on its biological nature, sexual union in marriage, propagation of children, etc., and on its economic and
juridical or contractual aspects, but overlooks its historical
condition, which is obvious in the fact, so elementary as to be
almost unnoticed, that its members are of different ages, that
is, that they proceed from different chronological levels and
thus belong to historically diverse worlds and to different
historical generations. This "unevenness," this simultaneous
presence of different time zones, is the motivating force of
history and the underlying condition of all the structures,
great and small, through which human life is articulated and
fulfilled.

4. Inseparability of Sociology and History

Sociology and history are inseparable disciplines, for both
consider the same reality, albeit from different perspectives.
History lies in the very heart of society, and only historically
can the latter be understood. On the other hand, it is impossible
to understand history without knowing the subject to whom it
happens, and this subject is society, a unit of collective life
with its own structure that is the theme of sociology. Without
a clear understanding of the forms and structures of collective
life, history remains nebulous; and without consideration of
historical movement, "sociology" is but a theory or a compilation
of unconnected statistical data that are unable to apprehend
social structures and thus fall short of social reality.

The difficulties connected with these mutual and dual demands
have caused sociology and history to remain for a long time in
a state of theoretical immaturity. In the historiography of the
past two hundred years nearly everything that is relatively clear
corresponds to exceptionally well defined historical realities
in which the subject society is unmistakable. This is true of
certain periods of Roman history and of portions of national
European history of the modern age. But apart from these happy
exceptions, the confusion is extreme, and more so in the case of
Oriental cultures. With Greece the difficulties are enormous,
and especially so as soon as one leaves the póleis, that is, beginning with the fourth century B.C. As for Medieval Europe
from its beginning and the history of the Moslem countries, they

12

present problems of origin that are anterior to any question of detail, but from which such questions arise. By a conscious effort or otherwise, contemporary historiography has been obliged to establish first and foremost the reality of its historical units. The thematic formulation of this reality is found, for instance, in the idea of Arnold Toynbee's "Intelligible Field of Historical Study,"[5] but the same problem is discussed in Oswald Spengler,[6] and in more restricted ways directed not to world history but to specific areas, in Paul Hazard[7] and Américo Castro.[8]

The lack of a clear understanding of the subject of history has inevitably led to the adoption of apparent units. It has resulted, for example, in the projection of present structures into the past or in the identification of political and real societies (since the two occasionally coincide), or, finally, in cases where there has been an awareness of the problem, in mere informative empiricism, that is, in the denial of history or in "historical irrationalism."

Viewed from the other side, sociology without history sinks into formalism, which considers only abstract relations and is far from any real knowledge, or else gives rise to an empiricism, parallel to that found in history, in which the compilation of data corresponds to an accumulation of deeds. If the custom in history has been to tell that many things have happened, but without knowing to whom they happened, conventional sociology identifies certain happenings but leaves aside the fact that they do actually happen, that is, that their very reality lies in their having happened. The result in both cases is the same: unintelligibility.

The problem becomes somewhat clear only if one bears in mind that historical "life" and social or collective "life" are two reciprocally involved dimensions and that both are incomprehensible unless one first knows what human life is. The analysis of human life in its effective reality reveals society and history to be rooted in life as its constitutive elements. It is by means of this analysis that the two realities and consequently the two disciplines are placed in proper perspective. The primary question that arises in regard to any reality is where to place it, that is, the zone or mode of reality to which it belongs. Sociology and history have either skipped over this problem altogether or have been too quick to accept inadequate solutions. The concepts of "occurrence," "event," "social fact," "social relationship," "reciprocal action," "culture," "civilization," "nation," "state," etc., have either been accepted gratuitously and inertially or borrowed from other areas of reality such as the natural sciences, politics, biology, etc. In 1934-35, when José Ortega y Gasset gave a seminar in the University of Madrid on "The Structure of Historical and Social Life" (Estructura de la vida histórica y social) (notice that it dealt with life adjectivized as both historical and social), he presented it as part of his course on metaphysics, the strictly theoretical content of which was entitled "Principles of Metaphysics According to Vital Reason" (Principios de Metafísica según la razón vital). All of Ortega's work follows this formulation of the problem, which he restated in his courses in Buenos Aires (1940) and in Madrid (in the Instituto de Humanidades, 1948-50), and which anticipated his book Man and People (El hombre y la gente), published by Revista de Occidente in 1957. From this point of view it seems to me that the relationship of sociology and history is made clear and the confusion surrounding them overcome.

5. Social Structures Defined by Tensions and Movements

A social structure is not a composite or arrangement of quiescent elements. Human lives are trajectories, projects, and pressures occurring in a certain direction. An arrow might serve as their symbol. Thus society is a system of directed forces, a "vectoral" system. The real elements of society are not static "things" but rather pressures, aspirations, drives, and resistances from which the "consistency" of the social unit is forged. All its ingredients "come from" and "go toward"; they are in real motion. Whenever motion is lacking, what occurs is not immobility but a brief period of rest or stabilization in a system of tensions. The fact that certain elements of a society are not changed does not mean that they are invariable but that they endure, that they are resisting and preserving their consistency by a series of combined efforts. This is precisely what happens when a living being is at rest, which is anything but inertia. However, at this point (or not far beyond) analogies of this sort must end, and when the subject is human realities all references to biological organisms must be taken with several grains of salt.

Yet it is not only the fact that social structure is a result of forces acting in a certain way but also the fact that, because these forces are variable rather than constant in intensity and direction, and because the real ingredients of a society change, the structure as a whole is in movement. By this I do not mean only that one structure succeeds another, but also something deeper and more important: that the structure as such also has a trajectory, that it is programmatic, and that it is always (and not only in moments of replacement or crisis) based on a dynamic distension, on a coming from a past and extending toward a future, both of which are present. Preservation and anticipation are two essential ingredients of any social structure and appear at any point at which we choose to intercept it. A time sample will show the intrinsic temporality of the structure, just as the blood circulating through a vein will flow out if we cut it.

This is why any social structure is "old" in the sense that it has been arrived at through time and that this arrival is

what explains it. It has been preserved, it has endured, and
this is what justifies it. Aristotle astutely pointed out that
in order for a community to exist, it is not enough for it to
last one, two, or three days; rather, it must "endure." This
is why all society is to some extent conservative. But at the
same time it is essentially unstable and based on the future.
For this reason it inevitably contains an innovative dimension.
At any given moment, a social structure is enduring and innovat-
ing, retaining time that flees from it and anticipating the future. Speaking more accurately, past and future appear societally as tradition and future (porvenir): tradition, because
the past functions as something inherited by or transmitted to
the present, which then acts as a depository; and future, because
the future is not only what "will be" but what is yet to be; it
is that which is coming, and even without having arrived it is
here already in the verbal present of "is." It is, at this moment, coming; it is by virtue of its being anticipated and pos-
tulated as expectation and imminence; in other words, it is by
virtue of its not yet being.

Only this condition renders a social structure understandable. Any functional structure, including biological organisms--
a dog or a bird--or even man-made apparatuses such as typewriters,
rifles, or airplanes, must be understood in the same way in terms
of the function itself and not according to its static, or better,
arbitrarily positioned, components. But the fundamental difference lies in the fact that once the machine or even the organism
has been given a functional structure, that structure functions,
whereas in the case of human reality the structure is never
"given," but instead is constituted by virtue of its own functioning. To put it another way, social structure is defined by its
own "plot." Yet this does not mean that once such a structure
comes into existence, a plot is then added, but rather that it
consists in that plot. A particular structure exists because
its plot is a certain one and not some other. From a new viewpoint, this brings us to our original theme: the co-implication
or mutual involvement of society and history and the intrinsic
historicity of societies. Only in this way are we justified in
speaking in a meaningful way (though still using question marks)
of collective "life" and of historical "life," or better still,
of historical and social "life."

6. The Problem of "Historical Situation"

At this point we can understand what is meant by "historical
situation."[9] Situation indicates a certain place or situs in
which someone is located. But despite the variation and historicity of situations (on which I shall presently insist), this requires a certain "permanence," regardless of how precarious it
may be, that is, a certain duration of the situation, stable or

otherwise. Soon we shall see the importance of this, and it is
well to keep it in view from the beginning. Furthermore, in
order to avoid what could be detrimental confusion, a distinction
must be made between "circumstance" and "situation," terms that
are often used synonymously and that in fact may be so used in
many contexts without any problem. Strictly speaking, they
differ in this way: circumstance is everything that is around
me, everything I encounter or can encounter about me. Situation,
on the other hand, does not include the circumstantial ingredients,
many of which are exclusively individual while others are universal and permanent, or at least exist on a very broad scale; rather
it contains only those elements that "situate" us at a given historical level, that is, those elements the variations of which
define each phase of history. Thus only a portion of circumstance,
that which is at once fairly general and labile, figures in the
historical situation. Yet whereas all circumstance is naturally
circumstantial, there is one element of situation that is not:
namely, the aspiration that constitutes my life and without which
there would be no situation, that is to say, I myself, in the
case of the individual life situation and the collective aspiration, an elusive reality that will be traced later, in the strictly
historical situation.

This situs of which the situation consists is one among a
plurality of possible ones. It would be meaningless to speak
of a single situation. Were there but one, it would not be a
situation but rather a simple determination. A situation exists
in binding relationship to others; that is, the one presupposes
the presence of the others but does not include them; without
them it cannot be, but it is not to be mistaken for them. For
this reason, to be in a situation is to be in one situation and
not in another; it is to be in one of several that are "present"
and possible as a virtual border around the concrete situation
in which I am.

But all this is purely formal and abstract. In a real
setting this plurality takes on a more precise character that
is not merely potential but real. Intrinsically historical in
nature, situations are subject to an essential instability.
Their mode of existence is transition. The decisive fact is
that man who is in a given situation leaves it in order to enter
some other. Why does he do so? Obviously he cannot remain in
a situation indefinitely because, first of all, its components
are very likely to change: some disappear, others appear, but
in any case they change their respective positions and their
perspective. But this is not the only reason why man leaves a
situation. Above all he aspires to be in some other situation,
and this aspiration is not only the reason for the change of
situations but also the basis of their existence, the reason
why there is something called situation in the first place.
Some time ago I demonstrated this with an elementary example:
if I am located in a room with the door closed, I can desribe my

16

situation as one of "being enclosed." But this description is accurate only if sooner or later I wish to leave, or at least could do so if I chose. If I had no desire whatsoever to leave now or later, it would be meaningless to say that I am enclosed; nor would I be. From earliest times man has been "tied" to the ground because he has had a more or less conscious aspiration to fly, until finally he has done so. On the other hand, it would make no sense to say that he is enclosed in this planet, though until now he could not leave it, because he does not wish to leave it. But wait, and within a short time one will see that after he has fully imagined interplanetary journeys, man will begin to feel growing within him an authentic aspiration (and it must be authentic) to leave the earth, and then his situation will be that of finding himself a prisoner on it. He will see himself as a slave of the terrestrial glebe, strictly enclosed on the outside of his convex jail. And probably he will go from a cloistral situation to one of interplanetary freedom.

Hence an isolated situation is unintelligible; it can be understood only by comparing it to others, and not with just any others but with those that really condition it and by their relationship form one of its components. Historical situations appear linked in a succession that exhibits four principal features: (1) Since time is irreversible, the succession of situations is not a mere series; rather, in addition to being ordered, it can be traversed only in one precise direction. (2) This time is not only successive but qualitatively differentiated; each moment of time is irreplaceable; it is not only "another" time but a different one. In other words, each situation is a concrete historical level. (3) Every historical situation comes from another, or rather from a series, for the same reasoning applies to each preceding situation. Thus a situation is the result of something prior to it and is incomprehensible without it. (4) Finally, since what constitutes each situation is an aspiration or project (and this is what impels the change from one situation to another), historical change always consists of innovation and invention. This concrete reason clarifies from another vantage point the features that earlier appeared as exigencies of the mere structure of temporality.

If we symbolize historical continuity by a batch of threads interwoven in the woof of life, we find that those threads are "long," that is, that they extend through time, coming from long ago and going on toward the future. Now then, in this image a knot corresponds to a situation. The threads are knotted, yet they do not end in these knots but extend beyond in both directions. It is not by chance that since antiquity men have felt that a situation is something that ends in a dénouement, literally in an "untying." It is a knot that one unties, or cuts, or at times is strangled by. The dénouement is the solution--the unraveling--of the drama. This "knotty" structure corresponds to the authentic nature of human life and of history.

17

But this brings up a final question to which we must presently turn our attention: if history is discontinuous continuity, knotted threads, then how is it articulated? How are these long temporal threads tied and untied? In other words, what determines the concrete succession of situations? Presupposing the necessity of their existence, which situations in fact do exist? Only by clarifying these points can we arrive at a rigorous understanding of the social structure, for as I have said before, the latter is intrinsically historical.

7. Analytical and Empirical Elements of the Structure

We could say that social structure is the form of collective life, provided that the word "form" is understood in a real and dynamic way, not as a mere scheme or static figure but as that which really informs and shapes life. But a new distinction must be added immediately: the form of all society is not the same as that of a _particular_ society. What I mean is that there are two kinds of elements that make up a social structure: analytical, that is, those which may be identified simply through an analysis of the requisites of any society; and empirical, that is, those which are revealed by experience with regard to a concrete society, but which nevertheless continue to be structural.[10]

A few examples will illustrate. All society is coexistence; it is a plurality of men who live together under a system of common _vigencias_. This much is valid for all society and arises from the analysis of the very notion of the social, or from any real society, in the form of requisites without which it would not exist. But the word "together," which I have just written and which appears so uncompromising, encloses a problem. Does it mean together "in presence" or not? The Athenians of Pericles were not together in the same way as the Americans of Eisenhower's time. Aside from its abstract and invariable core, its purely formal meaning, this condition or structural element of being together also has an empirical side. But do not misunderstand: I do not mean that it is an empirical "datum" that the members of a society are together in one way or another; rather, I mean that it is a _structural_ element, and that the structure in question differs as structure according to its empirical content.

The temporality of societies presents the series of formal and _a priori_ characteristics that I pointed out in the preceding section. But the empirical fact that human life has a certain mean duration and a certain rhythm of ages structurally conditions each society. The relationships of subordination or coordination between different societies, their isolation, the colonial relation to the mother country, etc., are decisive factors of structure. The apparently quantitative aspects—"apparently" because nothing human is ever solely quantitative—have immediate structural repercussions: the size of a country, the popula-

tion density (which does not coincide with what I referred to
earlier as being "together," though it does have some bearing
on it), the physical, technical, economic, and political means
of covering the territory, and the degree, regardless of the
causes, to which men feel bound to the place where they live.
Another structural and empirical element is the degree to which
a society is "closed." This can be understood in several ways:
it may be closed from without and from within (the problem of
emigrating or immigrating) because of geographical factors
(insularity, mountains, etc.) or linguistic, economic (poverty
or wealth), and political reasons. The combination of all these
reasons produces in each case a degree and form of seclusion
that affects the entire structure. Poverty, for example, necessitates emigration and causes people to emerge from a society,
but in another sense it does not permit travel and thus prevents
that emergence. Political persecution has sometimes occurred
in a centrifugal manner and has been the cause of great emigra-
tions, but in other cases, for instance, in many contemporary
situations, its primary consequence has been the "enclosure" of
individuals within the society. Imagine the differences of structure brought about by the element of seclusion in the France of
1910 and the Soviet Union of today, or between the United States
or Argentina of 1880 and Tibet during the same period.

Light must be shed on this question in order to determine
the nature of a society. This is what the present study has as
its overriding objective. It is not a question of formulating
a general theory of social structures but of understanding a
real and concrete structure. Having stated these adjectives,
however, we must also remember the substantive they describe:
they have to do with a structure, and this essential feature remains intact. Empirical data, including historical facts that
must be taken into account, are important only insofar as they
describe a social structure. And conversely, theoretical and
purely analytical considerations come into play only insofar as
they make feasible an investigation of the structure in question.

8. Macrostructure and Microstructure of History:
    Historical Periods and Generations

        Far from being a homogeneous continuum, historical time con-
sists in its qualification, for this and nothing else constitutes
the historical nature of things. But neither is this qualification "continuous," that is, merely a matter of gradients, for it
reveals "discontinuous phases or articulations." And this occurs
in two completely different ways that have been so misunderstood
or confused that many otherwise promising efforts to order historical periods have failed. In speaking of historical periods,
one must decide whether the term is used in a strict sense to
refer to regular and automatically recurring periods, or whether

it deals in a vague way with any historical time.[11] Clearly the former meaning is possible only if history admits of a fixed and stable structure—at least within broad spans of time—which justifies such repetition. Without such structure all strict periodicity would be arbitrary, imposing itself violently on reality and amounting to nothing more than pure cabalism.

Indeed, this occurs in efforts to establish uniformity in the macrostructure of history that lack a general principle of justification. However, it is not the same in the case of the microstructure, which is based on something that is highly precise and within certain limits invariable: the temporal trajectory of human life, with its mean duration and the rhythm of its ages. Here we encounter a rigorous and necessary structure in the form of generations, not generations in the biological sense, of course (that is, generations in the genealogical meaning), but generations as historical realities.[12]

As Ortega has demonstrated, the world changes every fifteen years, approximately, and he has shown the differences between things that change in the world and the world itself changing. The latter occurs with each generation. But it must be clearly understood that when we speak of "the world" changing, we mean the world of each man, and this means the society to which he belongs. For if we take the word "world" in an abstract way, there is no evidence that it changes every fifteen years, for until now the world has not meant a single society with a uniform system of vigencias, and thus "world" changes and generational transformations do not occur simultaneously in the world.

In the light of this fact, the process is unmistakable: every fifteen years, more or less, the entire system of vigencias of a society changes, though usually very slightly. In this way historical time is articulated and qualified in a precise manner. Instead of being "rectilinear," historical time is "ondulatory" with a fifteen-year wavelength. I hardly need point out that these images are only images and cannot be "exploited," that is, they do not allow inert conclusions to be drawn without, at the very least, confronting them with the historical reality in question. And, in fact, when several social units come into contact a type of "interference" is produced among these diverse wave movements or generational series that poses quite delicate problems, especially when it is not merely a matter of a "relationship" between societies that continue to be different but rather a matter of their transformation through fragmentation, incorporation, annexation, fusion, emigration, etc. Otherwise, coincidence or imbalance in the scale of generations can serve to determine within a fairly precise margin the boundaries of a society or the incorporation of several societies into a broader society. A detailed and precise study of the generations in the different European countries would make it possible to determine, with the rigor of a spectrographic study, the pace of the process of European unification, and it would reveal that process within the

20

different social strata, from the most abstract "societies" such
as intellectual groupings or their aspects, art, and so forth, to
the real and concrete society in its entirety. In the same way,
a rigorous application of this method could clarify the difficult
problem of the medieval societies from within that which later
was to be each nation, for example, Castile and Leon, or Castile
and Aragon within Spain, or, what would be even more interesting,
relations between the Christian and Muslim societies from the
eighth to the fifteenth centuries.

But in the case of the larger structures of history, "periods" and "ages" mean something quite different. The supposition
that a certain number of generations always constitutes a greater
historical period is completely gratuitous unless it can be justified, and so far it has not been. Attention has been called to
the surprising and paradoxical fact that the most arbitrary unit
of all, the century, has a certain reality despite everything:
there is an unmistakable appearance that sets the sixteenth
century apart from the seventeenth, and the latter from the eighteenth and the nineteenth, and so on. It seems that a very perceptible variation accompanies the transition from one century
to another. But I believe there is a clear explanation for this
"century rhythm," of which Karl Joël has spoken, this awareness
in modern man that he has moved from an old century into a new
one.[13] It is the experience of "New Year, New Life" literally
multiplied a hundred times over. Think of the nineteenth century,
which many have actually lived and others of us have experienced
to some extent in the vestiges it left on our childhood and in
the memories of our elders. During the last years of the 1800s
the "future century" was already being anticipated and heralded.
People spoke of fin de siècle, and the notion of the "nineteen
hundreds" (novecentismo) arose. Around 1916 Ortega proclaimed
himself "not at all modern and very twentieth century." Even
store signs emphasized the change. New styles sprang up; men and
women adopted new fasions, and this gave the feeling of being in
"another time." A rivalry grew up between the centuries: the
"old" and the "young" engaged in endless arguments over the excellence of the century that had ended and the other that had just
begun. They went so far as to personalize them, for indeed it
was a personal matter to them. Certain characteristics were
attributed to each century--century of lights, century of the
steamship and refinement. Their glories were recounted, and thus
a kind of "secular patriotism" arose with its resulting "xenophobia,"
its "chauvinisms," and even its epithets such as the "stupid" or
"damned" nineteenth century. Alliances with more remote centuries
were sought so as to discredit the present one, or more often, so
as to oppose the one just past. Thus the nineteenth century might
be condemned in the name of the sixteenth, and perhaps "from it."
All this has a comic and even grotesque side, of course, but
what has not been said is that the comic may not have importance
and effect. "Century awareness" is an obvious cause of the

21

unmistakable "century rhythm" in modern history, though it may be a superficial cause. We find the proof of this in the fact that before the fifteenth century it does not hold true. Earlier history reveals other analogous phenomena, but at other moments and at other turns of the road of history, because counting by centuries did not assume the same relevance in those times.

The minimal unit of variation, the generation, is based on the stability of the system of vigencias while a generation is in "power" and on its replacement when that generation is supplanted by another. Stability and discontinuity are, then, the features of this historical microstructure, and this is why it is an articulated structure. But to these features must be added that of periodicity. While human life has the same mean duration and the same procession of ages, the generation is a constant and elemental unit of historical change, and for this reason is the real unit of chronology. Consequently, it belongs to the empirical structure of human life; it is a concrete form of the circumstantiality of human life and, to this degree, is subject to possible variation. That the generation lasts some fifteen years is an empirical determination and thus valid only as fact. But it has a structural significance, for its validity extends over enormous historical cycles.

The principle of what I call macrostructure is totally different. Although it is true that the general system of vigencias, beliefs, ideas, usages, values, desires, and aspirations changes with each generation, this does not mean that such vigencias are exhausted within a generational span. Most continue "in vigor" for several generations. They may vary from one to the other; some weaken, others become stronger, some may disappear and give way to others; above all, our view of them changes; but the important thing is that they persist. Whole series of generations base their life on a system of vigencias whose essential features survive and endure. This is what we call a historical period.

But in stating this we are also saying that a historical period can no longer be thought of as a unilateral concept. Life contains very diverse planes and zones and the alterations that affect one stratum may leave others intact. In other words, partial changes occur within a way of life (which affect the whole structure, of course) and such changes may occur repeatedly and in different areas; the same way of life, using the term in the broad sense, may be modulated in several ways. Historical periods may be "superimposed" on one another at different levels, and not all of them are of the same importance or "order of magnitude." This would necessitate establishing a hierarchy among historical periods, and in fact this is what historiography does. Thus we make a distinction between Antiquity and the Middle Ages and between the latter and the Modern Age, etc. Furthermore, within the Modern Age, for example, we differentiate between the Renaissance and the Baroque or the Enlightenment.

The Theme of the Inquiry: The Social Structure

Yet the principle involved in these divisions lacks theoretical clarity. In order to begin to clarify the principle, it would be necessary to know the function of the different types of vigencias involved, their relationship to each other (and here almost nothing, not even the problem itself, is known), and the substructural connections that exist among them. Only with such knowledge can the relative autonomy of each regarding the others be established. It shows, further, how variation may appear in one while the situation continues unchanged in others, and consequently how the end of an era may occur within a larger cycle or age (or however one wishes to call it) that continues to exist.

The change from one period to another always means an important modification of structure that can occur in two very different ways. The first is what is properly called a crisis. Man lives within a system of vigencias, the most basic of which are beliefs in the strict Ortegan meaning of this term. Man's life assumes a certain form under the shaping influence of these suppositions, and it has a future horizon that is essential to it. As time passes and generations succeed each other, with each succession changing the situation to a greater or lesser degree, men undergo a series of experiences and efforts, some of which succeed while others fail, which partially undermine prevailing beliefs and diminish the future outlook. We must not think only of the failure of such experiences, however, but also of their realization: to the degree that the collective aspiration of a society is fulfilled and satisfied, it is also exhausted. The "horizon" comes closer, but at the very moment when it appears accessible, it ceases to be a horizon and becomes the wall of a prison. Such is the radical nature of crisis that has rarely been noted. It is a crisis of expectation. In such times man finds himself closed in without a future, and disillusion and melancholy invade his life. If this is all that happens, then something paradoxical occurs—for something is always happening in history, and the greatest event of all is when nothing happens, for then nothingness itself afflicts and extinguishes the period in question. Everything persists, everything appears to have been preserved and stabilized, even safe from destruction, but its function in life changes, its allure vanishes, and what was formerly in the forefront has now dropped back, perhaps even behind, fully possessed and inert. These are periods of discouragement but not desperation. In a state of desperation men are convinced that "things cannot go on like this," whereas in a state of discouragement they are persuaded that things may continue indefinitely as they are. This is why desperation, in this kind of situation, represents a ray of hope, for it puts an end to discouragement with the view that in a short time things must change. And with this limitation time again takes on a certain configuration, thus assuming its true function and, above all, its future dimension.

But there is another way in which social structure and with

it historical periods undergo change. A situation may be changed by the innovative appearance of a new and important element. Such an element can take many forms. For example, it may occur as a broadening of the geographical horizon with its concomitant economic, political, and historical alterations, such as actually happened with the discovery of America; or as economic transformation, as in the case of the Industrial Revolution; or as religious faith--think of the profound innovations of Christianity, and to a lesser degree, those of Islam; or as ideological enthusiasm, as "myth," such as that based on the new image of freedom that flourished at the dawn of the Romantic era; or perhaps as fear or a new relationship to happiness. A crisis occurs in all such cases not just because man does not know what to do with himself. For example, he does not know what his limitations are or how far he can go. He must explore himself, and he does so by leaving behind his world and his way of life and entering the future in an unknown and radical way.

But remember that everything depends on human vocation and aspiration. The same situation (ours, for example) allows two directions, two "exits," of quite different sorts to be taken. Consider the degree to which our present-day world may become static, inflexible, and uniform under the domination of a technology and administration that hold it paralyzed without dreams or promises. This is precisely the type of world that all kinds of prophets, great and small, have been predicting to us for decades. But it is equally possible that contemporary man is persuaded that this picture does not portray his true measure. And this is the most radical measure of all: discovering that life is committed to no fixed form. When this happens, man sees life as an inexhaustible enterprise involving risk, creativity, hope, and the fulfillment of reality. Hence, in speaking of crisis or the end of an era, indeed in speaking at all of a given situation, nothing has really been said so long as one forgets that the most important ingredient of that situation is man's free and open vocation or aspiration.

II
Generational Dynamics

9. The Articulation of Generations

If history is a certain discontinuous and qualified movement articulated in a series of successive and ordered situations so that each of the latter is tantamount to a given level, then it is clear that no isolated situation can be intelligible and that each temporal section—for example, a moment of time—encloses a plurality of levels, inasmuch as men of different ages coexist within it. This means that if we wish to understand a social structure we must study it as it appears during a greater or lesser "period" of time. And as we do so we discover that the latter appears as a drama complete with plot and actors to act it out.

In my aforementioned book Generations: A Historical Method I have treated this question in detail, and I refer those interested in the general theory to that work. Here I wish only to add several observations concerning the function of generations within a particular social structure. Generations have a double dimension: they are at once the "acts" and the "actors," the "whos" and the "steps" of history. Historical movement is not continuous, like that of a moving vehicle or an airplane, but is rather discontinuous, like that of a quadruped or a man. In other words, it proceeds gradually, by grades, or steps, or better still, by numbered steps. These steps, which take approximately fifteen years, constitute the elemental historical present. A generation is a period of time during which a certain view of the world remains relatively stable. But generations also represent the variations of that view and thus form the temporal rhythm of historical change. On the other hand, the true subject of history is a society, as we have seen, but a society that is intrinsically historical, that is to say, formed by the simultaneous presence of several different "times." This actually occurs as the coexistence of several generations, which may be otherwise described as the contemporaneity of men who are not coetaneous, in contrast to the fact that their own generation is based on co-etaneity. By this I mean that men of different ages coexist simultaneously and, therefore, that they are the contemporaries of men with whom they are not coetaneous. Yet the essential fact regarding each generation is that those groups of men born within what Ortega called à "zone of dates" are sociologically and historically the same age, i.e., coetaneous. Therefore, a generation is not only an interval of time, not only a concrete and real chronological unit, but also and fundamentally a group of men within a society, or better, one of the collective personalities that coexist in each situation. In short, a generation is one member of that plural subject of history we call a society.

Is it then possible to study a social structure within the boundaries of one of those so-called elemental presents, that is, within the span of a generation as a historical period? Naturally, the answer is no, because otherwise the different coexisting generations would then simply be juxtaposed or superimposed on one another without their customary dynamic articulation. The generations are in motion: they succeed each other in power, replace each other, and appear and disappear on the stage of history. The drama they represent cannot be understood by viewing only one act (or more precisely, one scene). Even the least significant historical period must extend over several generations, for without such temporal distension, we are left with a mere microstructure, which of itself is an abstraction. It is necessary, therefore, to examine the real articulation of several generations in a historical period in order to understand a social structure as dynamic reality rather than as abstract schemata.

I have stated that several generations were needed for such understanding. The question is: how many? We have seen that the principle of an era is never formal or structural, as is that of a generation, but is rather empirical and based on the content of that time period. An elemental period is determined by the appearance within it of "something"--leaving aside for the moment what that "something" might be--characterized by its ability to give a new appearance to life. Now then, if this new life style actually occurs, if a new historical period comes into being, it must needs do so by a historical process in which several generations participate, with each playing a different role. This determines analytically and theoretically the limits of what we could call a "minimal period" or, if you prefer, an "elemental period."

This new "something," which by its presence sets the style of the period, first springs into existence at a given moment as an element in the life aspiration of a generation. This generation will then attempt to impose on the world a view of life shaped by this "something." When the generation has completed its phase of preparation and begins the period of its assertiveness, that is, when it comes to power after some fifteen years, it will leave for the following generation this "something" already in existence. The men of the following generation are heirs to something that

26

in a strict sense is not theirs and which they did not create.
They simply begin to repeat and modify it. This "something,"
which began as a peculiarity of a minority and reached a limited
predominance only with the maturity of the first generation, is
now completely dominant. But this predominance in its complete
manifestation is encountered only by the third generation. Its
world is predetermined by this "something." This is the "inher-
iting" generation, the first one born into the world of the period in question, that is, born after the period is completely
established. This situation—mutatis mutandis—may be repeated.
A whole series of generations may live under the shelter of a
particular world form that continues to prevail, although each
succeeding generation may effect alterations. But it may happen
also in the case of the "minimal period" that the vigencia of
this world form weakens with the fourth generation. It is possible for the fourth generation to live within a world defined
by the "something" that has been the guiding principle of an
entire period, yet the collective aspiration of this generation
no longer finds expression in this world view. In this case,
the "world" of this generation is still affected by the older
view, but for the fourth generation this view is simply something
inherited and inert that it does not really feel. The social behavior of each man is conditioned by this inherited factor but
his private aspiration is different. There occurs, then, in
this generation the crisis of the period and the transition (or
at least the first steps) toward another period.

We see, then, that the first attempt to view things closely
reveals to us the structure and duration of what I have called
a "minimal" or "elemental" period of four generations, no more,
no less. Chronologically, the "intelligible field" at the very
minimum is four generations, or sixty years. Strictly speaking,
this period of time does not constitute an epoch, if by the latter is meant a way of life attained and shared by the entire
social body. In passing, this proves that the phases disclosed
by the history of abstract dimensions of life (philosophy, literature, art, politics, etc.) are not epochs, and that often they
last a much shorter time, since they are the work of particular
groups and not of the social structure in its full complexity.

Strictly speaking, four generations are not enough for an
adequate study of a minimal epoch, for the two generations that
flank it must also be taken into account: the first, so as to
show the contrast between the initial generation and its predecessor, certain members of which may individually reflect the
temper of the forthcoming epoch; and the following, in which the
epoch is effectively brought to an end, so as to place it in
perspective and to see it as a concluded and closed cycle. At
the very minimum, then, six generations act as the six characters
who make up and act out the most elemental drama of history.

10. Empirical Determination of Generations

It is anything but easy to determine specific generations. The analysis of human life in its individual and collective dimensions points to the existence of generations as well as to their function and dynamics. It is a consequence of the empirical structure of life that the mean duration of generations is approximately fifteen years (in round numbers not intended to be an exact figure). As for the real succession of generations and the precise time when these world changes that are the stages of history occur, these are matters that only an extensive and detailed study of historical reality can reveal. Anything less than this can offer only verisimilitude or approximation. Attempts to delimit specific generations—a common phenomenon of our time, especially in the area of Spanish literature—are almost all arbitrary; and when this is realized, it frequently leads to an attitude of distrust and skepticism regarding the possibility of determining in fact where generational boundaries lie. But it would be surprising if the first attempts were rigorously successful. Imagine the work that has been required for the most modest advances in our knowledge of the laws of genetics, the thousands of experiments and observations of Drosophila melanogaster or of peas, the years of patient research that the slightest increase of biological or physical knowledge requires, research that may absorb the energies of whole teams of experts, and then consider how incongruous it is to expect that in human affairs, which are much more complex, a few hours of improvised thought would be sufficient to clarify them. Only by means of a rigorous method of inquiry and after a series of very strict theoretical considerations made in the presence of ample empirical material that has been subjected to precise analysis could one determine the real succession of generations with any degree of certainty. Until this is done (and of course nothing remotely resembling it has been done) the inconsistency of those who make use of the term "generation" in an arbitrary and almost exlusively nominal way cannot be attributed to the theory of generations.

In Chapter Six of Generations: A Historical Method I outlined what Ortega has to say about the principle of an empirical determination of generations: the discovery of a "decisive generation" in which the world change is much greater than usual; the location of its "eponym" or representative man, taking as the central date of a generation the year he reaches thirty—or the equivalent, the year he was born, for the generational series would be the same in either case; and finally, the application of the scale thus obtained to historical reality so as to confirm or rectify it, making adjustments in one direction or the other until the theoretical aim comes into sharp alignment with the empirical data.

In the same context I propose a modus operandi that takes into account not only the mechanism of generations but our very

28

ignorance of their specific dividing lines as well. I shall sum-
marize it very briefly here, referring the reader to the work
cited for details. Take a certain number of representative figures who are fifteen years apart in age, if possible selecting
one or more for each date. We do not know where these generations
divide, nor indeed which ones we are dealing with. But we do
know that all generations are represented and that each group of
men selected belongs to a different generation. We may not know
which is which, but we have "captured" each of them in these unmistakable representatives. If we then take the names of men
appearing one year later than those given, probably in every
case they will belong to the same generation. Proceeding method-
ically, in this way, we shall obtain nuclei or groupings of names
in whom will be revealed and exemplified the common features of
the generation in question. But if upon adding another year, we
come to the "boundary" between generations, that is, if this new
year belongs to the following generation, an anomaly will be encountered that will be hard to describe in an isolated case
(there is a wide margin for individual differences that are irrelevant from the standpoint of generations) but that will be revealed sumultaneously through a whole series of representatives,
that is, throughout all the generations in question. It will be
found that upon adding a year to each of them, they have been
left behind. On the other hand, the representatives of this
new year will reveal an affinity with those names that we had
selected and grouped in the following generation in each case.
This amounts to a kind of "double entry" proof of the generational
division.

This method has two undeniable advantages: first, its universality, since it can be applied to any period, regardless of
whether or not any of the generations so treated are "decisive,"
and no matter how hard or easy it is to locate the "eponym" of
a generation; and second, its immediate effectiveness: in any
given case, even though we may not know where to separate generations, still we have them exemplified in a certain way by their
"representatives," who must necessarily exhibit the features of
their generations as well as the differences that set them apart.
Yet in spite of its simplicity and certainty, this procedure involves certain risks and must be approached with caution. This
is true first of all concerning the unity of the society from
which "generational representatives" are selected. In case of
doubt, it is better to stop short. By this I mean that it is
preferable to select them from a societal setting that is un-
questionably unitary, one in which the generational series is
undoubtedly uniform. Once this is done, attempts can be made
to extend and broaden the field. I shall clarify this with an
example: it seems highly probable that all of Europe, at least
Western Europe, since the eighteenth century—and perhaps earlier—
has formed a single society with the same generational scale.
But it would be a procedural error simply to select "representa-

tives" from this broader and in any case hypothetical society instead of restricting them to nations such as Spain, France, England, etc. Once the national generational scale has been determined, it would be proper to see whether the same thing happens in other countries, that is, whether the process coincides or reveals a certain décalage. And these two possibilities correspond to the existence or nonexistence of a supposed European society. Secondly, the matter of time must be handled cautiously. Inasmuch as fifteen is, I repeat, a "round number" based on the empirical structure of human life and for that reason approximate rather than precise and subject to variation, in principle it is not advisable to attempt to apply it to long chronological periods. If the latter are too long, an alteration in longevity and age rhythms may occur, causing the duration of generations to change within the elapsed time in question. This possibility is remote, but even in less extensive periods there is another risk: if the duration of each generation is not exactly fifteen years—a careful empirical investigation could show that the precise number is somewhat smaller or larger, though quite close to it. The resulting error is insignificant and easily discovered if several centuries were involved. Yet a third and more suitable precautionary measure is necessary. Our examination of representative "names" deals of course with individual lives. But upon examining their features, we must confine ourselves to those of a collective nature, that is, those traits that reveal in individual lives the presence of societal vigencias, which form the profile, as it were, of each generation. Regardless of their importance, strictly individual traits are irrelevant from the standpoint of generations.

The most reliable way to begin (and I expressly emphasize the word "begin") the empirical delineation of generations is to choose a specific and undeniable society, for instance, a European nation. Then within the history of that country one must choose a period that is long enough to include several generations and to allow their dynamic interaction to be seen, but short enough to be manageable and free of numerical error, in other words, an "elemental" or minimal period. Finally, once the society has been determined and delineated, one must examine the diverse dimensions of the social structure in which the collective or generational traits are active. Thus, if on the one hand it is not possible to study a social structure without knowing something of the real generations involved, on the other the best way to determine the latter is by investigating them within a precise structure. Once again, we find that circular movement of which the method of understanding human realities consists.

Generational Dynamics

11. Generational Coexistence and Succession

How many generations coexist within a society, that is, how many live simultaneously at a given moment of time? Leaving aside our own era in which the situation is changing and referring only to the <u>historical</u> coexistence of generations, meaning those that actually participate in the collective life of a society, we find that there are three, ranging in age from fifteen to sixty. Before the age of fifteen, in infancy and childhood, no kind of historical activity occurs. The period of receptivity and education generally does not transcend the area of private life. But why, one may wonder, should that participation stop at sixty? What about the elderly?

We find first of all a quantitative factor: generations are not only temporal intervals but also groups of men, or better, many men. The large segments of the population of a social unit are articulated in the generations. A relatively small group of men representing a mere fraction of the total population could not be so designated. One could say that these individuals belong to a generation, with the understanding that it no longer exists. Indeed, this is what has happened throughout history to men over sixty. Most of them have died before reaching that age and those who do live longer are regarded only as survivors. It is not only that there are fewer men over sixty than, say, between forty-five and sixty, but rather that there are so disproportionately <u>few</u> that the function of the elderly group is changed. In addition, <u>ad</u>vanced age causes the efficiency and activity of this group to be much less than is the case of younger men. Finally, these great "gaps" in the ranks of the elderly disrupt their formations and cause them to lose the articulation they have been forming all their lives. For this reason they no longer form a social <u>body</u> that acts as such within the societal mechanism. Rather, they <u>act</u> as surviving fragments, with individual functions that are qualitatively different.

In the twentieth century, and not before, this situation is changing. Increased longevity has added to the ranks of the elderly, and it means that they are not so old as before. In other words, they constitute a socially coherent fraction, even though numerically speaking it is inferior to the others. It has been decimated by death and decrepitude, but its ranks are still intact. This means that the older generation, those persons over sixty, persists still. And this poses a very delicate problem that lies beyond the scope of this study, but which I should at least like to formulate. The presence of another generation is no trivial matter, for it means an alteration in the social structure. Generations have precise functions, and the active intervention of four instead of three modifies their relationships to one another. Since we are dealing with a drama, it means that a new character has appeared on the stage, and inasmuch as he must play a part, the roles must be redistributed. To what degree is the function of the three younger generations changed by the presence of a fourth and fully active group? The fact that the role of "survivors" has been assumed by individuals of a fifth generation (at the present time, by the Generation of 1898 in Spain) means that a broader historical time is present at a certain moment of history. It also means that the retentive capacity, which is essential to any society, has been enhanced. We are thus facing a profound transformation of the social structure and the generational scale. For if this greater longevity is confirmed and stabilized over a long period of time (as it must be to be effective), we do not know whether it will be consolidated into a new intergenerational scale—four generations and a "surviving remnant"-- or whether the former relationship will be reestablished by readjusting the "roles" of the generations at the price of altering their rhythm and increasing their time of duration as well as the interval between them. It may be that the time span of prevailing world modes will approach twenty years in the near future. Certain phenomena such as infantilism, prolongation of adolescence and youth, etc., would seem to warrant this idea. But it is too early to evaluate the structure of societies that will follow our own.

As for the succession of generations, a final note must be added. Ortega distinguishes between cumulative periods and eliminative or polemic times. During the former periods, the younger generation essentially continues the tendency of its predecessor. During the latter, on the other hand, the younger generation disagrees and rebels. These are, respectively, times of the elderly and the young. But if we take a period in the strict sense, i.e., a minimum of four generations, and frequently more, we have what may be a quite varied rhythm. In fact, the cumulative tendency may be repeated at every change of generation; or it may occur in only two generations and be reversed in the form of disagreement with the one before it; or it may consist of a series of successive innovative disagreements that subsequently lapse. Thus, in studying a given period, one must determine the nature of this rhythm, which forms a certain historical profile. Continuity, stability, the preservation or loss of balance, and the speed of variation are other factors that are conditioned by the manner in which generational succession occurs.

But in using the term "succession" we must keep in mind that we are referring to generations in power--or in any of its roles or functions--and not to their succession in the world and in history. For in this sense they do not succeed each other, as Ortega and François Mentré saw quite clearly.[1] Rather, as Ortega says, they overlap or overlay each other. They fit together like tiles in a roof; in other words, they are partially superimposed on each other, coinciding in time but with different functions and at different levels. Thus, coexistence and succession form a single property of generations rather than two: their form or existence is successive, that is, historical, coexistence.

32

12. Generations and Their Expression

One of the most delicate and difficult problems in the investigation of generations concerns their presence and the way
in which it is manifested. How do we go about finding them? In
the case of contemporary generations, I find individuals about
me, and in them I can discover certain features that set them
apart as a group and above all situate them at a certain level.
As far as a contemporary is concerned, either I feel that he is
coetaneous, a man of my time and age, or that he is not. In
the first instance I say that he belongs to my generation. In
the second case I assign him to another either prior or subsequent to my own. But naturally this "impression" is not enough
although it should by no means be ignored. It must be justified,
and the purely individual traits that it involves discounted.
In other words, it is the result of individual observation, and
until it transcends the personal element and reveals transpersonal
structures, it can never be sufficient of itself to justify a decision regarding the generation to which a person belongs.

For this reason, there is less difference between investigations of present and past generations than would seem to be
the case at first glance. In both cases one must turn to the
forms of collective life that do not "appear" in the same sense
as a particular person. In other words, generations manifest
or express themselves, and I must proceed from this expression
to the reality expressed.

Of the countless men who live during a given period, only
a few are remembered, perhaps one in a thousand or ten thousand.
This fact presupposes a qualification of the individuals who for
one reason or another—including chance—are "accessible." In
general, these men are remembered and mean something to us because they did something concrete. Their deeds are marked by
the common quality of being evident; they are directly or indirectly expressive. To write a book, paint a picture, give
speeches, win or lose a battle, govern or try to govern, revolt,
commit treason, and create are forms of expressive actions; whereas
to make it possible for another to write or paint is to perform
a "passively" expressive act.

But this means that history is always concerned with exceptional material. This is so true that originally and indeed for
centuries the topic of history was the exceptional per se. It
was the memorable, that is, that which was worth remembering
simply because it did not happen every day, that which was worth
snatching from oblivion and preserving. From the time of Herodotus
until the eighteenth century, history concentrated on the exceptional; since Voltaire it has tried to overcome this limitation,
but its bondage to the exceptional continues because of the fact
that such is the nature of the material at its disposal. Therefore, one must accept what appears as an indication or expression
of what does not appear except by this means. The idea of intra-

33

history on which Unamuno insisted so much is entirely correct, though insufficiently elaborated.[2] Although it is not an adequate solution, we could say that it is the title of a problem. Unamuno stresses the notion that we speak of the "present historical moment," and this formula implicitly states that there is another moment present that is not historical. If one were to inquire into its nature, Unamuno would reply that it is intrahistorical. Yet this term is ambiguous, for if it means, as Unamuno was inclined to believe, that it is not historical, then it is an error, since all expressions of human life are historical. The formula that I have used so many times, "intrinsically historical," retains the essential and positive aspect of Unamuno's idea without attempting to elude historicity.

This means that we cannot stop with an accessible manifestation of one kind or another. We must refer it to a certain level, situate it in a certain zone of reality, root it in the interpretation of the underlying assumptions that made it possible. That is what I call the interpretation of the expressive aspect. Beginning with the exceptional aspect of the historical, this constant recourse to the forgotten substratum that gives it reality is the basis of the method of investigating generations.

Let us consider the clearest example: a writing. Its strictly personal content is sustained by a more ample foundation of prior elements that derive from its circumstance: the language in which it is written, the literary genre, that is, the kind of writing it is, the title, specifically, the type of title, the stylistic devices brought into play, that which is not said because "it goes without saying," the ideas that it effectively touches, the "authorities" to which it appeals automatically, presupposing the effect they will have on the reader's mind, and so on. All this is impersonal—or at least transpersonal; it does not come from the author and cannot be explained in terms of him alone. Rather, it comes from his "world." But here is where the specifically historical problem begins, especially from the concrete point of view in which we have placed ourselves: the viewpoint of generations. I shall explain.

Before the advent of historical consciousness (which is not the same thing as historicism, since the former is a real situation and the latter, a theory), man felt that he was installed in a present time the duration of which was vaguely defined but quite considerable in any case and which was called "the present day." Bear in mind how long it took to reject the idea of "contemporary history" begun in 1789: the assumption of a "modern-day period" has easily lasted more than a century. The reaction to this belief, growing out of a historical awareness of human things, has led in turn to the other extreme, to the atomization of time and consequently to the fragmentation of the present. According to this view, the present time would be each year, or, if one insists, each instant of time. But both positions are false, for time has quality and structure. This means that the

34

first duty of the historian is to establish that structure,
meaning that he must "date" the elements that coexist in a situation. Not all the ingredients in a given circumstance or world
that have a personal or transpersonal bearing on a manuscript
belong to the same temporal stratum or the same level. If we
take a certain writing as the expression of something that transcends its author, then that something must be positively ascertained. Furthermore, only a portion of these ingredients (or
perhaps certain of their aspects) belongs to the author's generation and thus may be considered his expression. Within the
general framework that constitutes the patrimony of a period,
each generation makes its particular contribution which must
be isolated and distinguished from what is common to several
others and from what is the author's own mark. All kinds of
structures affect the concrete and unitary reality of a given
writing, from the most universal and permanent to the unique,
irreplaceable, and irreducible personal vocation. The same is
true of a painting, a political intrigue, or the manner in which
one is wealthy or in love. As we examine specific acts of certain men, we must identify in those acts that which is the expression of many men, though not just any men, but rather those
who live in the same world, or what amounts to the same thing,
those who belong to the same generation. One must delve into
the most intricate structures which because of the wealth of
detail they offer can justify the various relationships of expression.

13. Masses and Minorities

As Ortega pointed out more than thirty years ago, all society is the articulation of a mass and a minority. Although
these terms tell us that the first is composed of many men and
the second, few, they do not concern quantity primarily because
the functions are reciprocal. The masses are organized and
structured by a minority of select individuals. There can be no
minority without a mass; the minority is the minority of a mass
and for a mass. Conversely, life for the masses is impossible
without a guiding minority, and in one way or another, all societies organize and form such minorities. For without this mutual
interaction, collective life is not possible. Ortega has devoted
many pages to this articulation to show that the health of a
social body depends in large part on the normality of this reciprocal action and that the demise of the ruling class because of
apathy or reluctance to fulfill its function, or because of the
unwillingness of the masses, causes a state of societal sickness
as well as disintegration.

But since it is a question of a reciprocal social function,
the two social elements, mass and minority, do not necessarily
coincide with social estates of a people. It is normal for them

to coincide grosso modo, because social stratification originates as a result of the dynamic articulation of mass and minority. Yet even in the most normal and well-adjusted case, social groups, not individuals, interact in this way. I mean that even in cases where the aristocracy really is the guiding stratum of a society, this is not evident in each of its members. Analogously, even in the most stable societies, individuals from the lower strata assume positions of leadership, which the collectivity always seeks to justify through certain channels. Consider, for example, what it meant in the medieval or Renaissance world to have access to the ecclesiastical hierarchy, or the significance of the royal privilege of bestowing nobility.

All this is quite clear, but one must take into account two other viewpoints that complicate the question considerably. The first has to do with the confusion between the concepts of mass and select minority on the one hand and mass-men and outstanding man on the other. Ortega insisted forcefully that the mass is not always made up of mass-men. The mass-man represents the degeneration of the men who form the mass. He is the wayward and inauthentic individual who does not recognize his condition; he is the "spoiled child," the smug "playboy," who collectively makes up the rebellious mass, rebellious, that is, against himself, against the very idea of being mass. Mass-men exist in every social class, says Ortega, because it is not a matter of classes of society but of classes of men. In this regard three points of view must be identified: the two necessary social functions, the directed mass and the directing or leading minority; the "solidification" of these functions into classes or estates that normally and statistically exercise such functions; and the kind of individuals who belong to each of these social classes. Ideally, the mass of a society would not contain a single "mass-man," although in fact the latter is found at all levels of society, even at the highest ranks.

The second point of view is still more delicate. One might think that because of their excellence, effort, or talent, certain men belong to the select minority, or elite, while others simply make up the mass that is guided and directed by the elite. Yet things are not that simple. "The barbarism of specialization" did not escape Ortega's astute scrutiny. The man who is eminent in a certain field and who enjoys a legitimate authority in it feels an impulse to behave in general as though that authority extended to other areas of his life in which he has no especial qualifications. In other words, he behaves like a mass-man because he does not accept his function as mass, that is, his passive and directed function in those areas where he can have no other role. Except for scattered cases, this means strictly speaking that the guiding minority is not made up of individuals, at least not in the full range of their activities, but of the acts of certain individuals, of the specific functions of certain persons in areas wherein they are truly qualified to act.

36

The famous politician, who is a part of the guiding minority as far as politics is concerned, is just another man when he is ill and cannot tell the doctor how he must treat him. Rather, he must obediently follow the doctor's instructions or change doctors—which of course is his inalienable right. The well-known physicist who knows only physics cannot tell a director how to stage a performance, although he is within his rights not to attend if it does not please him. The talented painter may not offer opinions on his country's foreign policy, at least not in the active sense of stating what must be done, although of course he may reject the political program offered by one party in favor of another. In other words, belonging to the directing minority is not a permanent privilege of certain men but a function that each one exercises insofar as he is qualified to do so; and as soon as that function ceases, the individual rejoins the ranks of the mass and thus becomes docile. Claiming that aristocratic status authorizes one to make political decisions, that economic influence confers literary taste, that an ecclesiastical rank allows one to speak out on philosophy, or that scientific knowledge gives license to interfere in foreign policy are different forms of the "barbarism of specialization" and, therefore, examples of rebellion by the masses as well as indications that those who so act are mass-men.

Thus, the distinction between mass and minority takes on a dynamic and concrete aspect. To repeat, it is a function, and the fact that society crystalizes, solidifies, and stabilizes its functions in the form of magistrates that coincide only in a statistical way with their primary purpose should not cause us to forget the fundamental issue of the matter. This solidification is necessary, being based on the very nature of society; and the margin of inadequacy and "inexactness" that it always implies only indicates the greater or lesser degree of inauthenticity present in all forms of collective life. At times it may be negligible and almost inconsequential, while in other cases it can be overwhelming. Therefore, in studying the social structure of a specific period, one must pose two questions: the first, which social groups are titularly responsible for leadership, that is, which are the select minorities?; and the second, how true is this designation, to what degree are these titular groups really select and qualified, and thus, to what point do they really exercise leadership? And if they do not do so to a sufficient degree this poses a final and delicate question: is the society vigorous and healthy enough to have created a "vicarious" and alternate guiding group, which may be quite different from the one that apparently exercises leadership, or is the responsibility vacant and unassumed and the society leaderless, confused, and inert? A precise diagnosis of this situation is absolutely indispensable if one wishes to understand the internal structure of a society of a certain period, the significance of everything that occurs in it, and beyond that the horizon of its immediate possibilities.

14. The "Representative" Structure of European Societies

The articulation of the mass and the minority follows a
fixed pattern, but it is only a pattern. The way in which it
is ca-ried out can vary considerably. The first and most fundamental fact to consider, but one often overlooked because it is
so obvious, is quantitative. The terms "mass" and "minority"
have an immediate reference to quantity. In a slightly different
sense but in the same direction, Aristotle spoke of "the many"
and "the few." To what degree is the minority in the minority?
Is this minor portion of society minimal or quite numerous?
Each society or each period has its own ratio that conditions
the reciprocal functioning of its two components.

But regardless of the ratio between minority and mass, there
are very diverse forms of connection and adjustment between them.
One form in particular that is characteristic of, though not exclusive to, European societies is what I call their "representative" structure. I mean that not only do the minorities rule,
guide, direct, and invent, but they also represent the majority.
But the word "representation" can be taken in two different ways
that are not mutually exclusive, and European societies are representative in both senses. First, there is representation in
the sense of "delegation," substitution or lieutenancy. The minorities are "for" the majority, they act as its delegates and
are empowered by it; for, of course, it is the majority that
confers power on the minorities that govern it. However, this
is not the most important or peculiar fact. There is a second
meaning, that of "scenic representation"; for the minorities
embody, stage, and act out the majorative drama of societies.
"Person" means face, or mask, and in this sense representation
personalizes or personifies collective life. This fact is fraught
with meanings.

Let us point out a few of them. First of all, consider the
existence of a "stage setting," that is, the establishment of a
perspective within the society. There must be a stage whereon
minorities meet each other, and it must be visible. In many
different ways, attempts to meet these two conditions, stage
setting and visibility, have been made throughout history, leading to the creation of a "capitality," the existence of which is
less obvious than it would seem to us today. Think of the function
of the sanctuaries or sacred sites, the games of Greece, the special assemblies, all of which were partial or transitory stages.
The existence of a social stage setting is linked to the size of
societies. If the latter are very small, they are visible to
themselves. Strictly speaking, there is no stage but rather
participation in the same experiences. When the statement is
made that Athenian democracy was not representative but direct,
one must understand that the basic reason for it was not a political system but a social structure. The entire Athenian society
was the stage setting, or _agora_, and therefore it was not properly

38

speaking representative or "staged." If societies are too large
geography and communication make the chances of visibility and
meeting somewhat problematical. Compare the European situation
to that of the United States. The "visibility" of Washington
does not compare to that of Paris or London. The "representatives"
go to Washington as "delegates" or substitutes for the citizens
who send them, but their activities have only the barest scenic
representation. This function is enhanced in two quite different
ways which I shall not go into here because they do not have a
bearing on our topic. Nevertheless, it is a fascinating topic
that has received little attention. Suffice it to say that it
has to do with the significance and success of television in
North America.[3]

The second consequence is the public nature of life in these
societies. The fact that life may be public in nature is neither
obvious nor necessary. The public aspect arises from the staging
or representative condition of society, and mere visibility of
the stage does not assure its existence. In one sense or another,
the spectators must also be present. I mean that what is public
must not be confused with what is merely known. All Spaniards
know many things which nonetheless are not public. For example,
information is never equivalent to publicity. If tomorrow all
Spaniards receive a news item sealed in an envelope, it will be
a matter completely different from reading it in the newspaper.
Actually, it is not even necessary for us to read it; it is enough
that we can read it. In fact, only a fraction of the people of
the country read newspapers, whereas in the hypothetical case
everyone receives the envelope with the item sealed inside. Yet
even though everyone may know it, it is still not public knowledge,
as is the case with the same item in the newspaper. Hence the
disturbance that the loss of publicity causes in the societies
of Europe; its absence is not merely a lack of something but a
real deprivation. In other words, when a certain way of life
has to be public and is not, it becomes clandestine. It is no
accident that for centuries European politics has displayed a
tendency toward parliamentarianism, and it is a mistake to interpret parliament strictly from the viewpoint of sovereignty and
therefore of democracy. The primary (and most important) function
of parliament is associated with "parlia," to speak, and to do
so publicly and on stage, as it were. Whether or not parliament
legislates is an important though secondary matter; the decisive
point is that it speaks in public of public things. This function
as a stage setting for the collective life of a society (which
at one time was exercised by the Spanish Cortes) in time passed
to the Court. Notice that the decline of the former was in fact
offset by the development of the latter. The establishment of a
capital, the fact that the Court became permanently fixed in a
city is important for two reasons: for one thing it made possible
its splendor and plenitude as well as the development of courtly
life by giving it the "theater" in which it consists. Furthermore,

as the European countries achieved more stable and rigorous structures, it became less necessary for their personification, royalty, to travel about the nation, appearing in each area. As the kingdom assumed a precise figure, its parts fell into place and its head, i.e., the capital, appeared. A whole system of reference and communication, material and social, established a relationship between the capital and the different territorial points. In this setting—Madrid of the Hapsburgs, Paris of the Valois and the Bourbons, London of the Tudors and Stuarts—the national dramas are staged, and the different European peoples attend the staging of their own history.

The third consequence is more immediate: the need for a collective "argument" or plot of life. Understand this well: all life, individual or collective, needs an "argument" and without one it is not life in the human sense. But the fact that the life of a society is representative means that this argument or plot must be expressly clear and that it must be lived and felt as such by individuals. This in turn presents two requirements: the argument must be understood, which means that it has to be intelligible to people, and it must be shared. What are the consequences of these two requirements?

The first is that individuals must be able to understand what is happening so as to be capable of foreseeing and anticipating to a certain degree the movements on stage. In other words, they must know "what it is about" and "where it is leading." French supremacy in Europe for almost two centuries was due in large part to the fact that its history was the most intelligible of all (compare this with its present situation and you can see where its greatest danger lies). The enactment of the national argument enhances the projective dimension of any society, makes it essentially forward-looking, and prevents it from sinking into the routine exercise of its traditional resources. It is from this perspective, and not by means of the relatively superficial reasons of mere politics, that one can understand the resistance of all forms of traditionalism to effective parliamentarianism and, what is more revealing, to the flowering of courtly life. I do not know how much study has been done of this aspect of the European monarchies, but it seems to me that this would be a very fruitful approach to investigating them.

The second requirement, that the collective life argument be shared by all, means that individuals are "a part of it" and that they feel personally affected by what happens, even though events may not touch them directly. Of course there is nothing odd in the fact that taxes, levies, and regular recruitment do affect individuals and it is to be expected that everyone would have a personal stake in war or peace and in public order and services. But it is much less clear and certain in what sense merchants can speak of "our" musicians, or how farmers are aware that there is something called "our" writers, or how both groups refer not only to "our" customs but also to "our" history. This requires an active participation in the drama of the society. But notice that "active" does not mean "intervention." Farmers take no part at all in the advance of letters or science; workers and laborers do not decide the directions that painting, music, and national rhetoric take. Their participation is that of the spectator, the viewer who feels involved, though perhaps uncertainly, with what is happening on the stage (except for occasions on the stage and in history when they burst in on the scene with the result that the play ends at that point).

This brings us to a point that I should like to touch on. I have deliberately chosen examples from what is public life by antonomasia, that is, from political life (in Rome it was called res publica and had to do with politics and authority) because they are the clearest and simplest. But it must be strongly emphasized that the representative structure of societies also affects other, quite different areas. Art and science, social usages and styles, spectacles and language, all bear the mark of this representative quality wherever it is present. A society cannot be understood without ascertaining the degree and forms of that representation.

These forms assume a precise cast within a given period. Once this occurs, they function automatically, so that people know what each thing "represents," although that knowledge is of course implicit rather than formally acknowledged. In the same automatic way, this condition allows one to calibrate the relative importance of things, events, and people. Under these circumstances, the course of life is easy and mechanical for the most part. This is what is called a "normal" period. This appraisal of relative importance, which is crucial in all areas of life (as well as in the life of organisms), is then performed naturally and without problems. One knows what the look on the king's face means, the queen's smile, a preacher's sermon, a bishop's pastoral, a popular revolt, the retirement of an ambassador, a dance, a party, the publication of a book, a hike in taxes (taxes always go up), an editorial, a general's actions, a change of ministers, a theatrical triumph, a prize, an execution, a parliamentary speech, an auto-da-fé. Life spontaneously regulates its reactions to things and in principle at least behavior is predictable. But at times this certainty about things disappears. A person, event, or thing appears which "represents" something unknown, and therefore people do not know what it means, or, since we are dealing with human realities, what it "is." Each component of common life poses a problem because there is no clear idea of what lies behind it, no certain knowledge of what is expressed by its appearance, no inkling of how things are linked to other things or substrata to other substrata. This accounts for the disorientation, the perplexity and the great likelihood of blundering that threatens all individual behavior. When the patterns of the play are altered, almost all the players bungle and play their roles badly. The impression is

one of dullness stealing over and dominating the entire society.
The collectivity lurches out of kilter, and only a few men know,
or better, do not know but can find out, what everything represents. But because other men do not have this knowledge, one
cannot determine one's behavior by theirs; and for this reason
an apparent "paralysis" overcomes the outstanding members. The
situation could be compared to the collective movement of several
pedestrians or vehicles along a street or highway. It is not
enough for me to see and make my way adroitly. My movements depend on others also seeing and regulating theirs. It is not
enough for me simply to see a man wandering distractedly along
the street, reading or with his back turned. I have to stop
and step out of his heedless way if I wish to avoid a collision.
This picture sheds light on what happens in society when the
pattern of representation is unknown.

15. The Problem of Assumptions

     All this brings us to a procedural conclusion: the need to
appeal to the underlying assumptions of each social reality.
Nothing is fully real in isolation. Each ingredient of human
life, and in this case collective life, is nourished, or better,
shaped, by the system of its references to other ingredients and
above all to the total structure. The need arises, therefore,
to look beyond the limits of any specific element in order to
see its real connections to others. In other words, each element
is sustained by other realities, which in principle are not apparent but which confer on them their real significance.
     This has its principal effect on those expressions that
make it easiest to know a social reality. I refer to what is
said. To say is always "to mean to say" something. Hence, we
can never simply take what someone says without knowing in advance or asking ourselves what he means. Likewise, we must know
the context of his words, the reason for saying them, the person
to whom they are addressed, the repercussions they may have, the
degree to which the person himself is revealed in them, and the
amount of truth contained and intended in them, that is, how the
speaker intends for them "to be taken." These factors have a
bearing on the significance of any human utterance, spoken or
written, just as they shape it and cause it to be what it actually
is.[4]
     An example may help to clarify these points. Consider the
customary way of writing the history of literature and the demands
that are imposed by the true explanation of literary phenomena.
Naturally it is not possible to limit it to a catalogue or repertory of authors and works. On this point everyone agrees; but
neither is it enough to investigate the origins, sources, ante-
cedents, and influences. Indeed, not even the thematic and stylistic analysis of literary works is sufficient. Of course all

this is necessary but it stops short of the most important and
critical factor that justifies all the rest.

The understanding and utilization of a literary text, especially if one wishes to grasp its historical function in order
to write a "history of literature," or history in any form, for
that matter, raise the serious question of what literature is
in each period. One must determine just who creates literature
in a given period, by what group or groups and for whom it is
created. Thus, one must describe the social personality of the
writer and determine the factors, which are neither accidental
nor constant, that cause him to be a writer, just as the range
of his readers must be ascertained both qualitatively and quantitatively. Who it is who does the writing is no small matter;
monk or layman, noble or bourgeois, whether or not he makes his
living with his pen—or perhaps supplements his income by writing—
are all pertinent factors. Nor is it a matter of inconsequence
whether something is written for two dozen courtiers or for the
masses; and in the latter case, one must ascertain which masses.
The approximate number of readers at any given time must be established and calculations made as to how many of them read each
literary genre or certain representative works. Similarly, esti-
mates must be made of those able to read, those who could read
because they could buy books or otherwise have access to them,
those who are readers because of their social status, the relative number of women readers, and so on. Also, the number and
volume of the editions of certain works, the frequency of reprint-
ing, the increase or decrease in readership over a given period,
the time during which a work is "read" as compared to the time
when it becomes the subject of "study" (these are quite different
functions) are matters that must be clarified in order to understand the literary phenomenon. And because they have not been
cleared up except in rare cases, this means that the majority
of literary data are not even remotely understood.

Furthermore, the purpose of each literary work must be
rigorously considered, whether it be to teach, entertain, indoc-
trinate, initiate followers into mysteries or create a "cult,"
stir feelings or convey a sense of exquisiteness, or perhaps
abêtir. And in every case, the means of serving that purpose
must be taken into account as well as any other activities that
also share that purpose, for example, oral narration, religious
worship, spectacles, science, politics, social gatherings, and
the like. In each case also the proportion of rivalry and alli-
ance must be calculated. The distance of literature from life
must be accurately measured and the degrees of authenticity,
sincerity, and spontaneity and originality (which are quite
different things) determined for each period and each genre.
As for the latter, they must be explained and accounted for in
terms of their prominence or decline, their relative strength at
each juncture, the degree to which they predetermine the content
of the literary work and the room they leave for individual dis-

cretion and variation. One must also ascertain the weight and influence of literature on life, as well as the status of literary genres (and authors) in the society, ranging from works addressed to the most exclusive minorities to the literature of the newsstand, the attributes and sources of which would have to be investigated for each period.

Finally, once we come to the literary work itself--and the road to it is quite long--we must ask preemptorially what it consists of, how it achieves its purpose, what its possibilities and resources are, and how it makes use of the language and previous literary forms in order to achieve its end. The analysis of the literary work that includes stylistics and much more must respond to such questions. It is not enough, for example, to study rhyme scheme, the structure of strophes, and the origin of metaphors used by the poet. One must inquire as to the area of their origin so as to determine the type of speech they spring from, the prevailing conventions affecting them, the "rules of the game" in force, and the repertory of basic literary forms belonging to the public domain at any given time as a common fund of literature. This repertory must be inventoried to see what it contains: perhaps popular sayings or "topics" such as are found in Renaissance lyrics, or "mythologies," or a falsetto tone reminiscent of 1790, and so forth. These features, which are relatively simple in poetry, are present in other genres in more complex forms. As for the theater, one must identify the part of it that represents "literature," as compared to other elements that are also present in it. In our own time, one must consider the place of radio, television, and the cinema, not only regarding the adaptation of these media to literary works and the problems this presents, but also in view of the effect that may derive from the fact that ours is a world where authors and potential readers alike go to movies, listen to the radio, and watch television.

Likewise, literature remains unintelligible so long as one has no clear idea of the importance of literature (and writers) during a certain period as well as that of each individual author and work. The true will to understand obliges one to appeal to the latent assumptions of apparent phenomena. Before the usual practice of examining existing writings and writers during a given period, one would have to pose not only the prior questions enumerated earlier but others as well. For example, what can a writer accomplish in each case? What does he intend to accomplish (and this is the only way of determining the concrete meaning of success or failure in each case)? Which literary genres prevail and what is their phase of popularity? What is the real function of each of them? What degree of innovation marks literary production, and to what extent, for social reasons, is such creativity emphasized or even exaggerated, or disguised and concealed? To what degree is there or not a dominant style? What are the actual relationships (of writers and readers) to ancient or modern foreign literatures, and what is the nature of their role (lineal, imitative, competitive, inspirational, etc.)? What portion of the national literary past endures, and how vigorous is that legacy? How is it regarded, as a weight, a cause for pride, a resource, a chain, or as a cause for shame? To what degree can--or should--literature be unpleasant or dull, or are these legitimate features at all? Many other questions of this type could be posed with a great deal of precision.

It happens, therefore, that utterance of any kind is based on a series of assumptions that make it possible, intelligible, and meaningful. I have insisted on literary utterance because it is the type preserved from the past and because it allows one to make general observations. These assumptions are basic because they exist in mutual foundational relationships, that is, they form a structure, which is only a fraction or partial outline of the social structure that we are examining. Once again we find a circle; yet as I have shown elsewhere, it is not vicious but a circle of virtues called a system. And in turn it must be said also that utterance is only an example, albeit of gigantic dimensions. In general, things could be formulated in these terms: our investigation encounters and considers diverse data; but these data are "given" by someone, to someone, in a given situation. These ingredients constitute the reality of the datum as such, that is, as a given. Thus, data inexorably require an interpretation or hermeneutics, and it must begin by determining the ambit in which these data function. We have seen that the generations are in turn the "who" and the "stages" of history, the characters and acts of the drama that is history. Consequently, any hermeneutics, the sine qua non of understanding data, requires an explanation of generational dynamics.

III
Social *Vigencias*

16. The Idea of Vigencia

The word vigencia is a technical term in the sociology of
Ortega that I find very hard to replace. Its etymological origin
is clear: in the normal use of the Spanish language, vigencia
is the state or condition of being "in force" (vigente); that
which is vigente (Latin vigens) is quod viget, that which is very
much alive, that which has vigor. In a secondary sense, it means
that which is awake, in a state of vigilance (Latin vigilia). In
Spanish, the word vigencia is used especially in juridical language:
a law in vigencia is "in vigor"; it has the "force of law" and
is presently binding. This same law loses vigencia when it ceases
to have such force or vigor. A law of the Partidas is still a
law, but it lacks vigencia and is invalid or dead. Ortega introduces two new meanings to the use of the term. The first is an
extension of its application; instead of restricting it to the
juridical sphere, he uses it in its full range. Secondly, he applies the substantive vigencia to any reality "in vigor" insofar
as it is in force. Thus, he speaks of the vigencias of a period,
of the various types of vigencias, that is, of their content;
and he pays attention to the nature of their prevalence and for
this reason to their function in collective life.

A vigencia, therefore, is that which is in force, that
which has vitality, vigor, or strength; it is everything I encounter in my social environment that I must take into consideration. The power of vigencias resides in this feature. If a certain reality within my social world does not require that a stand
be taken with regard to it, if it can be ignored, if, in short,
it need not be taken into account at all, then it is not a vigencia. For example, in society there are individuals and groups
of individuals who are vegetarians. But there is no reason for
me to concern myself with them and their vegetarianism; I am
under no obligation either to agree or disagree with them. In
fact I may very well not think of them at all, not even to consider

whether vegetarianism is good or bad. This means that vegetarianism is not a vigencia. On the other hand, I must take into account the fact that other individuals and groups like football: on the day of a game I discover that I cannot take the bus because it is loaded with those who wish to see the match. I open the newspaper and find many pages devoted to the sport. An office-worker does not heed me because he is busy predicting the results of Sunday's games. If I am a theatrical impresario, I see that football cuts into my audiences. In other words, football is a vigencia that requires of me that I take a stand and come to grips with it in one way or another.

Regardless of its importance, however, the fact that something is "in force" does not mean that I must agree with it. I may very well disagree with it. But the important fact is that I must disagree. If I am not a vegetarian, I do not disagree necessarily with vegetarianism. I simply am not a vegetarian and there the story ends, which is to say it never begins. As for football, on the other hand, I have no alternative but to concern myself with it, because on its own or through its consequences it touches my life and forces me to do something with it. This may take many forms: invitations to attend a game, crowded public vehicles, the lack of taxis when I need one, distraction of employees, a conversation about the topic by the barber, pictures of football players assailing me as I open the newspaper, which may delight me or perhaps annoy me if I prefer to see pictures of an actress or the winner of a Nobel prize, pages of prose that I must read or skip over, football terms that become part of everyday language. Disagreeing with a vigencia is the best proof of its reality, its resistance and coerciveness, with which I either comply or reject with effort.

This means that the authentic mode of social reality is not a simple "being there," but instead consists of pressure, coercion, invitation, and seduction. The characteristic of the social is not merely "to be there" but to be acting. For this reason nothing is more appropriate than the expression vigencia. The common feature of the ingredients that make up collective life is their vitality, their vigor. But at the same time stress must be laid on the fact that they are not actions; their vigor is exercised by their presence, or at times by their simple inert resistance, like a wall that blocks my way.

Here we must anticipate a misconception. To say that I must take vigencias into account might lead one to surmise that such an accounting is necessarily active and that I must consciously and expressly heed them. This is the case in only two instances: when the vigencia is not fully accredited or when I personally deviate from it. In other cases, I conform to, and am informed by it, behaving in accordance with it, submitting to its influence that is as automatic as it is imperious. Just as I am subject to the law of gravity or to atmospheric pressure, so I am under the power of vigencias. As a rule, I do not think about gravity

or air pressure, yet in my behavior I take them into account:
I do not leave a book in the air, because it would fall; I do
not place a heavy weight on my foot, for it would crush it; I
do not attempt to carry a piano because it weighs too much; and
I fly in an airplane, counting on the wind resistance to keep it
aloft. Normally I walk along the sidewalk of a street without
thinking about it, my direction being determined by its prior
structure. When I take a drink of water, I presume it is cold
without thinking about it even for an instant, and I notice its
temperature only if by chance it is hot. Likewise, whenever I
speak to a passerby in the street, I assume that he will understand the language of the country, and I am reminded of it only
if by chance he is not subject to the general linguistic vigencia
that becomes evident simply because it is not applicable in this
case.

This means that we dwell in a social world made up not of
things but of certain active realities, which, as we shall see
shortly, are stranger and more mysterious than they appear, which
exert active or passive, positive or negative pressure on us and
which we must consider willy-nilly, knowingly or unknowingly.
The pressure of vigencias is exerted along certain lines that
are structural rather than amorphous; but from another viewpoint,
what we call structure consists mainly of the disposition, content,
intensity, and dynamism of vigencias. As always, we find it impossible to explain ingredients apart from structure, and structure, without ingredients. From this it becomes apparent that
the habitual notions—matter and form, individual and species,
elements and movement, etc.—deriving from thought about things
are hardly applicable to human realities. At best they can be
"translated" analogously and with exceptions. If we understand
individuals as "things" in a "space," or society as a great thing
"composed" of elements, we shall never understand what collective
life is, and thus it will be idle to attempt to delve into a
social strucutre at all. We need to bring into play all that we
have learned up to this point in order to shed light on the nature
of vigencias and therefore on the makeup of our social surroundings.

17. The Boundaries of Vigencias

Vigencias exert themselves on individuals; but while the
latter must take them into account, vigencias are never of an individual nature. The pressure they exert is not the direct result
of an individual action, but rather arises from the society, or
in any case through it. I mean that a strictly individual imposition never has the force of a vigencia, as, for example, the arbitrary decision of a despot, unless a social vigencia exists in
the form of a belief that the caprices of the despot have the
force of law, that is, unless a peculiar "sanction" is bestowed
by the society on mere force, converting it into a real vigencia.

This is very important in trying to understand power structures and leadership.

Vigencias arise, then, within a given area and presuppose a social ambit within which they are dominant. This "within" is essential to any vigencia, and correlatively, so is the "without," i.e., the area lying beyond their influence. Thus a vigencia has certain boundaries which, in turn, have much to do with the composition of the vigencia itself. When Pascal wrote Vérité en deça des Pyrénées, erreur au-delà (Truth on this side of the Pyrenees, error on the other), he formulated an exact condition of vigencias. The same could be said of time. In the juridical sense, which is the normal use of the word, a law is "in vigor" in a certain territory, beginning at a certain moment and continuing until it is abolished, repealed, or ignored.

However, the essential difference is that social vigencias are not promulgated or repealed, and for this reason it would be wrong to infer from the limited character of vigencias that they are "conventional" in nature. Vigencias are not conventions, because they are not something agreed upon, nor are they based on a decision of individuals. We have just seen that even in cases where the content of vigencias arises from an individual decision, in order for it to assume the status of a vigencia another force, which is rigorously collective and impersonal, must act in support of the individual will in question. When Classical man noticed the limitation of many things, for example, their restriction to certain times or places, he interpreted them as conventions (such is the history of cynicism and to a large extent of all Hellenistic thought). But this notion was due to the almost total blindness of the ancients to the social. Their interpretation of society as pólis, as a "political" community, caused them to understand everything that was not natural in terms of nomos, convention or law. In other words, they extended to social realities traits that were properly political. With an astuteness that is seldom recognized, Aristotle realized the nature of the social, to the point that he was not far from creating an authentic sociology. Yet the dominant vigencias of his time prevented him from taking full advantage of his intuition, and in the end he posed the problem in terms of a politics, without developing his deepest and most penetrating ideas.[1]

Vigencias are not things agreed upon; they do not emanate from individual life as such. But neither are they natural. They are specifically social, which means that they are historical. But the most important thing is that the limitation of vigencias is not only negative, in the sense that "beyond" such limits they are not valid, but also that vigencias as such are constituted by that limitation when it is taken positively. Vigencias "prevail" within a certain enclosed area, and these pressures are exerted "from" the limits by a social mass determined by them. This means that the limits act on the individual subjected to a vigencia, and insofar as he is aware of it, he is also dimly aware of its limits. If one asks who exerts social pressures, who gives vigencias their power, the question can be understood in two ways: if an individual is meant, the question is meaning- less, and one would have to answer that nobody does, that is, nobody specific and personal; but if the question is in reference to the subject of vigencias, then it is perfectly legitimate and demands a precise answer. A man does not feel the pressure that comes from his family in the same way as that exerted by a wide social circle. He may accept a family decree that "alcohol is not drunk in this house," but such a prohibition would be an intolerable insult if imposed from without. A woman does not feel as obligated by a style that began last autumn as she does by the age-old social stipulation that she must wait for the male to take the initiative in love. If she shortens her skirt out of season or wears her hair en chignon while others of her social circle wear it short, she will have to face the reprisals of a "society" of minimal temporal density; whereas if she decides to declare herself to the man with whom she has fallen in love, she must overcome the pressure of hundreds of superimposed generations.

It is not only a question of more or less pressure. How pressure is exerted, that is, the quality of the vigencia, depends in large part on its limits. The pressure of a vigencia may be "slow" and the reprisal for its violation long in coming, while the response to an infraction of a recently constituted vigencia is fulminating, such as, for example, that which forbids giving a political greeting or using a certain linguistic expression that has fallen into disrepute because of being considered vulgar or trite. Yet it is quite possible that in the long run the older, slower vigencia cannot be disobeyed, while the newer one concern- ing salutations and ways of talking may be reversed a few years later and replaced by its opposite: what is at first an impera- tive will shortly be prohibited, and vice versa.

In the same way, these limits act on what we could call the "point of application" of the vigencia (mechanical images are un- avoidable in dealing with forces and pressures, though of course they must be taken only as images). Depending on their origin, vi- gencias affect one dimension or another of individual life and one or perhaps all social groups. This means that we cannot under- stand the phenomenon of the vigencia unless we acknowledge its several species and see the connections that link them to each other and to the social structure. In summary, it is a matter of ascertaining whether the vigencias in question form a single aggregate, sum, or repertory, or whether one may speak formally of a system of vigencias as the component of a given society and as the necessary condition for a social structure.

18. General Vigencias and the Boundaries of a Society

By general vigencia I mean that which extends throughout an

entire society and which is binding on all the individuals who
compose that society. But since we saw earlier that a society
is not primarily a grouping of men or a certain territory but is
defined by certain common vigencias, we seem in danger of being
caught in a circle: shall we define the generality of vigencias
by society, and the social unit by the predominance of vigencias?
This difficulty does not appear easily avoidable. On the other
hand, if we select a vigencia, must we then consider as a single
society the entire area wherein it prevails? For example, shall
we define as a society those areas of humanity in which the male
takes the initiative in love or those in which monogamy is the
rule?

This consideration is enough to show that a society cannot
be defined by a single vigencia. If that vigencia is general,
it must encompass the whole society, but this does not exclude
the possibility that it extends to different societies as well.
Thus, several vigencias are necessary in order for the area of
a social unit to be delineated. The question is: how many?
Naturally, this question cannot be answered. The important
thing is not their number--aside from the fact that numerically
isolating vigencias is an operation that may be procedurally
necessary but that involves a considerable amount of abstraction
and schematization of reality--but the function and importance
of vigencias. A society is defined by the collective application
of certain basic vigencias, which means that in general they determine conduct. But the term "conduct" is in turn quite vague:
it can mean having a monogamous family or several lovers, earning
money by working or by robbing, dressing in a certain way or going
about nude, working in science or metaphysics, writing poems,
having friends, conspiring, . . . Nevertheless, the conduct in
question here is of a very specific kind: we are interested in
those aspects of conduct that affect collective life. In this
regard, vigencias must be commonly applicable within the society,
else there is no society and living together is difficult or altogether impossible.

But two other things must be noted. One of them, the simpler,
is that it does not matter that vigencias may be violated (as long
as such violations are not too frequent) so long as they remain
viable. The thief who flouts the rule that property is to be
respected confirms it by his very act, specifically by the type
of conduct (illegal, furtive, exceptional, etc.) that marks his
act. The man or woman who is unfaithful to his or her mate implicitly posits the vigencia of fidelity to the degree that he
or she is unfaithful, and insofar as they behave as such. Fidelity, of course, is the sine qua non of unfaithfulness. Specific
conditions affecting the collectivity and requiring a series of
common vigencias are not the same in every case. For example, in
the Spain of the Hapsburgs the Catholic religion was mandatory,
because coexistence with the heretic was out of the question.
By way of contrast, in the United States of today religious

51

diversity is no obstacle to living together. On the contrary, the accepted view is that one may belong to this or that religion, whereas the intransigent person, by attempting to establish a single religion, would violate a basic vigencia and place the normal process of living together in jeopardy. In other words, what we call "living with" (convivencia) always occurs in a specific way; people live together in such a way that the "with" affects various dimensions of living. This proves that vigencias cannot be taken as something inert. Like everything human, vigencias depend on a project or aim, on an outline of life that one aspires to realize. Let us not forget that being in force (vigente) means being alive, or better, "very alive," and full of vigor. At first glance I seem to encounter vigencias passively within my world, much as I might come upon a mountain range. But if I ask why they are in vigor, I can find the answer only in their origin as a part of a certain aspiration of collective life. But this is not all; their present force, the fact that they are still in force, is based on the continuation of that project, or the existence of another that coincides with that previous aspiration in this dimension.

Thus, the first attempt to find the precise meaning of the term "general vigencia" invalidates the hypothesis that vigencias appear as a simple repertory. Their real nature demands a series of "enlivening" relationships (constituting the most rigorous and profound kind of "grounding," for the rooting of things occurs in a way that is not merely logical but real) that emanate from the concrete structure, coherent in terms of life, which often implies logical incoherence, as, for example, from the viewpoint of the "irrationality" of usages.[2] A skein of basic coinciding vigencias thus constitutes a society. The area in which some of these apply extends beyond these boundaries, and at times not one but several (though not enough to form a compatible social unit) spill over the society in question and are in force outside its limits. This means that social boundaries are not rigid and strictly linear, but rather reveal a certain flexibility that is especially important in allowing other societies of a more abstract and tenuous nature to be superimposed on the society sensu stricto.

If we take what is unmistakably a society—for example, a European nation—we see how it contains a commonwealth of basic vigencias. But we also notice that many of the latter are not exclusively Spanish, French, or German, but common to several if not all the nations of Europe, perhaps as well to several or all American countries, with some probably pertaining to certain groups and others affecting different groups of diverse configurations. This shows that in addition to the national societies, there are others of a broader and less compact nature whose boundaries can be recognized and drawn by studying the area in which the vigencias are in force. If we imagine a map and draw a different line on it to represent each vigencia, the superimposition of the latter will cause each portion of territory to be more or less

52

densely marked. In this way we would obtain a plastic and intuitive image of what we could call the "density" or "consistency" of the diverse societies. A social cartography--sit venia verbo--is perfectly possible, although the difficulties this would involve are all too obvious. Yet difficulty has never been an objection of science, and I fail to see why it should be so in human sciences, those sciences that some seem to demand should be easy.

Thus, the decision as to whether or not certain human groupings belong to the same society can be made only by an application in depth of the idea of vigencias and by a rigorous evaluation of their status in each particular case. (In passing, consider whether international relations and the theoretical disciplines that attempt to facilitate them could benefit from this point of view, and then bear in mind how far they are today from posing the problems in these terms.) But now a different question arises: along with those vigencias that spill over from an evident society into other more "tenuous" ones, there are others that do not apply to an entire society, but only to a fraction thereof. Are these also vigencias? And if they are, what are their traits? And thirdly, how are they articulated with each other and with the so-called general vigencias?

19. The Concept of Partial Vigencias

The simplest case of partial vigencias is that of societies that I have called "insertive," for example, regional societies. Without a doubt, there are particular Andalusian, Catalonian, and Navarrese vigencias that do not extend over the entire Spanish society. One might think that their relationship to the national vigencias is similar to that of Spanish, German, or Italian vigencias to the European. But this is not quite true for two reasons: the regional societies are felt to be insufficient, and besides, they are lived as though they were "open." By these statements I mean the following: that the man of any region whatever knows from the first that the majority of vigencias that exert pressure on him are not exclusive to his region and that they do not originate within it (unlike the member of a nation, who takes all its vigencias to be national and then discovers almost always with surprise, if indeed he discovers it at all, that such vigencias extend beyond the national boundary); and in the second place, that not only is it normal and not at all exceptional for men of other regions to be in his own, and who, therefore, are not subject to the same vigencias as he, but that in addition he himself must often come in contact with other regions. Our language distinguishes quite well between a "stranger"--one who is alien to the local society--and a "foreigner"--one who is alien to the entire society.[3]

There is one unmistakable criterion by which the belief

53

regarding whether an individual belongs to one's society may
be tested: the irritation or indignation provoked by an infraction on his part of the prevailing usages of our social unit.
If a neighbor of ours appears wearing earrings, it arouses keen
indignation and brings on immediate social reprisals. Yet we
view with perfect aplomb the same rings in the ears of a Papuan.
Furthermore, if we are told that this same Papuan eats human
flesh (something much more serious certainly than the inoffensive
wearing of earrings), this might seem atrocious, but it would not
"irritate" us or arouse our "indignation." We might find the
practice horrible or repugnant, but these are quite different
feelings. Until a few years ago it irritated many people in
Spain to see a woman smoking. The phenomenon still persists in
certain circles, and I shall have more to say about it later.
Yet that irritation automatically vanished if they realized the
woman was foreign. Then she was excluded from the prohibitive
vigencia and for the same reason her conduct became acceptable.
The growing irritation aroused in many countries by the usages
of foreigners, just at the time when they are much more familiar
due to the constant presence everywhere of peoples of different
nationalities, only proves that these usages are now felt to be
much less "foreign," more a part of a common society, and hence
subject to a system of corresponding vigencias. This was already
true among Europeans some years ago; now it has been extended to
Americans also, for they have been "adopted," and far from thinking that what they do is "their business," Europeans are beginning
to feel that they are members of the same society. This irritation
(which is itself at times so annoying) includes, among other things
of quite diverse origins, the real affirmation of the West as a
social unit.

Yet as I said earlier, the case of the "territorial" partial-
ity of a vigencia is the simplest. Things are much less clear
when we deal with vigencias the fragmentary nature of which with
regard to the total society is nongeographic. Such fragmentary
or partial vigencias correspond to different ways of organizing
the ingredients that form a society, and they have a conditioning
effect on the most delicate part of its structure, on its specific
form of articulation. Here we reach an area of delicate shades
of meaning which obliges us to move with extreme care and to make
inevitable distinctions among them.

The first of these, apparently rather subtle, is basic:
there are two ways of taking a vigencia into account: in a plenary way, which consists of being subject to it, and a secondary
but highly important manner, which is to be acquainted with it,
to be aware of it and hence to know that other members of society
must also heed it. An example will illustrate. Vigencias that
are specifically masculine or feminine in content are of course
binding only on men or women, as the case may be, and the other
sex is, respectively, exempt from their pressure. But most of
these "restricted" vigencias are matters of public knowledge.

Social Vigencias

This means that men know that women are subject to them, and
thus the pressure they exert on the distaff side of society has
at its disposal the "force" of both sides, although not in the
same way nor to the same degree, unlike the case of a generic
vigencia applicable without regard to sex. In contrast, let us
consider a vigencia that is not only restricted but also acknowledged by only one sex. Its pressure arises only from the sex it
affects; its sphere of application or predominance corresponds
to the "within" wherein its pressure originates. For instance,
there are certain vigencias that regulate speech, determining
topics that "can be discussed," expressions, vocabulary, and
even intonation and expressive gestures. Aside from the general
usages of a linguistic area, the way men and women talk is regulated by peculiar usages: the woman may resort to a stock of
diminutives not permitted the man, her repertory of adjectives
is not exactly the same, she may not always use the same images
or expressions, etc.[4] But the differences do not stop with these
exclusive vigencias that are known to all and that concern the
masculine or feminine use of the common language. There is also
"man-talk," or "woman-talk," in which quite different usages prevail that are known only to the sex in question. This is an
especially pure example for the very reason that it formally excludes the intervention of the opposite sex. Men do not know
what women alone talk about, for if a man is present, they do
not talk that way; and insight into the way the other sex talks
can be gained only by exceptional means: "treachery" on the
part of a member who tells (directly or indirectly, let us add
in passing), infiltration or spying, etc. In our society all
this is quite limited, but in others it has been or is a powerful
and highly important phenomenon.[5]

Viewed in detail things become still more complicated. Let
us consider any given social segment, a social class such as the
aristocracy, or a professional group, say the clergy or the military, restricting ourselves to well-defined groups. The vigencias
that are exclusive and peculiar to these segments can be divided
into two kinds: the first, strictly internal, are those exerted
on each individual within his group; a trivial but especially
clear example would be the military salute, which is obligatory
for all army members as such as well as for certain members with
respect to others. But since it is normal for each group or segment to coexist with the rest of society and to interact with
other elements that make up society, there are other kinds of
particular vigencias which we could call external or relational
that affect the members of a group insofar as it affirms itself
as such among all the other groupings; for example, the usages
that regulate the behavior of priests with women, the impression
the military man is expected to make on civilians, the types of
behavior proper to an aristocrat when he is not in "high society,"
le grand monde, but simply in the ordinary "world," that is, in
general society. Few things are more important than such behavior.

On the health of such relationships, that is, on the appropriate-
ness and vigor of the corresponding vigencias, depend in large
part the smooth functioning, the ability to live together harmo-
niously, and the equilibrium of a country. The disruption of the
"internal" vigencias of a group demoralizes or degrades it, causes
it to lose personality, disarticulates it, and thus deprives society of its specific function. Such is the case when aristocracies
relinquish their role. On the other side of the coin, when such
"internal" vigencias are automatically extended over the whole
society instead of being replaced by "relational" ones, the structure of society is broken, either causing some groups to infringe
on the territory of others and to impose patterns and styles on
the latter that are not proper to them, or else withdrawing and
isolating themselves in their aloofness. Nearly all social "-isms"
--militarism, clericalism, laborism, plebeianism, functionalism,
etc.--are consequences of this spillover of "internal" vigencias
into collective life sensu stricto; and the responses--the corresponding "anti-isms"--usually consist of negating not the unwar-
ranted spillover but the internal vigencias themselves and thus
the legitimate peculiarity of each group.

When studied from this angle, European social dissensions
are quite revealing, especially those since the eighteenth century,
when the ancient system of vigencias developed over centuries of
friction and struggle was disrupted. A period of particular
interest to us, the transition from the ancien régime to our time,
was the crisis of this readjustment which required the creation
of new forms and new relationships. In Spain there was a constant
imbalance in both areas and consequently a lack of social articulation that is quite visible even today.

Finally, the most serious matter is that partial vigencias
are not only fragmentary, belonging to certain areas of society,
but also exhibit frequently, though not necessarily, a polemic
tendency. Certain groups assert themselves not only with other
groups but also in confrontation with them. And most important,
an individual who belongs to one group may also belong to a different one--an aristocrat may be a military man or financier, a
priest may be an intellectual--and of course he forms a part, and
radically so, of the entire society. How then are these diverse
dimensions of collective life articulated?

20. The Diverse Dimensions of Society and
     the Clash of Vigencias

We would find the most extreme case of a partial vigencia
in a caste society. Each caste is subject to certain vigencias
that are not only proper to it but also exclusive. By this I
mean that not only do they not apply to other castes, but that
they are forbidden to them. Each caste must conform to a certain
pattern of conduct that is forbidden to the others. The vigencia

has then two aspects: it is at once affirmative and negative, imperative and prohibitive; it defines a social boundary both inwardly and outwardly. In such cases, there is no clash between vigencias. Perhaps groups have their differences, but each remains fixed within its vigencias. This situation lasts until in other types of societies the articulation of estates or classes is quite pronounced and each of them can relax within itself: patricians and plebeians, nobles and villeins, perhaps even still with the usías and majos.[6] In a different way it leads to a point where relationships between men and women are clear so that there is no question about which are generic human vigencias and which are particularly masculine or feminine. But one must not think that this distinction between social segments necessarily implies separation. They may live together, but each individual remains automatically and unmistakably attached to his particular system of vigencias.

This situation begins to change when each individual belongs to several social segments or when the lines between them are no longer clearly drawn. The latter has been happening with social classes for a century and a half, and one might add that this has occurred not by chance but because of intrinsic factors. The phenomenon is so important that it will need special treatment later. Let us take some less extensive examples that are clearer because of their simplicity. We shall consider the military, the clergy, and women in order to see how the general scheme of vigencias may be altered in their respective cases.

Being a member of the military can mean a "condition" or only a "profession." If the first alternative is the case, the military then constitutes a certain social group defined by a system of vigencias that is sufficiently "dense" to set it clearly apart from civilians or clergy. Belonging to the military group therefore involves almost all dimensions of the person's life, since even those areas not directly linked to it are affected and colored by the miliary status. Bear in mind that for centuries a military career was almost absolutely predetermined by a social situation (for example, nobility of blood, at times second-son status, and later as a passing phase, family tradition) and was not a simple private decision by an individual. Arms represented, therefore, a partial and limited world with very clear functions and with a repertory of rights and obligations, prescribed and authorized modes of conduct, in short, with the vigencias that constituted it. On the other hand, if the military is nothing more than a "profession" which any individual may choose (the underscored words are essential), then it has no primary qualifying effect on him. The individual is first defined by a whole series of dimensions—country, sex, age, social level, etc.—together with which and with their corresponding vigencias are found the more tenuous professional influences. A man belongs to the military in the same way that he might choose to be an engineer, professor, mechanic, mason, lawyer, doctor, or merchant.

Such is the case in the Anglo-Saxon countries where, for this
very reason, the military career can be very easily abandoned,
as for example, when a war ends, in order to return to civilian
life and take up another profession considered more interesting,
adequate, or remunerative in peacetime. And the strictly professional military man is aware of his complete and absorbing dedica-
tion to a profession that is but one among many others, such as
the businessman, the full-time professor or researcher. In this
case, belonging to the military has a minimal effect on the repertory of vigencias, for they are generic and hence civilian, and
those proper to each profession, including the military, are
added in only a marginal way to them. Things are more complicated when the situation is neither of the two described above.
In the first case, the military man, in principle at least, does
only certain things in keeping with his role and is subject to
its statutes. In the second case, he does more or less the same
as everyone else and has no exceptional or disparate role to play.
But it may happen that in the absence of sufficient activities,
interests, and forms of conduct of a specifically military nature,
he emerges from his world and begins to act in society at large.
But unlike the second case, he does not act as a civilian, as a
member of that general society, but as a military man, we might
say, outside the armed forces but without shedding his uniform.
Let us imagine a military man who writes; he may write militarily
of military topics in keeping with his knowledge and experience;
or he may momentarily set aside his military status and relax or
amuse himself in literary activity. (Ocios de un soldado [Soldier's
Leisure] is an old title whose author I cannot recall.) It is
also possible for the professional military man to have a side
profession, that of a writer, which he pursues like any other
writer, subject to the vigencias imposed by the activity itself
and to those of the literary craft in general. Everything is
clear enough up to this point; but whenever the military man attempts to write from the military standpoint not about military
matters but about scientific, political, philosophical, and literary topics, basing himself on the military and projecting it and
its vigencias over his new activity, there is interference between
two different orders of vigencias, and the upshot is confusion at
the very least. The same holds true in politics, social behavior,
and so forth. In Spain of the Romantic period not one word can be
understood unless one pays heed to such phenomena, which require
an examination of their specific historical content.

Going on to the vigencias of the ecclesiastical group, we
discover matters to be even more acute. This can be indicated
simply by pointing out some differences in comparison to the
previous case. The priesthood cannot be simply a profession;
it is an inalienable condition (I refer of course to the Christian
priesthood, the only one of interest in the societies under study)
but one freely chosen by any individual, that is, one belonging
to any social stratum. (The dual fact that in certain periods

58

the clergy is preferentially recruited from some particular class
and that the decision comes, at least initially, from the family
due to the extreme youthfulness, or better, childhood of many
seminarians, gives a decisive coloring to the sociological function of the clergy and its participation in collective life.)
In the second place, from the social point of view there is an
essential difference between those clerics who in principle constitute a separate group, often defined by a literal "cloistering,"
that is, a "closed world," and the secular clergy, i.e., those
who are out in the world. In the latter case, which is the one
that interests us here (if the first group is included it is precisely to the degree that its members abandon it and are assimilated in the world), the peculiarity of the ecclesiastical status
only rarely ends in the formation of an ecclesiastical "group";
rather, it involves the special way in which the priest lives in
a lay society. Indeed, pastors do not form groups together, or
if they do, their meetings are occasional and due to exceptional
causes. According to a Spanish saying, reunión de rabadanes,
oveja muerta (A gathering of shepherds, a dead sheep). Instead,
each pastor with his flock forms a group, and he assumes a very
precise function with them that, naturally, is pastoral. In
this normal form of priesthood the "internal" vigencias are essentially linked to the "relational" ones, since the latter make up
and regulate the priestly function or ministry. By this I mean
that the diversity of vigencias does not imply a clash between
them; on the contrary, this diversity conditions and defines the
relationship of the priest with the faithful. The difficulty
arises when the priest assumes functions of any other kind analogous to those of laymen—for example, intellectual, educational,
political, economic, artistic, literary, social, or those connected
with labor—and assumes them not as marginal occupations apart from
his position but as part of it. For instance, the case of the
French prêtres-ouvriers (worker priests) has attracted attention
only because it was an unusual phenomenon. Linking the priestly
status to the exercise of other duties or ministries is not surprising because it is common, but it poses the same problem: the
mutual interference of two different areas of vigencias. Consider
this very revealing detail: the intellectual "market value" of
ecclesiastics within a society and the difficulties involved
therewith, the constant fluctuation between what we might call
the "open market"—sit venia verbo—or particular markets. Notice
that the latter have been the more common and have a multisecular
tradition, so much so in fact that after intellectual life had
been clerical, or mester de clerecía,[7] "humane letters" or "humanities" arose marginally as the particular market of lay writers
and thinkers. When the secularization of European culture changed
intellectual activity into a largely secular interest governed by
"civil" vigencias, the domain of "ecclesiastical sciences" remained
as an autonomous area and private market. The serious point, which
poses a problem of vigencias—and therefore of collective life—is

found in what we could call a transference of market values: instead of one value in the open market, or a private quotation in the restricted market, a value is determined in the latter and its result transferred to or projected for the total market of an entire society. (The fact that similar phenomena are produced today in economic life, from which this comparison is taken, reveals particularly well a social situation of which the intellectual and economic factors are only aspects.)

Finally, let us consider the system of vigencias that affect the female portion of a society. Normally, women are subject to three groups of vigencias: the general or "human" ones that prevail in the society; the "internal," or those proper to the regulation of feminine life; and the "relational," those which determine relationships with men. In most social situations there is not the slightest misunderstanding concerning these categories, whereas in others there are certain alterations (in general involving transitions from one situation to another) that produce a clash of vigencias. In fact, a displacement of the boundary between "human" and "feminine" vigencias may occur. In Chapter I of my Introducción a la Filosofía (English title: Reason and Life) I insisted on the central fact that marks the new status of women in Europe: the vigencia that holds that women may not do more than that about which there is social agreement is being replaced by the heretofore "masculine" vigencia according to which one may do anything not expressly vetoed by society. In other words, whereas before woman was restricted in her actions to certain things which she was "authorized" to do, soon she will be able to do anything, provided it is not specifically prohibited. But this situation, which is surely coming, is still not here, at least not in many societies, and what is occurring in them is the broadening of the jurisdiction of "human" vigencias to include many more possibilities for women. And this, in turn, does not happen simultaneously nor to the same degree in all segments of a society. To cite a small but significant example, for centuries the vigencia has been that smoking is an exlusively male prerogative (a fact, let us note in passing, that is highly curious). In this century this custom has been "neutralized," and a woman may smoke without invoking social reprisals. But since this has not come about suddenly and universally, when it was already acceptable in the large cities and upper classes, it was still prohibited in smaller cities and in other segments of society. And a woman who smokes a cigarette naturally in her customary surroundings encounters the opposing vigencia when she is in the presence of other parts of society, in a provincial city or in the country. This is a minimum example of the way vigencias clash between diverse social nuclei. Job possibilities, social intercourse, traveling, the capacity for taking the initiative (especially the latter) are other areas in which the same situation is manifested.

It goes without saying that in a clash between vigencias,

the deciding factor is the vigor they possess, for this is precisely what decides or settles the conflict. But we must consider another apparently paradoxical aspect of vigencias that
can easily lead to error. I refer to dissension as a social
factor.

21. Dissension as a Social Factor

Within the general phenomenon of dissension it is necessary
to point out several dimensions that are surrounded by so much
confusion that social facts are all but obscured. Ortega has
shown quite effectively and forcefully that men are at once so-
ciable and unsociable, that they are full of antisocial impulses,
that society taken as something purely positive is utopian, and
that in reality the human collectivity is a struggle between
sociality and dissociation.[8] Later I shall have more to say
with greater emphasis on this matter, because it is of the greatest importance and explains one entire portion of any society.
However, for the moment I shall confine myself to pointing it
out as a reminder that society is far from meaning unanimity,
indeed that it is also based on dissent and therefore is always
problematic and uncertain, and that its existence consists of
creating and defending itself.

But dissension admits of other facets that must be considered
in this context. Vigencias exert pressure on individuals in the
sense that the latter must take them into account and take some
stand in regard to them. But this does not mean adherence, or
even acceptance or submission. There are many possible attitudes
regarding vigencias, and one of these is, of course, dissent.
What characterizes vigencias is not that they require submission
but rather that if they are not observed, then one must dissent.
I do not wear a tunic or practice the Koranic ablutions, but no
dissension is involved because neither of these customs prevails
in the society in which I live. But if I decide not to wear
mourning attire, it is not enough for me simply to go on wearing
color when a member of my family has died; instead, my decision
has a certain violent note, for I have to perform a positive act
that implies an effort to overcome an impersonal and collective
resistance. In short, I must dissent. Dissension is, consequently, one of the possible modes of behavior regarding vigencias
and one of the aspects of their social function. Moreover, without dissension it would be hard to realize that vigencias exist.
The latter make themselves felt when the reaction of the individual is not submissive but rebellious, when dissent puts vigencias
to the test and at the same time reveals their vigor.

Going a step further, we find a third aspect of dissent that
is more easily overlooked: it is what I would call the polemic
vigencia of elements not in force. Let me explain. Probably no
one believes the opinions, behavior, and attire of the surrealist

61

groups of Paris, or the existentialists of recent years, to be
binding. On the contrary, their charm lies precisely in the
fact that they are not predominant, that, indeed, they are in
opposition to current vigencias. Is this then a case of simple
dissent? Is it the same thing to be an existentialist in the
Café de Flore as to eschew mourning, to favor German rearmament,
to wear a derby hat, or to favor the works of Dumas over those
of Gide? While in the latter cases it is a question of individual
disagreement with certain dominant vigencias, and as such is socially inconsequential, the existence of dissident groups within
society is in itself a vigencia. In other words, their ideas
are not predominant--whether such groups have a certain way of
painting or of understanding poetry, whether they wear beards
or frown on makeup, whether they believe that everything in
existence is superfluous, etc., none of this prevails in society
at large--but what is socially accepted is the fact that they
affirm their views polemically over against the general system
of prevalent vigencias. This is tantamount to saying that one
of the vigencias holds that they must be challenged, violated,
and denied by means of certain rites and formulas, for instance,
with publicity, novelty, and subjection to a particular style
(a vigencia) and to certain esthetic norms (which are also predominant).

When society is very firm and stable, that is, when the
vigencias are solid and fully vigorous, polemic dissent of this
type not only is tolerated but even required, imposed by that
particular vigencia that seeks its own infraction. In contrast,
weak societies that are dissociated and in discord neither demand
nor accept these dissenting elements. A good barometer for judging the stability of a society is the normality of this kind of
phenomena. The eccentrics of Victorian England, the Hollywood
world in the United States, and similar phenomena that marked
life between the eighteenth and nineteenth centuries are good
examples. When societies lack sufficient health and flexibility--
sufficient vigor in short--two things may happen: when the state
apparatus is strong or at least has the appearance of being so,
the luxury of polemic dissent is suppressed by violence or smoth-
ered; when this is not the case, the phenomena of dissent arise,
but they lack "style"; they are not amusing or tonic because in
the absence of a strong society when vigencias have no real force,
then neither does the sport of disagreeing with them. When one
can do "anything" more or less, one thing is as good as another.
The pliant wall does not bounce the balls back that are stroked
against it, and of course this makes the game impossible.

22. Implicit and Explicit Vigencias

As I stated earlier, dissent makes vigencias apparent.
When there is no dissension, it may be that there is no knowledge

of which particular elements are predominant. This shows that vigencias make their presence felt in two ways: explicitly and implicitly. In the first case, the individual knows that he is subject to a particular vigencia, and this is the most important point: that it is particular, that it exists as a unit numerically different from all the others, that it is formulated or at least can easily be formulated, and that it exerts its force, basing it more or less clearly on some reason. This means that it is less compelling than other vigencias, for when reasons are given, the ascendancy is not absolute. No doubt justification corroborates a vigencia, but it does so externally. Once again it is like the case of the flying buttress that supports itself against an outer abutment. Consider the plenary case of explicit vigencias: existing laws. It is no accident that this is the normal use of the words vigencia and vigente ("prevailing," or more literally, "in vigor"), that is, before Ortega extended their semantic area to its fullest meaning. The vigencia of law is an example of explicit vigencias; a law is passed, presented as such, and "put in force" by a concrete power, and this means that alone a law has no power and that such power as it has must come to it from the outside. What are called "unwritten laws"—the most important laws, as Aristotle knew very well[9]—are not laws at all in the strict sense. In other words, they appear as laws when it is realized that they have power without anyone knowing it and without having been legislated. Common law takes on the appearance of "law" only when it is recognized as such, i.e., when it ceases to function in the customary manner and is "promulgated" in some fashion, when it assumes the nature of an explicit vigencia that formerly it did not have.

The strongest, soundest, and most deeply rooted vigencias do not appear as such; they are neither announced nor stated, and this is why it hardly ever makes sense to "enumerate" them. They are not catalogable except in two cases: first, retrospectively, that is, when they are no longer operable and therefore may be traced, or secondly, from any theoretical attitude that suspends the force of the vigencia and correlatively "exempts" the observer from its effect. It suffices to keep in mind that negative vigencias do not normally consist of formal prohibitions but of an expression that automatically regulates conduct without explicit awareness that this is happening.

The pressure of implicit vigencias, the purest and most important vigencias, those in which the phenomenon of vigencia is free of other influences, is a diffuse pressure, for example, unlike the restriction of law, a religious commandment, or a moral principle as such. Yet the fact that it is diffuse does not mean that it is vague (which it certainly is not), because this pressure is exerted according to certain lines of force that determine a form and outline of conduct. This is the same way in which the pressure of water or air determines the course of a moving body by acting upon it.

This idea becomes even clearer if we keep in mind that in
the implicit vigencias that I have just named it is necessary to
distinguish the imperative force of each example—law, commandment, or precept—of the generic and almost always implicit vigencias that sustain them. These may take several forms, such as
respect for the law, reverence for the divine will, or regard for
moral order. Later we shall see the repercussions this holds for
types of vigencias which, because they have an "ideological" or
"intellectual" content, are more directly affected by the balance
between implicitness and explicitness. I refer to beliefs, which
are so affected by this equilibrium that their dynamics consist
in large part in the degree of explicitness they reveal at any
given moment.

This explains why the investigation of vigencias is so difficult and why so little is known about them. They can be determined
only by observing them in real life, that is, in the real patterns
of conduct. If we analyze the "trajectories" of these patterns,
they allow us to see the active forces that have created them.
Such an analysis is by no means an easy matter, and it should
come as no surprise that the results will be misleading unless
it is carried out with a rigorous and adequate method. Fortunately,
there are simpler cases than the investigation of current vigencias.
Systems of vigencias have acted in the past; generally they did so
implicitly, but when viewed from the present they appear explicitly.
What accounts for the difference? The answer lies in the fact that
they originated and ceased. In comparing different situations, I
find that at a certain date a new force begins to act on men that
earlier had no power and that was not apparent to the men affected,
though it is evident to the observer who views two situations
characterized respectively by the absence and presence of that
force. Analogously, when a vigencia weakens (loses its vigor)
and is finally extinguished, the situation is altered and the subsequent modification reveals that it has ceased to act. Once again
we discover, this time by a different route, that it is impossible
to study a single situation, for its operative elements are revealed
only in the transition from one situation to another; and of course
because of the interlocking nature of their elements, the two situations between which the transition occurs are themselves transitory.

With this observation we have broached a new aspect of vigencias. Up to now we have considered them as certain realities or
forces defined by quality or content, area, intensity, direction,
and positive or negative sense. But this way of looking at them
is still abstract. These forces have a specific point of applica-
bility: the individuals affected by them. Only insofar as it exerts itself on real individuals is a vigencia concrete and specific.
And the way men react to them is also a part of the reality of vigencias; their functioning consists of their action complemented
by the personal reaction they arouse. The explicitness or implicitness of vigencias is an aspect that refers not to their intrinsic
vigor but to the manner in which they act and primarily to whether

they appear to the individual or remain concealed. But this is
only the first step toward their concrete nature; the implicit-
explicit alternative is too schematic. To begin with, there are
many degrees of implicitness. Is complete implicitness therefore possible? And if it is not or at least not necessary,
where is the dividing line between partial implicitness and unmistakable explicitness? But secondly and much more important,
to say something is explicit is still saying very little. How
is it explicit? In other words, what are the possible and real
relationships of the individual to vigencias in each historical
situation?

23. The Relationship of the Individual to Vigencias

The highest form of implicitness within vigencias is unawareness of them; and unawareness is possible only insofar as
the vigencias to which the individual is subject are "unique"
in the sense that they appear as automatic demands and not as a
particular kind of pressure among other possible forms. This
is why it is possible to be unaware of vigencias--at least for
the most part--only in an isolated society. The individual immersed in a social body that seems to him to be simply "society"
tends to consider its pressures to be reality itself and thus not
to notice them, as we are not usually aware of the air around us
unless it is turbulent. As soon as men realize that other men
are subject to different vigencias, their own take on a precise
outline and are experienced as such. The immediate consequence
is that the individual must take a stand regarding them, he must
behave in a certain way, no longer in response to their pressure--
with submissiveness or rebelliousness--but with respect to the
very idea of vigencias, to the mental profile they present. In
other words, to the strictly social reaction to the force of vigencias is now added a reaction of a mental sort that consists
of having an opinion about them.
But we cannot proceed too cautiously. The existence of the
element of opinion should not induce us to think that vigencias
are opinions. I am not referring to the fact that opinions are
expressed about the contents of vigencias (for when this happens
we are no longer dealing with vigencias at all), nor do I mean
that they derive their force from that opinion; rather, I mean
that given the social phenomenon that we have studied at some
length, then the individual is in a certain state of opinion regarding his vigencias; that is, insofar as they are his, he feels
linked in one way or another to their totality and to each of
them separately. This implies a certain way of feeling himself
inserted in a society and for that reason it affects his sense
of belonging.
The normal situation is one of "adherence," i.e., adherence
to the whole repertory of vigencias. It reveals the collective

personality and properties (in this sense we say: this is the way "we" are; these are "our" customs, values, preferences, etc.). Such adherence does not preclude dissent, which to be exact, is nourished by generic conformity. In the name of the sum total of our vigencias, we may disagree with a particular one that seems improper or false, perhaps a degenerate form or an unworkable innovation. When the social group asserts itself in the presence of others in a more or less polemic way, this adherence often becomes a source of pride. This is true whether we are dealing with the generic society, for example, the whole country, or with a social class or segment of any kind. In such cases, presumed superiority is stressed more than uniqueness. But it should be noted that this superiority is not, as a general rule, concrete and if you will, a posteriori, but rather a priori and generic. Such vigencias are better because they are "ours," and this reason takes precedence over any consideration of their content. So true is this that often there are men who declare that things in their country are the best in the world, that their nation is admirable and incomparable, yet when it comes to the actual details that make up national life, these same individuals frequently reject everything. We all know people who lapse into hyperbole in praising Spain, but who reserve the right to pulverize implacably each of the Spanish values on which their proud assertions could be founded. Whenever this happens a note of uncertainty invades this unilateral loyalty, rendering it wary and insincere. It then becomes excessively emphatic and aggressive and feeds for the most part on denying the merits of others.

Satisfaction, or better, self-satisfaction, is another kind of relationship altogether. Individual enjoyment of the vigencias that make up one's fragmentary or total society, one's feeling of being "at home" within it, like a fish in water, even vain pleasure, are phenomena that affect normal social adherence in a quite different way. Such, for example, has been the reaction of the Andalusian to his repertory of regional vigencias, as it was of the Madrileño during nearly all the nineteenth century—probably from the middle of the eighteenth century until the first decade of the twentieth, reaching its zenith during the Restoration—and of the Frenchman for a very long time, at least since Louis XIV, until a few decades ago. It would be profitable to follow the changes in this attitude with some care and observe the variation in the different social classes and in the more flexible particular groups.

All the foregoing are positive relationships, but they are far from being the only ones. One of the most interesting relations is that in which the individual feels "bound" or confined by vigencias; it is a relationship in which the latter function as a limitation. This attitude may exist along with a greater or lesser degree of adherence to one's vigencias. Indeed, at times the adherence may be deep, though more often it is residual, but its dominant feature is the awareness that the vigencias act

66

as a brake, a hindrance, or a restrictive force. Social pressure
takes two directions: pressure "against," and pressure "toward";
it is a barrier or an impulse. The regulation of individual conduct by vigencias includes both dimensions in a healthy society,
with an emphasis of course on the second. Pressure is always
more a spur than a rein, because the object is to move, and the
main purpose of the rein is to guide the movement. However, on
occasion vigencias act more as inhibitions and shackles, and to
the men subject to them they lie in the background without any
relationship to the future, appearing as holdovers from the past.
The feeling of alienation intensifies, often taking the form of
resigned conformity. The vigencia seems to be an inevitable
destiny that one must accept. At other times vigencias are re-
pudiated with varying degrees of intensity and determination.
When this happens, the vigencias continue to make their sanctions
felt, but they do so with a strong negative flavor. This attitude
generally arises in regard to specific and isolated vigencias,
and at the most to certain clusters located within the total horizon of collective life. Whenever the repudiation is generalized
and, above all, lasting, when vigencias give the appearance of
dragging along without losing their power (at least not to any
major degree) but to the inner discontent of individuals who
firmly reject them, then their relationship becomes one of shame.
This is an extreme situation that is quite revealing of the way
vigencias act in human life. For this sense of shame comes from
the feeling the individual has of being involved in such vigencias,
implicated in them, complicated by them, if you like; they are a
part of him, of his life, to be sure; they are his and he could
not entirely do without them, could not totally free himself from
them, for his world and his being, insofar as they are social
realities, are formed by them. In the face of a purely alien
restriction of some sort, the individual may feel hostility, aversion, or disapproval; shame arises only when something that is
in some way his causes it.

And because things are always complex and intricate, the
relationship of individuals to vigencias is almost never unilateral. Usually within a society there is a variety of attitudes
according to the groups and levels of vigencias in question. On
the one hand, it is absolutely necessary to isolate and classify
these diverse attitudes; and on the other, we must determine which
is the predominant vigencia, the one that lends its emotional tone
to each social body and determines the manner of belonging to a
society.

24. Grades and Phases of Vigencias

Taking an overall view of vigencias from the standpoint of
an individual life, we notice first that the pressure exerted
on one is not homogeneous. In their negative aspect (what I have

called pressure "against" as well as in the positive pressure "to-ward") vigencias betray differences of degree or intensity. This intensity has very little to do with the importance of their con-tents. Men who have no excessive scruples in committing an act of marital infidelity or in appropriating another's goods would not for their life go out in the street with a bow in their hair or in a yellow suit, use poor spelling in writing, or go to a party in sandals. A few decades ago such a man would not have gone on the street without a hat except in the case of fire or something similar. A woman would not wear a long skirt in the morning. In many cases she would rather tell a lie than utter a vulgar word, or prefer slander to being left off the guest list.

This shows clearly the nature of vigencias as such. When an individual expresses opinions or judgments, he assigns impor-tance to them in keeping with principles of another kind. When it is a question of the primary regulation of conduct that lies in having to come to grips with a system of pressures, the deci-sive factor is the nature of the vigencias. Basic vigencias are so forceful that one hardly thinks of violating them, though for that same reason neither can one imagine complying with them, for they simply exert pressures. At the other extreme lie the tenuous vigencias that are felt only as differences of density in the social environment. In some cases, they represent easier avenues to follow, in others, resistance to one's direction, or as gentle currents that push one along in a certain way in the case of those vigencias whose pressures are toward something. Just as gravity keeps things on the ground and orders the position of objects in the world, fundamental vigencias establish a general disposition of collective life, and diverse forces act on this foundation, creating a whole system of force fields.

These force fields of course have their own structure that is primarily dual. In the first place, there is a structure cor-responding to the generations; as we have seen, each of these has its own peculiar vigencias in addition to those common to all gen-erations coexisting in a society at any given time. Only one other thing need be said of this, but it is important: looking at things from the other side, we cannot say that the vigencias of a society are exclusive to any of the contemporary generations, but rather that only those of fully, i.e., historically, active generations achieve this status during their two phases of "ges-tation" and "activity" (gestión), to use Ortega's terminology. In other words, this occurs between the ages of thirty and sixty. (In the twentieth century one would also have to grant the status of general vigencia to the characteristics of the older generation, those individuals between the ages of sixty and seventy-five.) To take a specific example, it would be necessary to include the three generations whose birth centers around the dates 1886, 1901, and 1916. The vigencias of the generation of 1898 (i.e., of 1871) as well as those of the youngest to come into the world—those born around 1931—either are no longer or not yet predominant

68

in Spain.[10]

Secondly, vigencias are affected not only by generational phases but also from the point of view of age. I mean that in addition to the vigencias belonging to each generation and accompanying it throughout life (it would be correct to say that they constitute each generation), there are others that disappear after a certain age, possibly so as to exert their influence on the next generation. There are youthful vigencias that lose their vigor after youth, and others characteristic of maturity that weaken and give way to different ones as old age approaches. Likewise, just as there are "internal" masculine or feminine vigencias, so there are those within every age group, and analogously, others of a "relational" nature that regulate the behavior of men and women toward one another during each age.

Some of these vigencias (which exert their power according to phases) are ascribed to a phase of one generation—to the youth of generation X, let us say, or better, to its youthful phase—and are thus fleeting, while others possess a schematic nature and are therefore "iterative," that is, they are typical vigencias of youth, or old age, etc., and reappear in each new wave of men of the corresponding age. They are, then, renewable rather than continuous in nature, and in every case they exert their pressure on different human groupings. What we find is not the persistence of these iterative vigencias but a peculiar kind of recurrence in the form of discontinuity.

Yet the phasic quality is not limited to those vigencias that are exclusively phasic. Even in the persistent vigencias that are not ascribable to either a single age or a generation but rather affect an entire society at times over long periods, the form of historical existence is not strictly uniform and homogeneous but rather is modified by successive generations. This happens in two different senses: first, because each vigencia coexists with a repertory of vigencias that are partly variable, it assumes a different role in each case within the overall pattern of life; and second, because its own history affects its content and vigor. I mean that the very duration of a vigencia colors and modifies its meaning. Vigencias, as well as men, have "ages." A young vigencia that has barely begun its influence is not like one already rooted and established, or another that is "immemorial." This brings us to a new matter: the process of vigencias.

25. Origin, Decline, and Replacement of Vigencias

A vigencia is a characteristic affecting certain components that originally belonged to individual life. Ortega has shown quite well that all collective or social realities originate in individual life. But there is no social reality sensu stricto

69

until the purely individual is transcended. This means that for something to exist socially it must affect a considerable number of people. But numbers alone are not enough; mere frequency is not sufficient cause for something to be social. Moreover, in many cases the vigencia precedes frequency and is the cause of it. Because a certain behavior is predominant, the majority of men accordingly adopt it and it becomes frequent. This introduces a qualitative point of view that is essential. In social things, it is not numbers that decide but the function that each man or each action represents in collective life.

Let us consider the relatively simple phenomenon of fashion. First of all, fashion must not be confused with the usage of dressing in a particular way. Fashion is not a simple usage; the principle of the latter is that one wear something in particular; it is not the same as something being in style. Things that really are in style are not used very much, and when they are, they cease to be stylish. This is not, as one might think, the case of a usage restricted to a group, for the reverse is true; the acceptance of the vigencia admits one to the group constituted by it. The vigencia of fashion is intrinsically linked to a very precise desire: to be in style. Without that desire, the pressure exerted by fashion is automatically inoperative. Such is the case of innumerable mature women who are devoted to running their households and for whom fashion simply does not exist. Yet the usages of dress do apply: they wear dresses of a certain length, wear a hat or not according to their social status, dress in mourning, etc.

Fashion originates by virtue of an individual act prior to it that is not yet fashion but innovation. This innovation presupposes the disruption of a usage or at least of a fashion in case this is already a general phenomenon. Thus it has a marked negative, polemic, and dissenting character that presupposes a certain audacity. For this reason, fashion has originated almost exclusively in certain high social circles such as the aristocracy or in fringe groups, for example, the theatrical world, or women of loose conduct. In other words, it has nearly always had its birth with individuals capable of showing initiative who often seek to stand out and attract attention. But this still does not explain fashion itself, not even when we go a step further to individual imitation, a well-known topic on which Simmel insisted in his penetrating study. In order for fashion to exist, a dual condition is also necessary: a sufficient number of people within society must adopt the style in question, and this group must be recognized as the arbiters of elegance, style, good taste, etc. Then and only then does fashion as such originate and achieve predominance over the society, beginning with each and every individual of the social group in which it arose. Then it extends to those who wish "to be in style," that is, who wish to participate at a greater or lesser distance from the creative center. Finally, it extends to the rest of society as

70

something "in style," though without individual acceptance of it. Fashion functions for the entire society, but for many people it does so only as a relational vigencia.

I have chosen this example because it shows with especial clarity the quantitative and qualitative nature of the origin of any vigencia. This becomes even more evident in the case of contemporary fashion, which differs in mechanism considerably from the traditional. In our time, fashions are "imposed" and "launched" by certain professionals. It originates in a medium wherein initiative and innovation are anticipated beforehand. Paradoxically, innovation is taken for granted, and by a certain date. One knows in advance that there will be a fall fashion, that certain styles will be created for people to follow. This means that in such cases the authentic vigencia is that something called "fashion" exists and that it has different and well-defined social organs at its disposal. No longer is it based on individual inspiration, nor a posteriori: on certain prestige, nor on a social group capable of converting a given kind of behavior into a vigencia; but it rests instead on a reciprocal process: professional and planned "creations" and automatic acceptance of the same. Here what I said earlier becomes clear: the vigencia precedes fashion and is the cause of it; for something called fashion appears and is accepted by many people. Its force comes from a factor that is prior both to its content and to the opinion people have of it: the prestige of those who create fashions. But it would be erroneous to presume automatic acceptance in every case. Not every fashion proposed catches on or imposes itself. And the reason is that the underlying vigencia sustaining it may clash with other vigencias, for example, those concerning esthetic criteria, national prejudice, or religious or moral resistance. In such cases, the individual is subject to the opposing pressures of different vigencias, and the resulting direction is problematical. Consider also a secondary but very revealing detail: in order for the vigencia of fashion to be effective, it must preserve a mask of impersonality. Earlier we saw that the "example" of an individual elegant person was not yet the fashion itself. Likewise, the professional who launches a fashion also creates a certain fiction in prophesying, announcing, and guessing what will be fashionable, what will be "in" next season. His authority is more that of the discoverer and predictor than dictator; he does not order but rather knows and foresees what will be in style. When a fashion designer confuses the area of his real prestige with that of "power," he commits an error and the usual result is failure. Fashions that are simply ordered without being previewed, revealed, and announced in advance are usually resisted and at times determinedly rejected. For they represent an attempt to transfer fashion to another arena where it is not predominant. As a historical affirmation of this, think of the failure of all kinds of fashions imposed authoritatively: ordinances against luxury, proposals for a national dress code, prohibition of certain items of clothing or of makeup, etc. And when one of these ordinances does prevail (nearly always for only a short time), it does so as an imposition, never as a fashion. This was true of the uprising against Esquilache as it is with attempts to legislate bathing suits or sleeve lengths.

The only purpose of this example is to draw attention to a certain point in order to understand better the process of vigencias. It is important to be aware of the constant reciprocal relation between individual and collective life and the function of the former in the genesis of any vigencia. But its insufficiency must be also considered, which implies the existence of others, for it can arise only within a society, which is to say within a series of vigencias that are variable and partially successive in relation to one another. All vigencias derive their power from the remaining prevailing vigencias. For this reason, their effectiveness depends on the stability of the general system, not on the degree of "socialization" of a social structure (for that is another matter), but on the degree of sociability.

But this is only the beginning. Once conceived and formed, vigencias exert their pressure with variable intensity for a more or less extended period of time. Finally, they begin to weaken and decline. Why? And how does this phase of the process occur? Notice that individual dissent means very little, and almost nothing if it involves a minority. Yet even when the majority of the people dissent as individuals, the power of the vigencia in question hardly loses any power. Once again, in order to have social effectiveness, things must pass through society. Returning to the previous example, picture an unsatisfactory and bothersome fashion. Until some fifteen years ago, in the summer we Spanish men wore woolen suits only a little cooler than our winter clothes and quite dark in color. Given the temperatures of the country, nothing was more absurd; and of course a coat was absolutely required. The end result could not have been hotter and more uncomfortable. If one had asked each Spaniard individually all would have called the custom deplorable, as they wiped the perspiration from their brows. Yet the practice lasted for years and years with monolithic firmness. What caused it to decline? The reason is so close that we all remember it. The Civil War had abolished not only the fashion in the strict sense but dress codes as well; the majority of Spaniards had worn military apparel, trenchcoats, hunting coats, fur-lined and Saharan jackets, and shirts had either been used together or in succession. In other words, the vigencias having to do with dress had been suspended. As life returned to normal, quite literally few had any civilian clothing. For all practical purposes, the custom of wearing military items persisted. Lighter and brighter-colored fabrics were introduced after the example of summer uniforms. The commercial availability of silk or rayon jackets for men and similar items were enough to bring about a new vigencia: that of "dressing for summer." Thus the Bastille

of severe blue or gray woolen suits was successfully assaulted
and taken. I emphasize these trivial examples because in them
is found the phenomenon of vigencia in its pure form. Respect
for private property, church weddings, the privacy of correspon-
dence, or the obligation to keep an oath, hold similar implications and would require a detailed study of all circumstances
related to them.

Finally, vigencias may "cease" in two ways: by dissolution
or replacement. In the first case, a vigencia weakens, loses
power, and exerts less and less pressure until none remains. It
becomes easier to break a vigencia; the reprisals of society are
milder, and the number of those daring to break them increases.
After a certain time, individuals are free to do as they please;
behavior in this area is no longer prescribed by social pressure,
or what amounts to the same thing, there is no longer a vigencia.
One may go out without a hat, though he may just as easily go on
wearing one. Now there is no vigencia regarding a moustache,
which forty or fifty years ago was almost obligatory. Since the
end of the First World War, a woman can wear her hair long or
short, because there is no single dominant hair style. In many
countries mourning apparel has gone out of style, while in others,
such as Spain, the vigencia remains, weak and residual in large
cities, still strong in the rest of the country. But in any case,
this softened vigencia has not been replaced by another, and it
is still possible to dress in mourning. Similar examples could
easily be given.

What usually happens, however, is that vigencias are replaced
by others. In general, one social pressure or another affects certain components, the important thing being that there always is one
to exert. Usually this is the way most vigencias decline. They
are relieved or replaced by others that in turn arose from individual life, and that after some time as the restricted vigencia of
a particular group, spread over the whole society. Bearded faces
and their clean-shaven counterparts have alternated in time periods
of a little less than a century, and always the exchange has been
one of true substitution. When dueling disappeared, it meant more
than the mere dissolution of the vigencia, leaving the individual
free to fight or not; the old vigencia that required combat in
certain cases was replaced by another that stressed "no fighting."
The strict rule that a girl could not go out without someone to
accompany her has been replaced by one no less forceful that expressly forbids going out with a "duenna," "lady companion," or
"carbine," names corresponding to the well-defined phases of the
custom.

As a last item, we must consider the meaningful case of what
I would call "vacant vigencias." As with everything social, vi-·
gencias are realities that must be "full" or "empty" (vacant);
and it so happens at times that certain situations call for a
vigencia and there is none available. An example could be the
social forms of address and the use of the vocative. Consider

73

what has happened in recent times in Spain to the manner of addressing a married lady. Until a few years ago one placed doña
before her given name, but then people began to think that this
made her seem older, and it sounded too ordinary. It became
difficult to say "doña María" or "doña Pilar" to a lady without
seeming to add years to her age and lowering her socially at the
same time. The use of the surname with señora, which is normal
in the third person, as for example in an introduction, has never
been acceptable in the vocative, and señora alone sounds too
ceremonious. There was only one way left: the given name without anything else. This is preferable but excessively familiar
and a bit too abrupt. Then the choice was to drop the name altogether at first and as soon as one gets on more familiar terms
with a lady to call her simply "Carmen," "Teresa," or "Lolita."
In other words, the lack of a sufficient vigencia is felt and
the lack made up for with expedients that as such turn out to be
unsatisfactory. Similarly, another vigencia is beginning to
disappear: that regulating the use of tú and usted.[11]

26. Social Structure and Its Formation through Vigencias

This is a suitable point for looking at the other side of
the coin. Once the phenomenon of vigencias has been minutely
analyzed, we must see how they fit together in a social structure.
After all, this is our purpose. At the beginning of this chapter
I pointed out that the social world is composed not of things
but of very strange realities that consist of positive or negative action exerted according to certain structural lines. But
immediately thereafter I was obliged to add that this structure
consists mainly of "the disposition, content, intensity, and
dynamism of vigencias." This expression is quite exact, but
then not completely intelligible. Upon re-reading it in the
light of subsequent pages, one finds in it a clarity and fullness
of meaning that it could not have originally. Now the same expression may be replaced by a shorter one: the system of vigencias, with only one other condition--that the word "system" be
taken literally as a complex of mutually necessary elements that
sustain and support each other by means of an ensemble of operating tensions. And abruptly this clarifies something of greater
interest: social structure is not a society.
We might say that social structure is society minus people
and what they in fact do. For vigencias exist always for certain
individuals and are exerted on them. In turn, vigencias are partially formed by individual aspirations and they modify, limit,
or channel human behavior, though they do not determine it. By
this I mean two things: (1) that the social structure or system
of vigencias cannot be real--in any sense--except with people,
that is, by forming a society, by being the structure of a society;
and (2) that even with this structural system, the actual socio-

74

historical reality is not given, and though conditioned by that system, it is free, pliant, and, in short, unforeseeable. Earlier we saw also that a vigencia can never originate in individual life, but instead that the personal action of an individual must pass though the "matrix" of collective life before it can actually become a vigencia. Any vigencia presupposes society and thus other vigencias. Omnis vigentia ex vigentia, one might conclude. This is another way of stating its systematism, the utter impossibility of considering a vigencia in isolation from the others. This is why many vigencias are "inexplicable." Of course they are when viewed from the life of individuals and even from society itself if one restricts oneself only to its line of development. For the succession of vigencias is not linear in nature. It is the exception instead of the rule for vigencias simply to replace one another in the same order and in each aspect or dimension of life. Normally, each vigencia has its roots in the total social structure and its varieties spring from that totality, not from a "homologous" preceding vigencia. This is why it is impractical to attempt to derive vigencias along abstract lines; in a literal sense, a "history" of fashion, food, or law would be impossible. I mean that the changes of fashion do not come from fashion but perhaps from politics or culture. And artistic vigencias may very well depend more on eroticism, sports, or religion than on critics, academies, or expositions. Vigencias are understandable only within the total way of life from which they spring. Conversely, the smallest variation in them, sufficiently analyzed in all its connections, reveals a transformation in the whole of collective life. Taking the fact that on occasion the letters we receive have been read by others or that two thirds of the customers in a café are women, and examining the full implications of these two modest phenomena, we can reconstruct a goodly portion of our world.

This leads us to think that in order to understand the social, the only recourse we have is reason.[12] It seems pure jest to say this, but ten minutes of thinking about it will convince one that it is not, although in fact for years sociology has tried to get along without reason, often making a virtue and even a "method" of such efforts. The theoretical consequences now begin to stand out clearly; such practices have cost the lives of millions of people and threaten to do away with the rest of us.

Perhaps things will be clearer if we say that life can be understood only from within. If we are situated outside of a social structure, its vigencias are unintelligible because they lack their force, since each one acts in concert with the others—reinforced, accompanied, counterbalanced by them—and above all, on a point of application that is the individual. But because the latter is not abstract, not a mere grammatical or "sociological" subject, but defined by that matrix of positive and negative pressures acting on him and, to the same degree, by the pressure he exerts with his aspiration or life project, then understanding is inexorably linked to the presence of that actual situation in all its aspects. This is the same as saying that in the case of an alien society, foreign or past, the most exhaustive accumulation of materials, the most complete statistics, the most extensive information, will not allow us to understand social reality. The first thing needed--understand well, the first--is imagination. It is paradoxical and unfortunate that the father of sociology, Auguste Comte, tried to substitute observation for imagination and to base his own method on the constant predominance of the former. The only way data, information, and statistics serve a purpose is by "going to live" imaginarily in the society under study and in this way receiving the impact of vigencias. Thus, one can reconstruct the alien or past world with its tone of life; by imaginarily--novelistically--placing oneself in that world, one may assume vicariously and virtually what could have been the life of one of its inhabitants, and thereby bring a true-to-life pressure into play within that circumstance. In other words, one may achieve a hermeneutical transmigration to the situation in question. With this in mind, it is not surprising that the better novels have been the most effective means of penetrating other cultures. I do not mean to say of course that sociology ought to be identified with the novel, but that it should move closer (and in no case farther away) than is now the case. It must be joined to the novel and its many shortcomings, but naturally without surrendering the many possibilities of knowledge it holds.[13]

Thus, it is necessary to go a step further. In considering the social structure as a complex of vigencias, we must view them as they really function, i.e., exerting themselves in interaction with a human purpose. As a first step, this requires that we turn to the very peculiar type of vigencias we call beliefs. Secondly, we must study individual reaction to collective beliefs and delve especially into the problem of ideas. (I use both terms in the technical sense in which Ortega has proposed them.)[14] Thirdly, we must consider the crucial question of intention and the significance of a problematical "collective aspiration." Only in this way can we encompass the reality that is neither individual nor specific which we call social structure and thereby open the way to the study of the structures of real societies.

IV
Beliefs, Ideas, Opinions

27. Basic Beliefs

As Ortega has shown, usually there is not the slightest idea
about beliefs, especially in the case of those basic or fundamental beliefs on which our life is founded. These are radical (i.e.,
"root")[1] vigencias about reality and real things, our inherited
interpretations in which we are grounded and which to us are of
course reality itself. The fact that these beliefs have a mental
existence whenever they are formulated, which is to say, whenever
they cease to function sensu stricto as beliefs and appear in a
form analogous to ideas, has led to the confusion of two ingredients, or two realities, if you like, that function quite differ-
ently in our life. The distinction between ideas and beliefs is
one of the major contributions of Ortega not only to sociology
but also to metaphysics, where the distinction originates.[2]
In trying to understand a society, it is much more important--
and difficult--to ascertain its basic beliefs than to know what
ideas are present in it. Difficult, for one rarely speaks of them
because one rarely thinks of them, because, I repeat, generally
there is not the slightest idea about them. Beliefs simply function and act. We do not have them; rather they have or sustain
us. We are in them; they are not contents but rather continents
of our life. They can be revealed only by their effects. I mean
that what happens does so only because the predominant (vigentes)
beliefs are there, behind or beneath, making it possible. Men
think and do certain things and not others because they are immersed in certain concrete beliefs. What they say and do can
lead us via a prior analysis of the condtions and assumptions of
those utterances and acts, to the fundamental beliefs that generally are unknown. The problem can be stated in these terms: what
must the beliefs of a society be like in order for its ideas and
conduct to be what they are? I reiterate that seldom does one
speak of such beliefs. It is exceptional to find them announced
and formulated in the writings of a period. Rather they are mani-

fested by their alteration and movement. When beliefs change, the loss stands out, and usually what we see is their empty outline, the vacuum they have left in society. They are like an invisible boat of which one sees only the wake.

This means that if we heeded only ideas, their history would be inexplicable—hence the insufficiency of all attempts at a "history of ideas," unless surreptitiously one gives more than what the title promises. Ideas are not derived from each other, but from a total situation conditioned mainly by the basic beliefs. Indeed, ideas originate to supplement or complete beliefs; they come to fill their cracks, sometimes to shore up their leaks, only rarely to undermine them, because, in the first place, this happens only when one is outside a belief and, secondly and more important, ideas generally are ineffectual and inoperative in the face of beliefs. When they appear otherwise, it is because another belief has taken over and has effectively displaced the earlier belief. Later we shall see how, paradoxically, explicitly defending and stressing beliefs usually threatens and breaks them.

Beliefs are always a particular type of vigencia: those that refer to the interpretation of reality. Essentially, then, they follow the dynamics that we studied earlier. Unlike ideas, which always originate in individual life and are something I think, beliefs exist in the ambit of collective life; I find them in society and myself immersed in them, and in this way they constitute my life. Man, to whom society "happens" in his individual life, or to put it another way, whose lot it is to be social, in part is "made" of beliefs, which form one of the essential dimensions of his world. Hence the difficulty of penetrating to the deeper levels of his life, for only rarely do they come to light. The only relatively easy way of gaining access to basic beliefs is history, not only because inoperative beliefs leave behind their outline, which is then filled by others, or because certain structures that appeared to be reality itself subsequently are shown to be interpretations, but because of altogether different reasons. Historical changes, the movement of history itself, are the modes in which fundamental beliefs appear and are their normal form of manifestation. Because of their subterranean nature, they appear indirectly on the surface of collective life, and their active character means that they are evident only in movement, in the activity of life itself. In attemtpting to understand what occurs in history, it is necessary to reconstruct the actual situation of each period as well as the tensions that impel men from one situation to another. And if done primarily with visible elements, with what we could call data, this reconstruction will be deficient, as likewise will be the understanding of the situation, provided the word "understand" is used in the rigorous sense. These gaps in intelligibility, which must be filled if understanding is to be possible, reveal the location of other elements not manifest and apparent which we could call basic presuppositions or assumptions. Beliefs figure among these

in a primary way. If I wish to understand what a man does, I
need to know why and to what purpose he does it. I discover
that he follows a course of action in view of a whole set of circumstances, experiences, resources, needs, and projects. But I
also discover that he is moved a tergo by the fact of being lodged
(probably without being aware of it) in a series of basic beliefs
about which there is not the least question and which confer a
specific meaning on all the patent elements of his life. In summary, they cause him to be in a definite situation and not some
other that would be possible with the same visible ingredients.

The most important point is that the coincidence between
formulated beliefs and ideas leads to confusion. The "content"
of a belief is an idea when it is known and stated; it then becomes a mental and intellectual reality. It appears to be an
assertion, opinion, or thesis amenable to logic and open to inquiry as to its truth or fallacy. But it so happens that a known
and expressed belief does not function as a belief, for in its
true state, it is something else altogether, and whatever we may
say about it as an idea will have little to do with its authentic
operations. The difficulty, then, is that we know of beliefs
only by formulating and "ideafying" them, if I may use such an
expression. And once their intellectual operation has been performed, we tend to assign them to the world of ideas, mixing them
together and judging them from a point of view more suited to the
latter. We regard them first in terms of importance and second,
in the light of their internal relationships and connections to
other beliefs. Now then, judging them in these three aspects
from the standpoint of ideas can only lead to error. For the
importance of beliefs is not intellectual but vital. The degree
to which a belief allows a broad and deep understanding of the
real is not so important as the degree to which a belief has a
decisive effect on a life. And their soundness, or solidity, is
not a matter of "evidence" or "proof" but an indication of the
point of "implantation" in this or that level of individual and
collective life, or a sign of being old or new or perhaps of
passing through a phase, or else a suggestion of the ambit from
which (as we saw in a general way in the case of vigencias) it
exerts its pressure. Finally, the connections between beliefs
are not "logical" relations like those that link the different
propositions of a science, but links of vital foundation, or, to
use a term that seems more expressive, of vivification, of enlivenment. (Although one might add that at the last it turns out that
the highest form of logical foundation is precisely "enlivenment,"
or "vivification," using the term in its fullest meaning, which
as of now is still hardly known.[3] Without forgetting that it is
beliefs and not ideas we seek, we must inquire as to their importance, solidity, and connections. To put it another way, we must
ask whether beliefs constitute a system, and if so, in what sense
and in what kind of order or hierarchy.

28. The Hierarchical System of Beliefs

The decisive thing about beliefs is that they are believed. Pardon this trite but unavoidable introduction. What I mean is that any consideration that omits this intrinsic function skirts the topic of beliefs and in reality touches on something else such as the conceptual schemata that function as its components, or the residue they leave when they disappear, or their "contents," which may coincide with those of many other human realities that are not beliefs at all. In trying to understand the phenomena of beliefs, we must keep in mind two methodological principles: the first, to surprise them in fraganti, i.e., in their proper role of being believed; and the second, to observe relatively simple and elementary beliefs without excessive implications and interferences to becloud their reality.

This is why it seems to me highly dangerous to think about religious "beliefs" in investigating the reality of beliefs; for though religious beliefs no doubt exist, a great deal of the content of religion is not belief in the technical sense we give the word here. Of course it is not dogmas as such that are formulated, defined, and proposed for one to accept. Such acceptance, which is intellectual on the one hand and voluntary on the other, will be vitally activated by a belief to which one clings; of this there can be no doubt. But the dogma itself, exactly the part of it that is dogma, is not a "belief." It is not a belief to accept the thesis that "God is everywhere, by essence, presence, and power." On the other hand, it is a belief, and a decisive one at that, to feel ourselves living under the watchful eye of God, to be in His hands, to rely on the certainty that He is watching what we do and think, to feel that we are not alone, and to be tacitly turned toward Him in the sense that we presuppose His presence in doing what we do. Not only do many men share this belief who have never heard nor formulated the thesis stated above, but also others who "do not believe" in God, who deny this thesis and even the one that asserts the existence of God.

It would be preferable to use the word "faith" to refer to religious belief (the content of faith is made up of beliefs and other elements ranging from supernatural inspiration to free and voluntary acceptance, to persuasion) and to seek the peculiarity of beliefs in those cases in which they appear in their pure, simple, and elemental forms.

Beliefs have to do primarily with the behavior of reality. Fundamental beliefs are basic interpretations of the real insofar as they function and are not thought of as interpretations. This is why, strictly speaking, beliefs do not originate in the individual through persuasion; they are not really "convictions," but are "injected" by the course of life itself. The functioning of the reality that surrounds us from birth, the presentation of each thing as a certain thing, as "a certain way of being and behaving," infuses in us the corresponding subterranean belief.

80

The free and uncontrolled use of the air, as opposed to the restricted use of foodstuffs, causes us to have certain beliefs
about the inexhaustibility, certainty, and gratuitousness of
the former, and about the limitation, uncertainty, and cost of
the latter. The case of water is more revealing in this regard:
whereas in the large civilized cities of our time water is available just by turning on a spigot and is almost as plentiful as
air, in other kinds of culture it becomes a reality that is
scarce, improbable, valuable, and hard to come by. When the
supply drops and spigots no longer flow, the former belief becomes problematical and must be revised, and the situation is
one of minor crisis. Beliefs regarding one's fellow men--trust
or distrust, for example--do not spring from any ideology or
mental persuasion, but from the way they are dealt with; the use
of bolts, locks, and chains and the practice of checking the
windows at night instill in a child a set of quite different
beliefs concerning men than those acquired in societies where
doors are not locked, where change is not counted, and where
one's word is automatically accepted. Beliefs dealing with the
male or female status arise from the kind of relationship actually
found functioning in the society into which one is born. The
human origin of the belief in God is not a doctrinal argumentation
foisted on the child, nor even the formal proposition that God
exists, but something much simpler and deeper: the introduction
of God into his life, the presentation of another reality in the
panorama of his being. The child accepts in principle the realities of which his parents speak, he takes them to be actual, and
only later does he begin to disqualify some of them, and he does
so first of all with those that are not presented "seriously."
When God is discussed, He is automatically included in the child's
world according to the way the theme is treated: with veneration,
fear, love, frivolity, or "onesidedly" or "belligerently," as the
case may be. Negative beliefs, which are so important, owe their
origin to the aversion, fear, hatred, or scorn with which certain
realities are treated within the family circle. Thus, they determine attitudes toward the snake or the Negro, the bourgeois class
or the witch, the Jew or the prostitute, a storm or an eclipse,
and at times toward the one-eyed person or the sick--the tubercular
or leprous person--the heretic or the "papist," and toward the
communist or the fascist.

Beliefs, therefore, are the most profound and elementary
forms of incorporating different realities into life. They are
the broad functional interpretations of the real, those on which
men rely and by means of which they live credentially, i.e., on
"credit."[4] And this conditions their systematic and hierarchical
nature.

What I mean is that life, which is the real organization of
reality,[5] imposes a particular perspective in each case; it manifests diverse "amplitudes" and profiles and a distribution of its
elements that is not always the same. Consequently, the system

81

of beliefs is not theoretical but vital (of course theoretical systems—in the plural because historically there are many—are also vital, but only in certain areas of life defined by the basic assumption of the theoretical attitude). Thus the system of beliefs refers only to those areas of the real that intervene in human life, and exactly in the perspective and proportion of that intervention. Naturally this begins with space and time: to a primitive and sedentary society, for example the inhabitants of a valley, the "world" is the valley, strictly speaking, and everything else a vague "outer" world. For contemporary Western man—who in fact travels over the entire planet, is affected by everything that happens in the world, and is aware of the complex network that stretches from the sun and moon to remote galaxies— the spatial world has very different features. The same is true of time: in primitive man, and for that matter in the simpler areas of life today, the small margin of recall quickly vanishes in the shadows of the "immemorial," while the man with historical awareness, even with the historicist mentality, moves in a temporal and chronological world that is very broad and historically qualified. It should be understood that beliefs sufficient for one situation are inadequate for another. Furthermore, it should be noted that beliefs are regulated by a principle of "life economics" and thus are marked by sufficiency and necessity, unlike the essentially "luxurious" and vitally "excessive" nature of theory.

While beliefs are highly precise, compact, and effective regarding certain aspects or zones of reality, they may be vague and tenuous concerning some, and completely lacking in others. Beliefs are not a set of answers to a formal questionnaire and hence always the same; they are modes of interpreting the realities that are functionally present in each life. This is why in investigating a social structure the method cannot be to ascertain which beliefs a society holds about a series of points that seem important to us; rather, it consists of determining what it is about which society has beliefs. This will show the profile of the way of life and will give us an outline of the system of these beliefs which is more important than their specific content.

Clearly this system hinges on the actual and vital foundational relationships between its ingredients. This means that it is neither theoretical in the sense of responding to a logically coherent image of the world, nor determined by mere static connections; rather its articulation is sustained by a fundamental and constitutive project or aspiration of the corresponding way of life. Only as a function of the life drama that it serves is the repertory of beliefs systematic. But from this point of view it can only be systematic; otherwise life would not be possible. Clearly, by stating that it "is systematic," I mean that it "must be so." The failure or breakup of the system—which naturally can happen only because there is a

system in the first place--causes an alteration or interruption
of the normal course of life, or, in other words, it brings about
a crisis of beliefs.

This implies that the hierarchy of beliefs depends exactly
on that aspiration and outline of life. Because it is organic,
the system is hierarchic; and the functions determine that hierarchy. Beliefs about space and the locational structure of the
world are all-important to a nomadic people, less so to a sedentary and isolated culture, and hardly at all to non-seafaring
island people. Imagine the gulf separating the beliefs of the
Saharan Tuaregs concerning the mysterious animal world from
those of the dwellers of the Brazilian jungle. In the first
case, we are dealing with a conspicuous world, characterized by
visibility and thinly populated; in the second, we find the
latent world, by its very nature hidden and impenetrable and
defined by the swarming of thousands of unknown species of animals. Hence the enormous weight of beliefs about creatures
among the Brazilian Caboclos.[6] I have sought out these extreme
examples in keeping with the methodological simplicity that seems
essential to me. But if we look closer at hand, the same phenomenon will appear in the comparison of two national European societies or two historical periods of the same society, for instance,
Romantic Spain and our own.

29. Two Forms of Attenuation of Beliefs: Dissolution
     and Intellectual Adherence

The notion of an ideology that undermines and destroys the
beliefs of a society is rather childish. Ortega has insisted
quite adequately on this, showing instead that ideas are recourses
to which man turns in order to shore up beliefs in crisis or to
bridge their gaps.[7] Since ideas and beliefs do not appear on
the same level, an ideological attack against beliefs is difficult without the prior operation of "ideafication," of "translating" them into the terms of ideas, in short, of transforming
them into ideas whose contents coincide with those of beliefs.
But when this is done and before the attack has begun, beliefs
have already ceased to function as such in the strict sense,
that is, they are in crisis before being set upon. We shall see
how delicate this matter is.

The most frequent form of diminution, weakening, or attenuation of beliefs, of their disappearance if carried far enough,
is what we might call their "volatilization." A belief that once
had a decisive role in life, that shaped it at its deepest levels,
begins to pale, to be less and less intense, to have a decreasing
impact on behavior, until it dissipates, vanishes, and evaporates.
Remember that this does not mean necessarily that its content is
not believed. The disappearance of a belief leaves open the question of whether or not its content is also rejected, for it is far

more than a matter of assertions and denials. It took a long
time for the belief in pagan gods to decline to a point where
no one believed in the existence of such deities. The belief
in progress, which sustained Europe for more than a century, has
vanished as a belief; we no longer base our lives on it, but
this does not mean that contemporary Europeans deny progress.
Most of them would affirm it within limits; their "opinion"
would be that progress exists and that it determines to a great
extent the course of history. The same situation is found in
comparing the medieval belief in the sepulcher of Saint James
(Santiago) of Compostela with the current opinion of many that
indeed the Apostle is buried there: this opinion does not have
the repercussions today that the earlier belief had for Castilians
of the twelfth century.

If the "volatilization" of a belief does not necessarily
mean its negation, then what causes it to happen and what specific meaning does it have? We are dealing with a change of
structure, and this involves a shifting of its components, including beliefs. If a people goes from living in the jungle to
dwelling in cities, perhaps because of a rapid process of industrialization, its beliefs about the animal world become inoperative
as vestiges from its past, yet there would be no change of opinion
about any of their contents. Beliefs almost always dissipate because of a change of direction, a shift in perspective, which
takes attention from former interests. Among most modern men,
belief in the "evil eye" has been replaced by a belief in microbes.
Note that the important point is not that evil eye is impossible
(nobody has taken the trouble to demonstrate its impossibility,
nor is this the level at which to pose the problem). The disappearance of the belief in diabolical possession does not exclude
the fact that millions of people today think that it is possible
and even real in some cases. Yet this idea does not obviate the
fact that possession is not generally considered, and when someone
appears who exhibits the symptoms traditionally attributed to it,
the idea that comes to mind is not to exorcise but to send that
person to a psychiatrist. Quite often a new belief literally
eclipses other beliefs and in a vital sense annuls them, although
logically it has no effect on them. This is exactly the way the
sun makes the stars disappear, even though the latter continue
burning in space and thus shining with the same intensity they
have at night; and the moon, which does not disappear, pales and
fades to a secondary plane, and we do not depend on it to see as
we would in the middle of the night, even though it is there and
can be seen. When man begins to live on the basis of a new belief that comes into his world, that belief in no way acts on
his former beliefs, yet it alters their meaning and function,
enhancing, weakening, or obliterating them. This would be the
proper point of view from which to study the historical dynamics
of beliefs, as a history of the ways of life understood as complex
units and organically articulated and impelled by a certain

aspiration. As I noted earlier, and as Ortega has demonstrated, there is no "history of ideas." But it must be said also that neither is there a "history of beliefs," nor in general of any partial and abstract element of human life. What does have a history is life in its complete and concrete reality.

In some cases, beliefs weaken and decline not through this process of neglect and dissipation but precisely by the opposite road: through intellectual adherence to them. The phenomenon is complex and delicate. It is perilous to speak very much of beliefs, for in order to do so, they must be stated, formulated, and expressed in the form of a thesis or idea of their content. And this is the first step in ceasing to function as beliefs sensu stricto. Accurately speaking, beliefs are not affirmed; one is immersed in them, and whenever they are affirmed, whenever men begin to support their substance intellectually, they begin to act in another dimension of life at a level that undoubtedly is more superficial. Although it seems paradoxical, we might say that the explicit affirmation of beliefs is the first step in their decline. This is why I pointed out earlier that even before beliefs come under attack, their mere expression in terms of ideas places them in crisis. That is, this "ideafication" of beliefs is already a sign of their attenuation, and whether they are attacked or defended is a relatively secondary matter.

Ideas are much more than beliefs. In addition, they are unstable; they vary, modify, and correct themselves. Moreover, as intellectual realities, ideas move in the ambit of question and problematicity, while beliefs function as the "unquestionable." We might say that by the mere fact of being an idea, any idea is problematical. As soon as an idea is expressed, its questionability comes forth; the "goal of truth" that accompanies logical judgment as such makes falseness an impossibility in an idea and thus creates the need for its justification. Whereas a belief rests on itself, sure and quiescent, an idea has to justify itself at each instant and must always be proving its truth. To formulate a belief ideologically means intrinsically and inexorably to place it in judgment.

Furthermore, while belief is possessed of a certain vagueness (I mean vagueness from the standpoint of ideas, for belief can be rigor itself) its formulation requires intellectual precision and introduces a whole series of difficulties, possible contradictions, and variabilities, the justification of which becomes a serious and perhaps unnecessary problem. Let me offer what seems to me to be a revealing example. In Genesis it says that God took a rib from the sleeping Adam's side and from it made Eve. Given the religious assumption in which Genesis appears, this story presents not the slightest difficulty, and it contains a series of profound and wonderful meanings: woman, formed from man himself, flesh of his flesh and bone of his bone; woman, made also of finer and nobler stuff than the original clay, etc. There is no difficulty,

The Structure of Society

I repeat, provided that this account is not presented too much
as a "thesis," that there is no attempt to have this belief pass
for an idea or pseudo-idea, and that there are not too many questions raised in keeping with a presumed intellectual rigor about
"how" it happened and exactly what it was that happened: whether
Adam had an extra rib or whether he was left with one less; whether
God replaced the rib or whether the space was filled with flesh;
and how it was that the woman's whole body was made from the rib,
and so on. All these points have been raised in detail—and with
unbelievable frivolity—by many theologians, including the great
ones, thus endangering belief about this matter, and indirectly
the entire Christian faith. There are hundreds of similar examples,
many of them centering on serious matters.

Hence the evident dangers of apologetics. When the contents
of a belief are formulated as theses or ideas, they must then be
justified; and in order to do so, "reasons" have to be given.
But because the latter are often fragile, the belief, perfectly
justified as such within the life economy that is proper to it
and having no need of demonstration or proof, is invalidated and
destroyed by being "transplanted" to an inadequate terrain where
it is tended with insufficient intellectual procedures.

The consequences of converting beliefs into ideas are, to
begin with, that they are removed to a different and more superficial dimension of life; secondly, they are then infused with
problematicalness; thirdly, they become unstable and always subject to proof or substantiation; and finally, they are vitally
attenuated, regardless of their intellectual justification, because the latter always operates at a shallower level than basic
beliefs. Compare the vital intensity of our adherence to a perfectly demonstrated truth, for example, that in a right triangle
the square of the hypotenuse is equal to the sum of the squares
of the legs, and our belief, undemonstrated and undemonstrable,
that we are children of our father and mother. Whereas a decisive part of our life is normally based on the latter belief,
the intellectual certainty of the Pythagorean Theorem is, except
in unusual cases, a matter of complete indifference to us.

There is another consequence which though indirect is extremely important. "Idea-fied" beliefs weaken and in some cases
disappear and are lost. In other cases, however, when they are
sustained by a strong authentic belief despite their ideological
attenuation, or perhaps by a complex of independent life interests,
they replace the energy they have lost as beliefs with an exacer-
bation as ideas, that is, with an intensification of the type
that corresponds to the idea, such as partisanship, belligerence,
or fanaticism. A belief converted into an idea, but deficient as
such, degenerates into "ideology" and becomes an "-ism." It seeks
the power it lacks to sustain and impel life a tergo in the aggres-
siveness with which it is sustained. Hence the typical belligerence and polemic tendency of weakened and insecure beliefs, which
warily assert themselves against a backdrop of abstract hostility.

86

Beliefs, Ideas, Opinions

In considering all the beliefs of a society, it is of course
necessary to pay attention not only to the hierarchy they have
as beliefs but also to that defined by phase. By this I mean
that attention must be given to the state of "credit" in which
beliefs consist. Over against beliefs in full vigor, there are
others in an attenuated condition. A "quantitative" determination of the state of beliefs must be made regarding the degree
of intensity with which they affect life. But this alone is not
enough; another is necessary: to determine by what avenue this
quantum of intensity and solidity has been achieved, and consequently, to ascertain where the belief is heading. There is a
difference between a belief gradually fading away because of a
shift in perspective brought about by a growing disinterest in
the "theme" of the belief, and having been converted into an idea
and then undermined by a belief of an opposite sign, or finally,
having been invalidated by the zeal of its defenders so that it
now appears as a prepotent, aggressive, and explicit ideology
emptied of all content and substance as a belief. It is possible
for a belief (and such cases are especially interesting), having
been exhausted as a belief, to have another life as an ideology
within a society, just as it is possible after a period of time
for an idea that arose in an individual mind to become a belief
in the full meaning of the term. And this brings us to the relation between them.

30. Interaction of Ideas and Beliefs

Until now I have insisted on the distinction between ideas
and beliefs, on their relative independence, even on the difficulty of their undermining each other so long as they maintain
their integrity within their respective planes. But now we must
consider another aspect. The connections between ideas and beliefs
are many. Above all, both are found in our life, that is, they
coexist within it, having their roots and their development within
its boundaries. This points to the very elementary but for the
same reason very important relation of coexistence. Both function in human life. But in what proportion? There are types of
human life wherein beliefs constitute the basis from which one
lives. Above this level, a minimal repertory of secondary ideas
orient man sporadically regarding restricted questions of limited
scope. In other societies, or other individuals, life is determined by a complex of momentous and systematically linked ideas
and by a multitude of lesser ideas that touch on every imaginable
question and form a thick network around life. All this, of course,
is based on certain fundamental beliefs that remain in the background, silent, hidden, and almost unnoticed like a nourishing
subsoil. There are many intermediate degrees--and structures—
between these two extremes, and the investigation of a social
structure must clarify the precise state of that coexistence and

87

try to gauge its proportion. Consider, for example, the significance of this problem in an understanding of the Middle Ages.
In studying the medieval epoch, attention swings from ideas--
Scholasticism, ecclesiastical organization, political thought,
etc.--to the underlying beliefs, which are expressed and revealed
in a thousand different ways. What is the real weight of culture
in Latin compared to that of the common tongues? It would be
idle to attempt a strict evaluation here, to compare, for example,
the "value" of Abelard to that of the Chanson de Roland, Peter
Lombard to the Poema del Cid, the Summulae Logicales of Petrus
Hispaniensis to the Libro de buen amor, Duns Scotus to the
Romancero, Dante . . . to himself, that is, to discriminate between the weight of the ideas and the beliefs in the world of
the Divine Comedy. Naturally, such distinctions would be the
pathway toward understanding the epoch as a whole as well as its
diverse phases. For they imply an analysis of the respective
function of both elements in the life of medieval man carried
out independently of what might interest us were we historians
of philosophy, of theology, or of art, or were we trying to
trace the formation of the European peoples of our time from
the Middle Ages.

Such a study would unearth not a few surprises. Usually
it is thought that the Renaissance signifies a triumph of ideas.
It is not my wish to anticipate the results of an inquiry that
neither I nor anyone else to my knowledge has made, but considering as one must the final phase of the Middle Ages "bordering"
on the Renaissance, and not--as is absurdly done--the eleventh
century juxtaposed with the fifteenth, it is not unlikely that
the Renaissance would appear as a period of crisis of ideas and
as a time when two or three fundamental beliefs were fully prepotent. In an analogous way, it would be necessary to see how
the nineteenth century began with a restrengthening of beliefs
and what is more with a reversal of the process that I referred
to earlier as the "ideafication of beliefs," and that we might
call the "credential" functioning--sit venia verbo--of many
ideas of the eighteenth century.

The proportion in which ideas and beliefs function within
the order of a way of life determines a series of its characteristics. It establishes, for example, the rhythm of its historical change; a way of life in which ideas play a minimal role is
necessarily slow in its evolution, regardless of the nature of
its beliefs. Conversely, the preponderance of ideas means a
rapid rate of change. The cause of the prodigious acceleration
of tempo in historical change in the Modern Age, above all in
the past hundred years, can be explained to a large extent by
the shift in balance toward ideas. But it is not enough to
speak of historical change; we must also ask what it is that
changes, what zones of life are affected by change. When the
basic beliefs are very solid and authentic, when a person's
roots are deeply and powerfully sunk in them, it is still possible

to have a social structure in which change occurs quite rapidly, but this does not prevent great social stability. This seems to me to be the case of the United States. On the other hand, it is also possible to have a society of minor or slow change and yet be the picture of instability because the subsoil of its beliefs is tenuous and thin. Bear in mind that rapid movement and great edifices require a firm base, while only hovels can be built on shifting sand or mud, where movement is the most difficult.

The well-known fact of the relative stability of rural life in comparison to the urban derives from the different degree to which ideas and beliefs act on them, respectively. This would be the proper viewpoint from which to study the greater or lesser rate of change in the various social classes, the difference between the lower-class man and the proletarian, and the surprising inalterability of titled aristocracies when compared to other upper groups of society (intellectuals, professionals of the first rank, businessmen, etc.). This factor is also characteristic of different political movements, which spring from different sources and receive their impulse from certain subterranean beliefs that sometimes are not all apparent. Only this can explain many phenomena of political life that otherwise would be incomprehensible. But this is not to be taken in terms of the alternatives of traditionalism and revolution, for either may as easily be a question of ideas or a matter of beliefs as the other. The study of Spanish political life during the eighteenth century--and of course during the twentieth--is extremely revealing in this regard.

The process by which men go from an idea, which originated as such in an individual mind, to a belief is the same that we studied in our discussion of the origin of vigencias. But we must not conclude from this that beliefs necessarily must originate from individual ideas. This case is relatively rare and hardly ever happens with basic beliefs. Beliefs originated in this way always retain a greater similarity to ideas. They are formulated and explicit beliefs and for that reason more easily confused with ideas, yet different from them because of the way they function in life. Earlier I spoke of the idea of progress, which was born in the eighteenth century in the minds of Turgot and Condorcet. In the nineteenth century it became a sort of collective belief that engulfed Europeans and Americans, who found it to be predominant in their world as an inherited idea, as an interpretation that expressed reality itself. These two traits characterize beliefs arising from ideas: they appear as reality, but in an express form. The latter quality is missing in original beliefs, for example, in those having to do with the firmness of the ground, the inexhaustibility of the air, the fearfulness of unfamiliar places, the existence of higher powers, or the binding ties to a family or a tribe. These beliefs do not begin as ideas but are born of a particular experience of reality,

the formulation and intellectual expression of which is always
secondary. For this reason, with primal beliefs one always has
the impression that they are never exhausted in their formulas
or propositions. When an authentic belief is expressed, when a
person states what he believes in, he always tells something less
than the real belief. This explains the surprising fact (though
no one is surprised by it) that one may sing the Creed, whereas
it would be absurd to do the same with the Pythagorean Theorem,
Maxwell's Laws, the Kantian Categories, or the twenty-four Thomist
Theses. Singing the Creed is quite different from merely reciting
or reading it, for something important is thereby added to it, not
in the way of meaning, but as belief. It is a matter of the general meaning of the liturgy and worship, of the way in which religious beliefs live—and correlatively are endued with life.
By means of such recourses, compensation is made for the distor-
tion and mutilation brought about by formulation. The essential
"plus" that believing has over saying what is believed is "said"
or at least suggested by the music and in an overall way by what
we might call the "liturgical temper." (The nature of the latter
is another matter and not a simple one at all; suffice it to say
that the question is important, for often the degenerate forms of
liturgy destroy the content of belief instead of strengthening it;
many habitual forms of piety amount to supreme impiety: nasal or
dragging voice, or one that is disagreeably sweet, and intrinsically mocking singsong, abuse of the superlative, and likewise,
altars adorned like a candy store, mawkish images, etc. This is
expressed quite appropriately in the popular Spanish saying: El
Padrenuestro puesto en solfa es solfa (The Paternoster is ridicu-
lous when it is treated ridiculously).
     We have already considered how a belief becomes an idea.
The example of progress is excellent, for it serves to illustrate
both processes: from the idea of progress came the belief in it;
and from the belief in progress men have gone again to the idea
in its present phase. In religious life there are many cases
of beliefs that cease to function sensu stricto as such but which
persist as ideas or theses to which the faithful may cling intellectually. But this term is somewhat misleading, for it suggests
that everything the faithful adhere to is a belief, and this is
not the case at all. Because he is immersed in a belief, the believer affirms many ideas received as ideas, theses, or dogmas
with which he has no relationship based on belief in the strict
meaning of the term. The theological distinctions between explicit and implicit faith is accurate, but it is not sufficient
to explain this attitude. He who believes "everything the Church
teaches," believes it with in implicit faith, because he has ex-
explicit faith in the Church, and naturally he does not know what
it is that the Church teaches. Imagine now that the content of
those teachings is explained to him. One might say that as they
are stated and presented to him, he begins to believe them with
explicit faith, yet this does not prevent him from maintaining

belief in the strict sense, which, as we said earlier, was faith
in the Church itself. Consider, for example, a recently defined
dogma, say the Assumption. Prior to its dogmatic definition,
many Catholics (but not all) held the belief that the Virgin had
been taken up to Heaven, without very much insistence of "how" or
in what form this occurred. After the definition, all Catholics,
those who formerly believed it and those who did not, now believe
in the defined dogma, that is, they agree to the definition, support it, and abide by it. But it would make no sense to say that
now all "hold" this belief; and what is more, among those who already believed it, the vague traditional belief can be distinguished
from the precise adherence to the dogmatic definition, and even
though both refer to the same thing, they are not identical as
religious realities in the personal life of the believer. How
can the belief in Purgatory and the souls therein as it appears,
let us say, among the masses, be equated with the "belief" in the
rights of the Church in matters of teaching? The "belief" in the
Eucharist--that Christ is truly in the consecrated Host--is not
the same thing as intellectual adherence to the doctrine of tran-
substantiation because one holds that belief. All this, let us
say in passing because it is not our topic, holds the utmost
importance for the teaching of religion and for religious life
as a whole. So often the latter is dislodged and separated from
the dimension of belief by careless liturgy, by excessive treatment, by the proliferation of pious details, by involvement with
other things (politics, intellectual theories, etc.), by the addition of what we might call "ideological" crust formed by doctrinal elaborations obtained by means of an inertial way of thinking that operates automatically and vacuously with a dearth of
authentic religious data, and by the zeal to "demonstrate" what
cannot and need not be demonstrated, forgetting or scorning the
essential function of belief as such.

Yet aside from the possible transition of ideas to beliefs,
or vice versa, the understanding of a society involves another
decisive question: the actual interaction at all times between
current ideas and beliefs. Both beliefs and ideas are instruments
of certainty: the first, in their proper function of providing
the certainty "in which one dwells"; and the second, by offering
the certainty "that one reaches."[8] Thus, the total certainty
in which our life is grounded is the result of the experience
and interaction of the system of beliefs with the repertory of
ideas; for, paradoxically, whereas it is necessary that basic
beliefs constitute a system that is vital rather than "logical,"
the dominant ideas of a society may very well not be characterized
by system at all. This interaction is necessary because beliefs
alone are never enough, because situations arise in succession,
creating new things with which one must know how to cope. Therefore, the primary and normal function of ideas in all kinds of
societies, and not just in those exceptionally intellectualized
like ours, is to fill the gaps, breaks, or fissures in the system

of beliefs and to deal with new situations, against which beliefs
are relatively defenseless. As I said before, this is why the
function of ideas is sporadic and very limited in societies that
we call primitive (or for that matter in the "primitive" strata
of complex and intellectualized societies) and much the same in
the vast majority of societies, taking the total volume of humanity throughout all of history, although the situation is different
in the tiny fraction that for obvious reasons we know best and in
which we are normally more interested. The "autonomous" functioning of ideas with their own life and independence is an absolutely
uncommon historical phenomenon.

But the intervention of ideas is necessary even in the society
that is the most firmly governed by a solid and compact system of
beliefs. For inasmuch as they have not been formed logically,
among themselves beliefs exhibit vital not logical coherence; and
because not all are in the same phase or the same degree of intensity, their hierarchy is problematical. They displace one another,
causing gaps and cracks, and in the face of this situation, man
has no other recourse but to set himself to thinking in order to
know once again how to cope with things. In other words, he
mobilizes his ideas primarily to the degree that the vicissitudes
of beliefs have made it necessary to do so.

But there is more. Historical experiences and accumulated
failures break down beliefs, and encountering this failure, ideas
begin to operate on the new situation. It matters little whether
the critical action of ideas confirms the failure and hastens the
fall of the belief, whether it supports and sustains it, or finally,
whether it reaches beyond the belief to a new look at the question.
In any case, the intervention of ideas again becomes necessary
because of the situation thus created.

Up to this point I have been speaking of a schematic and
unreal situation: that of an isolated society. In point of fact,
the different societies are almost always in the presence of one
another, and the beliefs of one spill over into the area of another.
These alien beliefs are not those held by members of a society, but
they know that others hold them. This situation is decisive and
perhaps more than any other necessitates the use of ideas. If
one wishes to understand a social structure, especially the more
advanced societies, it is necessary to study carefully this aspect
of the interaction of beliefs and ideas.

One must also pay heed to another aspect, perhaps the most
radical of all: the total situation of ideas, that is, their
relationship to beliefs as seen from the latter. In other words,
this is the belief in ideas, the variable faith in reason that
each society has. Such faith conditions the different expressions
this reason may take. To put it another way, it is the belief in
each of the ways in which ideas operate: oratory, narration, poetry, dialectic, science, and in turn, the individual sciences.
There is no simple answer to questions about the effective function of ideas in history. Does one mean ideas that move the

world, or are they only the spare tire, or perhaps only "the
fly in the car," as Ortega once asked about philosophy? These
are the first questions to be answered, but bear in mind that
they must be asked for each society and each form or possibility
of ideas. Such is the decisive dimension in which the interaction
of ideas and beliefs occurs.

31. The System of Valuation

Because human life consists of preferring certain possibilities to others and of realizing itself by selecting a temporal
course that traces its trajectory on a field defined by each
situation, the world is not only an aggregate of elements endowed
with certain qualities but rather appears as a valuational structure. This is important because it affects the very appearance
of realities. This valuational system conditions the panorama
of the world that beckons to man almost as much as the human per-
ceptional apparatus. Notice that of the countless elements that
exist about us, only a few are really present, that is, only a
few are noticed as such. Of course the disposition of our sen-
sorial organs and our attendant habits in using them are the
primary factors in determing this selection. But secondarily
a series of valuations causes us to heed or ignore the sensible
ingredients of our world. Our surroundings seem to be curtained
off by an indifferent background against which objects are outlined positively or negatively according to a variable but real
hierarchy in each case. Human life is then conditioned by a
valuational system that varies historically and is one of the
constituent factors of a social structure.

Fundamentally this system is based on beliefs. From earliest
childhood things are presented valuationally to the child; his
food and pacifier, later his rattle and toys, are all shown to
him to be things of positive value, and he is encouraged to treat
them favorably, whereas dirty or dangerous things arouse negative
emotions, and he is motivated to have an aversion to them. On
the other hand, he is left with a neutral attitude about many things.
To be sure, this usually applies to remote realities, or those so
close that they do not function as objects: clothing, the cradle,
etc. As the child continues to grow and expand his perceptual
horizon, his world is enriched by new elements that bestow on
him a pattern of behavior determined by a valuational scale.
When, properly speaking, he enters the world, I mean the common
social world, he finds a predominant system of values, the body
of which coincides generally but not completely with those of his
family. There are private values received by the child from his
family that are neither original nor prevalent in society but
restricted to his personal surroundings. There are others of
limited scope--those of a social class, a political trend, a
religion, and the like--interspersed with private and social

values. Finally, the valuational capability of the individual begins to act, which modifies his inherited system, passively at first and then with a degree of independence that varies greatly. In fact, the amount of variation is one factor that must be determined in order to understand a social structure.

This system of valuation extends from material things to the most abstract realities. Each physical substance, from gold to "precious" stones to excrement, is affected by a valuational denominator that presents it as something "noble" or "vile." It applies especially, of course, to living realities, plant or animal: orchids and thistles, weat and darnel, horses and worms, sheep and serpents, doves and spiders, lions and hyenas, eagles and vultures, nightingales and bats, dolphins, sharks, sardines, or octupuses. Each appears within an emotional halo, with a certain prescribed value that arouses an initial reaction in us and conditions their usage and thus their reality.

This is true to an extreme degree with human beings. Races, physical types, professions, regions of a country, and religions are valuationally qualified. And the valuational scale is subject to historical change. An abyss separates the disdain for work evinced by the hidalgo of 1600 and the work cult of proletarian ideologies. Attitudes toward Negroes, semitism or anti-semitism, esteem or scorn for the military, veneration or contempt for the priesthood, the social assessment of being Castilian, Galician, Andalusian, or Catalonian in Spain (and with similar groups in other countries), the variable esteem in which the two sexes are held, and the wide range of attitudes about children; all human reality is directly founded on such valuation.

Imagine the distance separating the esteem for a Roman gladiator from that for a leading football player in our day. Measure how far removed is the attitude of a tenth-century nobleman, who would be ashamed of knowing how to read, from the nineteenth-century esteem for the homme de lettres or Herr Professor, and then compare both attitudes to their Spanish counterparts at the same time and for the same type of men. Compare the regard for priestly office in 1400, in 1580, in 1780, in 1900, in 1935, and in 1954. Consider what it meant in Spain as an advantage, initial esteem, and good will to be Andalusian around 1890, and the disadvantage of being Galician or perhaps Extremadurian. This situation has changed profoundly in a half century.

The study of a social structure must include a determination of its valuational system. Only in light of it is it possible to understand what happens, that is, to understand the real course of history, the social stratification, industrialization or decline in production, the caliber of patriotism, the religious tonality (which is decisively influenced by esteem or disrespect for the clergy), the selection of professions, and consequently, the composition of society, relationships between the sexes, tolerance of vices, and hence the moral format of that society, and so on. The scale can range from the harshest intransigence toward sins of the flesh to the greatest indulgence, from the acceptability of economic immorality to unbending firmness in money matters; personal cowardice may be tolerated or it may be cause for social disqualification; moral sensitivity toward the traitor may vary greatly; the situation of the homosexual may be atrocious or very comfortable, even privileged. Unless one is clearly aware from this point of view of what is happening in a society, nothing will be understood.

But I have purposely used the word "system," and indeed valuations necessarily constitute a system, because they are a regulatory mechanism of life. This is why it is impossible to understand the predominant system of a period and a given society by merely cataloging its particular values. Taken as a whole, they form a pattern that must be revealed and outlined, a pattern that expresses at one of the deepest levels what the verb "to live" means for those men. (For men, to live means in the main "to be worth living"; recall the Latin adage: Propter vitam, vivendi perdere causas ["Because of life, there is no reason to live"]); and if one prefers a less exalted text, then consider the popular Spanish commentary about a devalued and scorned way of living: Esto no es vivir ("This is not living"). Hence valuation always appears as an adjusted mechanism of compensations, and historical crises begin as a disarrangement that usually leads to disarray. As I see it, the social function of dueling, which prevailed in nineteenth-century Europe, was principally to maintain a certain need for personal valor in a world that was increasingly safe, peaceful, and settled, a world too lacking in danger (I refer especially to the second half of the century and perhaps up to the war of 1914). Dueling quickly went out of style when the world became perilous again, when it became necessary to have personal courage in order to live with medium dignity without seeking superfluous complications. In earlier times, from the Middle Ages until the seventeenth century, dueling represented part of the noble and chivalric education; it was an attribute of that status, a training school as was sport or the study of foreign languages in other societies. In a similar fashion, moral tolerance for certain vices and sins tends to compensate for excessive rigidity in other areas; and within the total system of valuation, it would be necessary to inquire seriously about the function of such severity or relaxation as a whole. One would surely find that within the economy of life they are compensation for other phenomena that have no reason to be directly moral in nature.

Since, on the one hand, valuation is a matter of keen interest to men, because it colors the world and lends it vivacity, relief, and drama, and since on the other, individual action counts for a great deal in it, it shows considerable flexibility. Not only remote societies but those close to one another as well differ considerably; and the variation may be great from one generation to another. This means, strictly speaking, that

95

one cannot "describe" or statistically trace the valuational
system of a society; rather it must be told. The attempt to
affiliate and demonstrate it leads one to tell its story. Even
in the case of what I have called a "minimal period" or "epoch,"
it is essential to unearth and narrate its valuational plot, or
argument, which thus projects, as though on a screen, the man of
that time and the profile of what in his view is understood to
be happiness.

32.   The Dominant Ideology or Intellectual Image
      of the World

    Each society has a dominant ideology that creates what I
call the "intellectual image" of the world (so as not to over-
burden the theory of reality to which I refer). I mean that
even when it is a matter of intellectual ideas or content, what
predominates in a society is not really an idea of the world,
much less what is usually termed a concept of the universe. Instead, that society will have a relatively vague picture of the
world—naturally not justified scientifically—and far removed
from what men think in that society who are endowed with theoretical knowledge. That intellectual image is not exclusively
scientific in origin; some of its important ingredients will
come from areas remote from science, for example, religion. It
goes without saying that a religion is not an ideology, but it
is no less certain that an ideology about reality accompanies
any religion more or less implicitly. To look at examples
closer at hand, let us consider contemporary Christianity as it
is taught in its most elemental forms in the catechism or in
any school text of "sacred history." From this teaching are
derived an imprecise notion of the created world in relation to
God the Creator, a cosmogony, an idea of man as a corporeal and
spiritual being, a minimal psychological doctrine (the corporeal
senses enumerated in the catechism, the "potencies of the soul,"
vices and virtues, notions of repentance, attrition, contrition,
"heartache," devotion, and the like), a hierarchical idea of
society (parents, teachers, those older "in age, knowledge, and
government"), a vision of history (Chosen People, prophecy, prov-
idential plan, Last Judgment), a very definite idea of man's
"place in the universe" in relation to plants, animals, angelic
spirits, and the Divinity, a notion of the miraculous and thus
of "natural order"—almost of "laws of nature." All this without
counting the specifically religious and theological ideas, which
have a general ideological cast and also contribute to forming
that image of the world: the natural and the supernatural, the
Incarnation, the idea of sin, the notion of efficacy (for example,
sacramental), the idea of spirit, the eschatological vision, the
interpretation of death and immortality, the principles of justice,
merit, reward, and punishment, the opposition of time and eternity,

etc. This and much more is the fabulously rich intellectual
repertory found in the catechism of Father Ripalda and the
modest summary of sacred history of Fleury or others and presented without the least scientific purpose to the child in the
remotest Spanish rural school. Thus he is informed about the
Deluge and sacrifice; Jews, Philistines, Babylonians, Phoenicians,
Macedonians, Greeks, Romans; Balthazar, Nebuchadnezzar, and Alexander the Great; the Nile, the Red Sea, the Sinai; idolatry and
the Golden Calf; social patterns--tribes, polygamy and monogamy,
concubinage--the Wise Men from the East; homicide--Cain and Abel;
seduction--Samson and Delilah; the world of dreams--Joseph; the
instability of empires, the passions of the soul, destiny that
is announced and fulfilled--mane Tecel Fares--.

This is only an example. My interest here is to show one
of the nonscientific ways of forming an intellectual picture of
the world. Other means would be stories, legends, novels, the
theater (and in our time the cinema and modern media of communication), proverbs and adages; traditions, family conversation,
café talk; travelers' tales, and newspapers, since these came
into being. All this contributes in varying degrees to forming
such ideology, and in comparison to this process, scientific
teaching turns out to be completely secondary: four-fifths of
our ideas do not come from scientific instruction, not even in
our archly intellectualized societies; in others, the proportion
of science might be 10 percent or one part in a thousand.

With this I wish to show that in any society there is an
idea or basic ideology of the world that is common to the whole
of that society and not restricted to educated classes or to men
of scientific background. For everyone in that society, including men of science, share the same image to which they add or on
which they superimpose certain elements proper to each of the
social groups. Therefore, it is possible to refer to this complex of common elements that constitute the basis of the general
ideology, which, in turn, is one of the most important components
of any social structure.

But after having forcefully emphasized this fact, we must
insist on a quite different aspect: the historical variation of
those ideologies and the differences between them, even with
closely related societies. Each country, for example, knows
its own things and has its prestigious doctrines, its familiar
traditions, and its authors whom "everybody" reads. But this
changes with time, and every few years new ideas and new styles
appear in a society, enhanced by the prestige of the unknown--
often the exotic or the forbidden--or by zeal for novelty, especially among certain influential groups that others then imitate.
This is why, against a stable background, the intellectual picture of the world changes and at a much faster rhythm than basic
beliefs.

Naturally, scientific knowledge in the broad meaning of the
term is a decisive factor in the formation of that predominant

ideology. If it seems that I have minimized its influence, it
was because I wished to avoid falling into the common mistake
of trying to derive the prevailing ideology from science. The
role of science in that ideology is not always the same, nor is
that of each of the sciences: theology, astronomy, philosophy,
biology, history, and physics have had a decisive influence on
the image the average man has had of reality, and this has occurred in the form of interaction among them but with phases of
undeniable predominance on the part of some over others. Add
to all this the influence of technics on the idea of the world:
it is not the same when man reacts passively in the face of
reality, when he endures it or at best uses it by docilely following its structures and dispositions, as when he modifies
those dispositions to suit his own personal ends, which in
principle are independent of the reality about them, or when
he goes further and produces those dispositions himself insofar
as they become necessary in order to carry out projects that
have nothing to do with the "natural" possibilities of things
that he has counted on traditionally. As a minimal example,
consider the "idea" of reality instilled in man by the fact of
donning the skin of a recently slain animal, a woolen or cotton
suit, or a fabric of nylon, dacron, or orlon. In the first place,
he does not even know what the latter are, where they come from,
or how they are made. The only thing he knows is that they are
made to order specifically to satisfy certain desires and conditions imagined prior to their existence. All the technology
of this century—but not that of earlier times, not even that
of the great technical period of the past century—possesses this
feature, and it is causing decisive changes in our concept of
the real.[9]

The science that figures in the formulation of that general
ideology is not, of course, today's but yesterday's science.
Notice that even scientific education always lags behind time;
college manuals represent the state of intellectual disciplines
of a generation or two ago. The wish "to know the latest thing"
usually is counterproductive, because it is not enough to "talk"
about or simply name the most recent facts; quite often, for
example, philosophic works that contain the latest existentialist
thinker but that have never reached the historical level that Kant
signifies are inherently "pre-Kantian," maybe even pre-Cartesian.
As the speed of communication and notification has been increasing
so that ideas reach us more quickly, a parallel acceleration has
occurred in the speed of scientific change, even without considering the fact that rather than simply appearing, ideas must also
undergo a process of penetration and assimilation, to which I
shall directly refer in detail.

Therefore, the investigation of a social structure must
include the general background of an ideological nature, not one
obtained or possessed intellectually but one that conveys a predominant "image of the world." As such, it must be reconstructed

98

so as to show its guidelines and boundaries--for such an image
is always limited, so that the effective reality of a society
and the direction it takes in history cannot both depend on it;
in fact, it is essential that it be oriented in one or the other
of these directions, or perhaps that it alternate equally between
them. Furthermore, in the pursuit of that investigation, the
affiliation of the different ingredients of that image must be
determined and an appraisal made of the weight and importance
of each one. And above all, I repeat, all this must be put
into motion so as to show what that image is at each moment,
whither it is moving, and to what degree it dwells passively
in men's minds or impels them toward the future. Reality is not
only what "is there"; it is always what "is coming" and also
what "is going away." And the heart of man is usually stretched
between both dimensions. One of the deepest and subtlest features
of an era is its attitude toward this: whether it watches with
melancholy as things disappear into the past, or whether the
imminence of coming things on the horizon stirs its desire. It
is a question of small changes in this indefinite and distended
sensitivity and the impossibility of renouncing either dimension
entirely.

33. What There Is to Know and "Who" Knows It

The social function of strictly intellectual and scientific
knowledge is conditioned by the nature of its object. Until the
eighteenth century, at least during its first years, knowledge
had a strictly personal cast: that which was known was known
by someone, by an individual man, who because of his learning
was learned (sabio); such was Leibniz, and perhaps with less
certainty the same situation could be extended to the end of the
century with Kant. Afterward, the ambition to know personally
what is known becomes problematical. And this suggests a question that would have been meaningless in earlier times: who knows
what is known?
Here I am interested not in the intra-intellectual aspect
of the question, that is, the area of specialization, but in its
social ramifications. As the sum total of knowledge becomes
ever more inaccessible, it grows more impersonal and becomes
more and more a matter of belief. "Faith in reason" is far
different from "faith in Science"; the first induces me to believe that I can know everything, or at least any one thing, if
I put my mind to it with sufficient perseverence. Understand
well: this does not mean that everything is known, but that it
can be known. On the other hand, faith in Science implies that
everything is known, or soon will be, even though I do not hope
personally to possess that knowledge. Science (always with a
capital) has the answer; it is an impersonal authority, the
depository of knowledge. It assumes an institutional character

in the form of universities, academies, and laboratories and materializes as libraries: for there in books is where knowledge resides.

The matter is a bit more complicated than it might seem at first. Bear in mind that throughout the history of the West most men have remained outside the general scope of Science. This was the business of a very few who had access to it, those who knew certain techniques and thus could develop and explore it. Let us begin with the ability to read, since too often we forget the universality of illiteracy for millennia. But without going that far back and considering only the Modern Age in which there has been a considerable increase in the number of those able to read, Latin still formed a dividing line between two enormously disproportionate segments of society. Even after the common languages invaded scientific disciplines, real access to centers of learning, libraries, etc. was restricted to a very few. Starting in the eighteenth century and especially after the beginning of the nineteenth, this situation changed somewhat. Many more people acquired direct familiarity with the world of higher culture and they had a new relationship to Science: instead of Science being for them a remote and higher authority, they began to know "what it was all about." In other words, Science came closer to them and became understandable in the sense that nonscientific people knew what it was and had the impression of taking part in it. A peculiar form of communication arose, consisting of broad groups of people associating themselves with something that exceeded their capabilities, that maintained a wide buffer of inaccessibility and thus preserved the greatest possible prestige. Science was a true "initiation into the mysteries," and one must stress the persistence of the mystery as much as the actuality of the initiation. It was a time when the social impact of Science was strongest and most effective and when European life was most profoundly influenced by the predominance of scientific knowledge.

Now the situation has changed, and for several reasons. Ortega had much to say on the topic, especially in Reforma de la inteligencia, Historia como sistema, and Apuntes sobre el pensamiento. He shows how the failure of Science in human problems has been a deciding factor in its decline. Here I wish to touch on the aspect concerning the "subject" of Science, a topic that seems to me to be of no mean importance. The growing complexity of scientific disciplines has caused them to be much more inaccessible than in the nineteenth century. Let us not forget that the latter was marked by popularization, which began in the eighteenth century but was especially dominant in the second half of the nineteenth. Yet after a certain date that varies according to discipline but is most pronounced around the beginning of the twentieth century, popularization becomes next to impossible. Whereas during the past century the physical concept of the world was easily translatable into elemental forms (consider what Ganot's

Física and its more succinct versions meant for over fifty years);
the theory of evolution and Darwinism could be expressed for use
by the masses, astronomy was perfectly compatible with Father
Secchi and Flammarion; and geological theories ("Neptunist" and
"Vulcanist") as well as their geographical counterparts could be
transposed without great difficulty to the books of Malte-Brun
or Elysée Reclus. A few decades later the pattern collapsed.
It may be that the last popularizable and popularized scientific
theory was Bohr's atomic model. The break came with the theory
of relativity. Probably with no other have so many attempts at
popularization been made. But it was too much, and every attempt
has come up short. Those who have been unable, because of an inadequate intellectual preparation, to understand Einstein's theory
from within have had to be content with the splendid brilliance
of its mysterious prestige and with the barely useful translation
that "everything is relative." Much the same happened (though
without brilliance) with the Quantum Theory, and since then
similar examples have occurred with increasing frequency. The
names of the great scientists have ceased to be popular, and not
even the Nobel Prize makes them famous among the masses. When
the newspapers indicate that it has been awarded them for their
work in a given specialty, the readers do not even know the field
to which it pertains. Although the case is different, a situation
has arisen in philosophy that presents certain analogies to the
one given above: positivism appeared to have been born precisely
of vulgarization (and nothing less than vulgarization was the
extraordinary thought of Comte in the hands of his followers!),
and it is no wonder that one of its slogans should end up in the
Brazilian flag--Ordem e Progresso (Order and Progress) or that
there are still positivists in several countries (for example, in
Brazil and Chile) who practice the "Religion of Humanity." The
vogue enjoyed by the philosophies of Schopenhauer and Nietzsche
because of their literary attractiveness maintained a certain
popularity of philosophic thought until the first years of our
century. But phenomenology gave rise to an esoteric quality that
resisted all attempts at popularization. The same has happened
with the symbolism of modern logic and all related epistemological
philosophy. (What has happened in recent decades, culminating
in existentialism, is a delicate topic about which I shall have
more to say later.)

Hence the masses feel alienated from Science. In writings
published today about its results, the reader is clearly aware
that what he has before him is not Science but a product manu-
factured especially for his benefit which underscores how far
away and inaccessible scientific matters really are to him. One
may recall the series published by the American magazine Life
under the general title The World We Live In, in which there is
a curious combination of a broad and serious scientific preparation of the material and an explicitly "nonscientific" manner of
presenting it as a published text. This is completely different

101

from the attitude of the readers of Flammarion or Echegaray who
had the impression of being in the heart of Science but without
the effort and mathematical apparatus. Aptly, it was termed
"science without tears."

But there is still something else. Science is alien not
only to nonscientists but also to scientists themselves. The
proliferation of intellectual production has been of such enormous volume and the knowledge needed to master it so specialized,
and becoming ever more so, that each man of science has access
only to a tiny part of the scientific bibliography. Science has
gone from personification and presence in the "learned man" to the
impersonality of books that are "potential" in nature. For though
scientific books exist, one must go to them and read them in order
for the knowledge they contain to be realized and actually present. Now the chances of this occurring to any marked degree are
rather slim and next to impossible as far as complete realization
is concerned. I mean that no one can absorb the scientific bibliography and master available books except in an imperfect and faulty
way. The question of "who" knows all there is to know must be modified: not only do we see that specifically no one person does so,
but also that absolutely no one can do so. This being the case,
the masses are no longer quite sure what to do with Science. While
it is all the more accessible and more apparent than ever on the
one hand (in the form of incredible modern technology, the awesome
reality of nuclear bombs, and recent medicine with its fantastic
advances, etc.), yet on the other hand, it is alien, incomprehensible, and hard to pin down. This is a delicate but very important aspect. If we consider the political implications of modern
physics, we can see how one factor in the situation created around
nuclear research is the perplexity felt by nonscientists--and by
many scientists, too--regarding the "personal" reality of Science
and by extension its conditions, demands, risks, possibilities of
development or stagnation, promises, and threats. Every society
represents a position with respect to the articulation of what is
known with its human subject, and ours is particularly unstable
and confused in this regard.

34. The Means of Spreading Ideas

There are at least four points of view from which to study
the process involved in the diffusion of ideas, which is a necessary condition of their social effectiveness and an essential step
in their transformation into an ingredient of a given social structure. The first of these views is what we could call the social
origin of ideas; the second, their avenues of communication and
penetration; the third, the speed and scope of that diffusion;
and the fourth, the changes in ideas as they spread over a society.

By "social origin" of ideas I mean the area of society wherein they originate and from which they spread. The most important factor is that this area may be within or without the society in question. Do not think it unusual for this area to lie outside a society: in many societies ideas are ordinarily "imported," and importation becomes the mark of their importance; indeed, in many societies ideas derive prestige from their foreignness. This was the case in Rome with respect to Greece, and the same thing has occurred among several nations of modern Europe regarding other countries. Thus it was that English political ideas were imported in the eighteenth century; French ideas were borrowed by almost all the rest of Europe during the eighteenth and nineteenth centuries; and German ideas were in vogue between 1870 and 1930. (Spain has had its phases of "exportation" to Europe, not strictly of ideas, but rather of ways of life, values, styles, etc.) Until well into this century, America received in enormous quantity from Europe, especially from England, France, and Spain, the ideas that spread over the New World. Now there is beginning to be a question about the "internal origin" of certain American ideas and their status and articulation with those of foreign extraction.

In cases where the origin of ideas lies outside the society on which they act, the second point of view—avenues of communication and penetration—is decisive, since those avenues are the very condition on which the reality of such ideas rests in that society. But we must not overlook another aspect. The thesis that ideas arise outside a society cannot be accepted without qualification. For if this is indeed the case, then it means that the two societies (the "exporter" and the "importer") exist within another "society" that is broader, no doubt more abstract and partial, but no less actual. (Hellas, the Greco-Roman world, Europe, the West, etc. are examples of such societies.) One can imagine how important this is in understanding such pehnomena as colonization and its different forms as well as processes like "Japanization," in which the nature of the abstract "society" of which the concrete societies form a part is problematical. A history of colonization could be written from this point of view, that is, on the composition of more or less tenuous societies that may include the mother country and each of the colonies, or these by themselves. In turn, this would shed much light on the social reality of countries that have once been colonies and on their current relations with their former colonizers. In passing, it should be added that this is another theme that would need thorough study in order to reach a proper understanding of the term "West."

In any case and regardless of whether the origin of ideas lies within or without the society proper, there is always an internal origin: that area of society wherein they arise or where the introduction is made from the outside. This area is always quite small and only a tiny fraction of the social body assumes this function. But aside from this quantitative indica-

cation (which in addition is not very precise, since the size
of that fraction may vary considerably), the most important
thing to know in regard to that creative or transmitting minority is the people who compose it and their social status. These
may be individuals working in isolation; or corporations such as
schools, convents, and university institutions; or possibly an
established system of relationships that create what is called
an "intellectual world," "literary circle," and so on. Not to
be overlooked is the fact that within the society ideas may
originate at a single point, at least to an overwhelming degree
(the case of Paris in France) or at several partial centers in
different locations, as happened in Greece and is true of modern
Germany. Another factor of far-reaching consequences is the
social level of the area in which ideas are incubated. This
may be considered in two ways: first, in terms of the social
stratum from which the individuals come who assume this task;
and, second, the social hierarchy to which they attain by carrying out that function. Consider, for example, medieval monks,
Renaissance courts, or the European universities of the nineteenth
century.

Beginning from the point where ideas have originated or
have been introduced from the outside, the means by which they
are communicated and the ways in which they penetrate the body
of a society differ enormously. There is of course a vast
difference between a society of minor dimensions, such as a
Greek city, and one of enormous proportions such as the United
States. The situation varies according to the degree of homo-
geneity of a society, but more especially according to its
structure: its distribution by cities and their mutual relationships; the existence of a guiding elite or intellectual minority
its ability to extend its influence, the prestige it enjoys, and
the amount of interference it encounters from public or ecclesiastical power; the margin of freedom, the number and importance
of institutions of learning, communication media--the press, books,
journals, newspapers, and today radio, television, and the cinema,
and the social function of each. A few examples will illustrate
the way in which these different factors act.

Most French books are published in Paris; Spanish books,
since the seventeenth century in Madrid and since the nineteenth
also in Barcelona; German, on the other hand, in many cities,
of which Berlin is only one and not the most important: Leipzig,
Munich, Frankfort, Hamburg, Halle, Tübingen, Paderborn, Heidelberg,
and Stuttgart. Turning to America, in the United States the publishing industry is spread over several cities (New York, Chicago,
Boston, Cambridge, Philadelphia, Washington, Los Angeles, Berkeley,
New Haven, etc.) but in Argentina it is concentrated in Buenos
Aires and in Mexico, Mexico City, so most Spanish American books
are published in these two cities. But it is not just a matter
of publishing centers, for the organization of intellectual life
does not uniformly coincide with them. Whereas in some places

104

the universities are in important cities and thus in immediate
relation to social life and what is called "literary circles"
(the best example is Paris), in other countries, witness Germany,
there are small university cities from which intellectual life
"radiates" over the whole society. Many universities of the
United States constitute a third form, while most English universities represent the intermediate stage. In these the university
itself with its campus, residences, etc. is the locus of the intellectual world. It is located in what is almost always a small
and relatively independent city that only in a remote sense could
be called a university city. This accounts for the fact that
while intellectual and literary life is public to the maximum
in France, less directly so in Germany, and decidedly less so in
England, in the United States it is professional and exerts its
influence on society through the prestige of its institutions.

On the other hand, while centers of learning number in the
dozens at most in the countries of Europe, in the United States
the number climbed into the hundreds some time ago and now far
surpasses a thousand. This means that in North American society
for a long time ideas have spread more in the form of college
instruction than through participation in an academic life, as
might be the case in Germany, or in a literary circle, as one
would find in France, Spain, Italy, or Hispanic America. Both
European forms are relatively diffuse, manifesting themselves to
a great extent in cafés and newspapers, which treat intellectual
themes and publish articles by non-journalistic writers. But it
should be added that American college instruction does not correspond exactly to that of continental Europe; to a great extent
it is education in another sense, that of personal development
and the cultivation of character. As one might expect, it performs a function that to a great degree has more in common with
the broad cultural stimulation of newspapers and salon gatherings
than that realized in European centers of learning.

Similar differences appear in the ways of achieving prestige,
which in turn is necessary in order for ideas to penetrate into
a society. It has long been indispensable in France for one to
enjoy triumph and acclaim in Paris; in Germany, the more closed
world of the Gelehrte has associated prestige with certain academic titles within a rigorous hierarchy; in England, it has
been linked in large part to political life (which in turn was
a school of manners) and the natural prolongation of the centers
of learning. I mean that while in Germany what really conferred
prestige was to be ordentlicher Professor (Ordinarius) in Jena,
Tübingen, Marburg, or Berlin; in England, it came more from
having studied at Eton, Harrow, Oxford, or Cambridge than from
teaching in those institutions, and the development of what was
acquired in them normally did not lead to an academic life, but
to Parliament, civil service, or perhaps to shaping the personality of a writer who combined classical erudition and purity of
style with an affected air of nonchalance and "humour" that were

105

totally contrary to the German professor's Gründlichkeit. In
Spain things have been too variable for simple characterization,
and it would require a careful investigation of its social mechanism during the transition from the eighteenth century to the
middle of the nineteenth when that mechanism was consolidated
along certain lines in this regard.

The characteristics and means of influence of publications
are closely connected to all this and to the amount of freedom
they have. In societies where freedom is shaky, the spoken word
assumes incomparably greater importance, but since the spoken
word tends to disappear after a time, it is extraordinarily difficult to do a later study of a society in such a condition. Before
the nineteenth century, the influence of journalistic publication
in the spread of ideas was very scant. Yet for some hundred and
fifty years countless journals and newspapers, many with a large
circulation, have become a primary medium and in certain countries
overwhelmingly superior to all the rest. Naturally, the type of
periodical publication that aids in the spread of ideas varies
according to society; in the Latin countries it is no doubt the
newspaper; in England, the "highbrow" review and some newspapers
of the same ilk, like the Times; in Germany, a few intellectual
reviews and a newspaper here and there, but on the whole they
lack the penetrating impact of books; and in the United States
it would be magazines, within a finely drawn hierarchy: at the
present time The New Yorker is different from Collier's, Time
from Newsweek, Life from Harper's Bazaar or the Atlantic Monthly.
During the past fifteen years in Spain the influence and effectiveness of newspapers—and journals—in spreading ideas have de-
clined rapidly, and this has been compensated for by a surprising
increase in the social power of books.

When public powers actively intervene in the dissemination
of ideas, that is, when they do not limit themselves to furnish-
ing the instruments for their diffusion (for example, establish-
ments of learning, libraries, museums, etc.) but instead control
positively or negatively the content of those ideas, the consequences are varied and upon close inspection, misleading. For
naturally that power assures and intensifies the mechanical propagation of ideas, that is, it makes people aware of them; but at
the same time its intervention undermines them as ideas, for it
places them in a dimension not proper to them and automatically
causes them to lose efficaciousness. Imposed ideas do not hold
up as ideas, and although they may circulate, they do so by spill-
ing over their proper channels, producing social effects of a
different order. An especially clear and interesting occurrence
is that of religious authorities, notably where they are ecclesiastical as well. When their intervention remains within their
own sphere, that is, within the area of spiritual power, it trig-
gers the system of prevailing religious beliefs and the ideas
connected to them and thus acts within the proper ambiance of
ideas and their social function (I use the term "prevailing

106

beliefs" because their effect extends even to those who personally
do not adhere to them). In other words, when ecclesiastical authority behaves as such, as authentic spiritual power, its authority extends even to nonbelievers. On the other hand, when by
virtue of its links to secular power it uses the latter's means,
then regardless of its power, it loses its authority over it.
It would be easy to accumulate concrete examples of all these
changes in societies defined by different religions and with a
variety of relationships to the diverse powers. At the present
time these appear in extremely differing forms, although the differences are moderated (or, above all, called on to moderate) by
the fact that today all countries live in the "presence" of others
and the connections among powers in one part of the world are evident in all the others where secondarily they exert an influence.

As for the speed with which the diffusion of ideas occurs
and their extent, the variation is, above all, historical. Both
have increased incredibly in volume since the end of the Middle
Ages, occurring in clearly marked stages: the invention of the
printing press at the end of the fifteenth century; the appearance
of learned Gazettes at the end of the seventeenth century, which
afforded a means of communication to the cultured men of Europe,
together with the founding of Academies and the publication of
widely read dictionaries (Chambers, Moreri, Bayle), especially
the Encyclopédie, and with it the formation of "enlightened"
social groups in all countries, the predominance of the common
languages in all scientific disciplines, and preeminence of French
as the language of international communication; the establishment
of a daily press at the beginning of the nineteenth century together with the general triumph of parliamentarianism in Europe,
industrialization, the formation of a prosperous and numerous
bourgeoisie, and the stepped-up tempo of communication in the
form of railroads and the telegraph; and finally, the active incorporation of America (and to a lesser extent other areas beyond Europe) and the swift technical advances in communication:
telephone, radio, cinema, television, aviation, and the automobile.

But it would be an error to think it sufficient simply to
acknowledge the means of communication. The use to which they
are put is the deciding issue, and this involves the attitude of
men. Think of the rapid spread of ideas by humanistic means up
to the middle of the sixteenth century, and compare it to the
growing isolation of Spain beginning about that same time and
especially after about 1640. It produced what Valera called
"the Wall of China," within which Spain enclosed itself in the
seventeenth century. Ortega referred to it as the "Tibetaniza-
tion of Spain in the times of Phillip IV." On the other hand,
it is not at all certain that prohibition and hobbles slow the
rate of spread. It depends on how people react to them, that is,
on the attitude of those on whom they are imposed. In the seventeenth century, especially during the second half, the restrictions
were effective, and they still persist a century later (think of

107

the misfortunes of Jovellanos and the incredible difficulties
he encountered in trying to import books and start his library
in Gijón), but they are circumvented, and illegally circulated
works compensate for the scantiness of their number by the ra-
pidity with which they pass from hand to hand and by the automatic credibility granted the clandestine. And from the third
point of view what communications achieved, nationalism destroyed
in large part; while the humanists and the enlightened formed a
single intellectual family throughout all Europe by writing
letters and avidly reading one another's works, in the following
century and in ours situations arise in which, because of nation-
alistic feeling, local vanity, or political partisanship, books
at hand are not read and those on one side of a boundary ignore
intellectually what happens on the other side.

All this, which has reference primarily to communications
among different countries, applies with minimal corrections to
the spread of ideas within a single society. With this in mind
especial stress must be laid on the extent of average culture and
the presence of prestigious intellectual minorities. In regard
to the comparison between the first third of the nineteenth century and the first third of the twentieth this could not be more
revealing. Thus, whereas during the first of these periods the
intellectual backwardness of Spain and its isolation from the
European community reached its peak, during the second, Spain
was reinstated at the "level of the times" at an almost incomprehensible pace.

Finally—and this is the most interesting and delicate part—
it is necessary to consider the transformation of ideas as they
spread throughout the heart of a society. This involves primarily
alterations in their total repertory and the appearance they give
as a whole. In speaking about the ideas of an era, we may tend
to think of all those associated with the mentality of some great
representative figure such as St. Thomas Aquinas, Erasmus, Descartes,
Locke, Leibniz, or Voltaire. Yet the ideas of a society during
their lifetime are always different. In the first place, they
are older, because the slow pace of collective life imposes a
décalage between the great intellectual and the social body
wherein he lives. But one must consider the time lag in each
case and inquire as to the "age" of the societal ideas in question.
Secondly, the creative intellectual does not transcend his society
in every regard, and insofar as certain lines of his thought fail
to do so, its perspective and hierarchy and thus the whole of its
relationships are modified, thereby forming another life "system."
Thirdly, there is a wide range of difference in their expression,
and expression is an intrinsic component of ideas. By expression
I mean two things: first, the necessary "vulgarization" or "popularization" of ideas, which must be restated in more accessible
forms; it is the difference between Philosophiae naturalis prin-
cipia mathematica (Mathematical Principles of Natural Philosophy)
and Newtonisme pour dames (Newtonism for Women) by Francesco

Algarotti; the second aspect of variation in expression is due
to all types of caution. Remember that intellectual freedom has
hardly ever existed anywhere, and therefore the difference between
what "is said" and what is "intended to be said" is normally very
great, naturally so in writings aimed at a broad public. Generally
the author does not say what he wishes but what he can say, which
is another matter. The reader who has traditionally known this
(only now is it being forgotten after a century, 1815-1914, in
which intellectual freedom has been a reality for the most part)
usually has not heeded what the writer says but what he believes
he is trying to say. But because it is highly unlikely that this
can be completely successful, we encounter three considerations:
(1) what the author thinks and means; (2) what he says; and (3)
what society understands by it. Unless we remember this, it will
be hard to know what the ideas of a society really are.

But even after considering this, the decisive fact is that
ideas do not have the same vital function for intellectuals as
they have for those who are not. For this reason, in the hands
of the latter, ideas lose their sharpness, precision, and theoretical rigor, and thus degenerate as ideas. And this happens
not only because of a lower intellectual level among the masses
but also because of a deeper reason. Theoretical rigor does not
interest the masses; they use ideas for other ends and in their
hands--more in their hands than in their minds--these lose their
sharp edges, their transparency and exactness, and almost always
their truth. But in their hands they gain something that men of
theory never had: power. In order for the ideas of Descartes,
Leibniz, Locke, and Newton to have power, in order for them to
become a historical force, they had to cease belonging exclusively
to these men and become the property of the average man of 1790,
in the process passing through the likes of Voltaire, d'Alembert,
Holbach, and Destutt de Tracy; in order that the ideas of Hegel
might be converted into the transforming factor of world political
and social structures, they had to be transformed themselves not
only through Das Kapital but also through the Communist Manifesto,
finally reaching the level of ideologies in Marxist and anti-
Marxist parties.

Earlier I said that the forms of current thought are so
esoteric and difficult that popularization becomes almost impossible, and I gave as examples the theory of relativity and phenomenology. But I also remarked that a very curious phenomenon has
been appearing in recent decades, and this is the place to say
something about it. The most recent forms of philosophy, which
certainly pose great difficulties--the names of Heidegger or
Jaspers suffice to show it, and L'Etre et le néant is not far
behind them--are blood brothers to certain literary forms, novels
and dramas, often written by the philosophers themselves, which
express the same general interpretation of reality. I believe
this means that doctrines which in themselves are rather inaccessible may be made available to broad segments of society without

their degenerating as they come into possession of the masses. The reason for this is that they are spread and transmitted in a "nontheoretical" form.[10]

35. Opinion and Its Dynamics

With what has been said so far no sufficient theory of ideas, beliefs, and their relationships has been formulated. What has been given is the outline of their functioning within a society, thus determining the systematic and effective possibilities of studying a social structure. But it is not enough to consider only beliefs and ideas as such; the phenomenon of opinion must also be included.

I said beliefs and ideas as such, for the question is whether opinions in themselves are different from both or just another manifestation of their functioning. Opinions are overt, and in this regard they differ from beliefs in the strict sense. When an opinion of something is expressed, it is recognized as an opinion. A person is not immersed in an opinion the way one is in a belief. Rather, one "has" an opinion as one has an idea. But it is symptomatic that the verb "believe" is often used to express opinions: "I believe the weather will be nice tomorrow," or "I believe that such and such a policy is more favorable." Opinions have something to do with ideas and beliefs at the same time, yet they are not identical to either. Where do the connections and differences lie?

In the full and rigorous sense, a belief is that which is unquestionable. Merely by being so, it is not stated and there is not even any overt awareness of it. It points life in a certain direction to the degree that it presents us with a certain mode of reality; in no way does it do so by means of pronouncements about objects. Opinion also has a guiding function. But far from being unquestionable, questionability is inherently a part of it and specifically so insofar as it is one among several possible opinions. One might think that it is a matter of an uncertain or weakened belief, but such is not the case: even the most energetic opinion counts on others which it forcefully opposes, and a single or exclusive opinion ceases to be one. In politics, for example, when an opinion is stated only about one thing, strictly speaking, there is no opinion about that thing, and the phenomenon disappears, replaced by submission, indifference, or boredom. The same is true of literary aesthetic views. Whenever these are solidly accepted and practically unanimous, they cease to be opinions. Thus it is an effort for us to say we "opine" that Velázquez was a great painter, that Napoleon understood war, or that Homer wrote some interesting poems. Yet, while opinions resemble ideas by being expressed and stated, the differences are also important. Compare a Gallup Poll to an examination. The first inquires about the opinions of those

questioned; the second, about ideas. When one asks who the "Man
of the Year" is or whether our Asian policy is correct, each
possibility may receive a percentage of the responses, and always
a certain percent will have "no opinion." As for the student
taking an examination, when the professor asks him the formula
for the volume of a sphere, the capital of Honduras, the characteristics of Echinodermata, the date of the battle of Lepanto, or
the laws of the syllogism, he either answers or not, but it never
occurs to him to say he has "no opinion." At the most he will
say that he has "no idea." Is this the same thing? The student
assumes that what is asked of him is known, even though he may
not know it. Thus it is something that could be known and probably he should know it; and he cannot say something else because it would be untrue, and he would fail the test. A person
asked for his opinions begins by assuming the "opinionability"
of the topics, that is, their uncertainty and the plurality of
opinions about them. In the opinion of some, Adenauer is the
"Man of the Year"; for others, it is Mendès-France; another group
would favor McCarthy; a fourth, Einstein; and a fifth, Gina
Lollobrigida. Any one of these matters as well as others (but
not all) are subject to opinion, and it would not even make
sense to think they had only one answer, as is the case of the
formula for the volume of a sphere or the date of the battle.
When someone states that he has no opinion, it does not mean that
he does not know, but rather that he has not taken a position
because of lack of interest or because it is not possible for
him to do so, or perhaps because he does not have enough in common
with the matter to move him to one side or the other. This means
that opinions are not held about just anything but only about
certain themes that are of interest in orienting one's life. When
I read the newspaper I may learn that a certain football team won
a game, and then I have an idea about it, but still I have no
opinion of sports, because my activity does not depend on them.
I do not learn about football because the pattern of my life
neither presents the need nor the benefits by my knowing what
to do in regard to the chances of this or that team winning the
championship.

The first thing that must be determined if one wishes to
investigate the function of opinions as a component of society
is what we might call their "area," using the term in several
senses. First and foremost, it is necessary to know about which
topics opinions are expressed in a given society. How many and
which ones arouse opinions? The differences are enormous; in
some societies opinions arise about relatively few things; by
way of contrast, others are dominated by a storm of opinion.
Many things are not subject to opinion, and not by accident but
because a prevailing vigencia has so established it. In other
cases, opinion is a social requirement in the sense that it is
expected and counted on. This is true, for example, of the
ideology of fashion, regardless of whether the tempo of the times

belongs to romanticism, naturalism, surrealism, or existentialism; and it holds for candidates in an election, controversial books, rivals in a match, the most celebrated beauties, the best speakers, the best actors, etc.

Secondly, we must know who expresses an opinion in each case. I do not mean the number of those with opinions, although this will vary between wide extremes. Instead I refer to their structure. (Naturally, when I say that the number of those with an opinion varies, I do not mean those who opine, because everybody has opinions sometimes, but rather those who in a certain way make a profession of offering opinions; I refer to those who normally have opinions about things and thus contribute to forming the predominant opinion in the society.) In fact, these may be either an amorphous mass of people, a group, or a series of joint groups. When people speak of the existence of the public, or public following, this is what they have in the back of their minds (though something else is involved as we shall see later). In some societies there are nuclei of "those in the know" or "connoisseurs" who express coherent opinions about politics, literature, music, theater, or elegance. There may be little communication between such groups, leading to varying degrees of articulation among the the opinions they offer. It may be that those who opine about opera have no connection with those who do so about literature, but are linked with those who shape opinion on feminine beauty or notions of elegance. In other times and other countries opinions about literature come from the salons. General esteem in a society depends in great measure on this structure of opinion, as does what Ortega has called the "social power" of each profession or individual, for instance, politicians, writers, the clergy, the military the rich, as well as each member individually. When opinion is divided into mutually exclusive units, a generic appreciation becomes difficult, and the overall social reaction is uncertain and clumsy, unless there is a general "appreciation" of what is esteemed in particular circles. I mean that restricted valuations arising from such partial circles are also assessed at a certain value in the society, and the one who is important in some field is appreciated by all. Thus the great physicist enjoys the esteem of those who know nothing of physics, the great musician by those who fall asleep during a concert, and the famous bullfighter by those unable to tell a Miura bull from a Dutch cow; and not because in their opinion these persons are great, but because their respective social circles have such an opinion of their greatness.

The predominant opinion almost always originates in very small circles; frequently it comes from individuals: a critic may shape literary or musical opinion, a lady may define opinion on what is elegant, a journal starts the intellectual opinion that will hold sway in great social segments, and a prestigious newspaper can shape a whole sector of public opinion. A larger nucleus adheres to these opinions in an active way. I mean that the individuals who make up these groups also hold that opinion because they understand the matter, yet they are led by that person or outstanding group. A much broader social zone then accepts this opinion as its own but without really getting into it. The balance of opinions depends to a critical degree on the greater or lesser degree of perfection with which this scheme works within a society. And this scheme depends on the presence of those prestigious catalysts—and on their freedom of expression—on one side, and on the tractableness of the rest of the social body on the other.

I have mentioned the balance of opinions, but I do not mean stability, because opinions should be unstable. Their essential multiplicity, the intrinsic uncertainty that affects them (there is a close association between opinion and appearance [cf. the Greek dóxa]), and the fact of being the object of acts explicitly subject to opinions, all serve to endue opinions with considerable mobility and flexibility. A rigid and immutable set of opinions is an indication of social decrepitude; whereas if they are extremely fleeting, it is a sign of inconsistency. The rhythmic change in opinions, the ease with which they may be opposed, the flexibility with which they may be discussed, confronted, and corrected, and the course of each individual from one opinion to another are phenomena that indicate the vitality and health of a social organism, like the pulsebeat in the wrist.

36. Private and Public Opinion

Opinion is one of the great regulators of collective life. Intellectual and artistic life, social coexistence, economy, and above all, politics are based on the dynamics of opinion. But now a further distinction must be made, the omission of which invites serious confusion and the likelihood of not understanding well how opinion functions as an ingredient in the social structure. I refer to the dichotomy of private opinion and what is called "public opinion."

Opinion consists of the fact that I opine. It is, therefore, an individual act that one executes as an individual. The same opinion may be shared by several others or by many, in an extreme case by every member of a social unit. In this instance we say that it is a general or common opinion. Of course it need not be the opinion of all, only of the majority. (I leave unanswered the question of what is meant by "majority" in this context. Is it something exclusively quantitative? Is it formed by adding one more person to half of the society? Is it necessary to have one more than half? And half of what? Of the total population or of those whom I have described as the molders of opinion? As one can see, it is not a simple matter; yet these questions cannot be answered here because other factors are involved that will not appear until Chapter VI.) But we must avoid an error that lies in our path: that of considering private opinion to be the equiva-

lent of individual opinion, or likewise, to equate the public
with the general. It is enough to remember that when there is
a public opinion, there are also several opinions, all of them
equally public. In other words, minority and even individual
opinions can be perfectly public. This means that the condition
we are trying to describe is not quantitative in character.

It is still not enough for an opinion to be social or collective, that is, it is not sufficient for an opinion to be what
"people" think, as opposed to what each person as such may state
as an opinion. Nor even is it enough to combine this feature
with common knowledge, i.e., that each person may know what
everyone knows, that each individual may be aware that the opinion of everyone else is the same as his. Another rather subtle
but extremely important condition is necessary: the matter must
be noted or recorded. In a meeting when someone asks that something be recorded in the minutes, what is he asking? That the
others be informed of the matter? No, because they have just
heard it. That they subscribe to it or support it? Not at all.
He simply wants it to exist publicly, instead of remaining a
part of the private world of each one's vigencias; he asks that
it become the property of everyone, that it be there in the open
in the common arena, in short, that it serve as a norm to which
all may refer. Everybody knows that many things have happened
or do happen that are perfectly well known and yet are not a
matter of record; they cannot be appealed to or counted on to
establish any kind of social action; they do not exist in that
zone of reality that is properly "public" life.

How something becomes a matter of public record is another
matter. The means of publicity or publication are many and
variable. In some societies it is enough that something be
uttered in public, although the expression "in public" does not
always mean the same thing. In other cases, something said in
a café becomes public, while in others, not even what is said
in parliaments or legislatures qualifies as such. Sometimes,
the town crier is the instrument of publicity. Elsewhere, it
may take the form of a pasquinade, a military decree, or the
ninety-five theses of Luther posted on a cathedral door. At
still other times, the press and radio must intervene, especially
the former: until something is printed it does not really seem
public.

Under many circumstances public opinion does not exist, and
this constitutes one of the most serious abnormalities that can
beset a society. It may have a repertory of predominant opinions
overwhelmingly accepted by the majority of people. Opinion may
be practically unanimous and still be private. When there is no
publicity in a social body, there is absolutely none; I mean that
even the opinions that are topically "public" are not, because
such publicity amounts to mere "notification." In other words,
when opinions cannot be a matter of public record, then those
that are so by exception cease to function as opinions. Political

114

life as a whole, especially since the beginning of the Modern Age, cannot be understood unless one has a clear grasp of this situation.

Finally, mention, at least, must be made of another process with very complex mechanisms: the publication of private opinions. At a certain moment an opinion is made public that was held by many individuals, perhaps the majority, but that was absolutely inoperative. And then a new reality comes into being that is different from what had been true before and that becomes effective in a new area, acting on dimensions of collective life heretofore closed to private opinion, regardless of the numbers subscribing to it. Only with this idea in mind can one understand the political history of Spain since the beginning of the nineteenth century, for it explains many phenomena that have not been correctly interpreted.

V
Aspiration and Happiness

37. The Collective Aspiration and Its Individual Versions

The aspiration, project, or vital program is the most personal and proper feature of human life. Being I consists of exerting a certain pressure on circumstances, compressing them so as to lodge in them—in the future—a programmatic outline of life. Thus it is the dimension of imagination and future that figures in the constitution of all human life.[1] This is why I have insisted throughout this study that a social structure is not composed of quiescent elements but is defined by tensions and movements. (And when these seem to be missing it is because the society is at rest, but never motionless.) But here we must proceed with caution. What is relatively clear in regard to individual life becomes highly problematic when we turn to collective life, and such is the case of social structures. The imaginary and programmatic I, the personal vocation if you like, is an established and precise reality, but the same does not hold for the collective aspiration with its ambiguity and difficulties as a concept.

To begin with, there is an intimate relationship between the personal vocation or aspiration and the forms of social life.[2] The preconceived plan of life toward which we launch ourselves is found—at least in outline—in our social surroundings, and it assumes the possibility of realization and the power to move us only if it is founded on the precise forms of a world, which naturally is our own except in very rare cases. Thus the individual aspiration is rooted in the collective structures that make it possible.[3] The fact that one is born into a certain society, country, and period limits the panorama of aspirations that are normally possible, enhances the probability of realizing certain ones, which would then be "typical aspirations" and often pursued, and finally underlays all possible aspirations with certain partial characteristics that basically coincide despite superficial differences.

Aspiration and Happiness

Furthermore, this point of view must be brought into focus
with two others. To begin with, an important distinction needs
to be drawn: the expression "collective aspiration" involves a
certain ambiguity that for our present interests needs to be
brought into the open, though perhaps it will not be eliminated,
because the connection between the two meanings is not at all
accidental. By "collective aspiration" or objective one may
understand the statistically predominant aspiration among the
individuals of a collectivity, and hence deduce a certain prevailing type or scheme that informs the aspirations of individuals as such. But one may also take the expression to mean the
collective aspiration in the strict sense, that is, the "aspiration" of the collectivity, of the social unit in each case, for
instance, the aspiration of Israel as the Chosen People, the
missionary aspiration of sixteenth-century Spain, or the revolu-
tionary zeal of France at the end of the eighteenth century and
the beginning of the nineteenth. These two meanings are different but not separable, for since the individual can project his
life only according to real possibilities, he does so individually
as a member of his respective social unit and in keeping with the
collective aspiration in the second meaning of the term, regardless
of his personal position regarding that aspiration, whether it
seems good or bad, whether he supports or opposes it, identifies
with it or considers it madness. The Spaniard of 1580 may very
well not have felt the least missionary or evangelical calling;
he may have been a Lutheran, or even a nonbeliever, but he could
imagine and carry out his individual aspirations only as a Spaniard,
and that meant in view of a pattern that included decisive factors
of the Counter Reformation and conversion of the Indies. He met
these vigencias in everyday life, and he knew that any foreigner
he met would consider him a member of a community marked by those
features, indeed, so much so that his own peculiarities could
only be added to them as a kind of rectification of the general
"Spanish" profile that would inevitably be ascribed to him. And
so it was in other cases. The idea of European national societies
has been formed in this way, based in large part on the image
held by foreigners which then has a strong effect on the internal
social structure. In fact, one of the most important differences
between those various societies is the degree to which this process occurs, the greater or lesser reciprocal presence of certain
units with respect to others and consequently the explicitness
and awareness of the aspiration of the collectivity as such. No
biography is intelligible without this dimension. But, in turn,
the manner in which this aspiration weighs on individuals, i.e.,
the state of its influence on them in terms of force, authenticity,
and adherence, must be explained. We know that the collective
aspiration of Castile, as long as it remained Castile, that is,
until national union, was the Reconquest, unlike Aragon to which
the Reconquest "happened" during its history but with which it
was never identified. But it is no less a known fact that from

117

the time of Fernando III—or at the latest from Alfonso XI—people only inertly felt that aspiration, which did not mean however that they ceased to dwell in it. Even the kings were affected by this attitude: witness Juan II.

This brings us to the other point of view which is to be joined to those discussed above. Given the collective aspiration sensu stricto, that is, what the social unit aspires to be, independently of individual reaction (for simplicity let us suppose that it is accepted wholeheartedly), we still would not have the individual objectives determined by it. We would have to say the statistically predominant objectives, for the collective aspiration cannot be applied uniformly and automatically to each individual life. I mean that the strictly collective aspiration is transferable to individual life only by means of a diversification into "roles." In other words, a new structure is interposed here that we might label "participatory." On the one hand, individuals "transfer" to their own program of life the aspiration commonly assigned to their age, sex, social standing, and personal vocation; but on the other hand, such patterns or models by which that objective is realized are not always the same. The differences may involve such items as the greater or lesser degree of uniformity, relative awareness by individuals of the collective aspiration, the degree to which life is public, and historical consciousness. As extreme examples, compare imperial China to the United States of today, or if you prefer, Augustan Rome to the Gaul of Vercingetorix.

Hence the collective aspiration in the strict sense exists in a way that is hard to determine precisely. First of all, it exists as a social vigencia with which each person must cope as he comes into contact with it, that is, as a system of usages, pressures, values, effective relationships, activities, etc., the foundation of which is the aspiration in question. At this point that aspiration is not yet "visible"; it is encountered as one lives and acts in the form of an impulse, resistance, or direction. To return to the previous example, the Spaniard of the middle of the sixteenth century found himself with an ecclesiastical organization. His world included very active religious orders, the Inquisition, the costs of wars in Europe, the coming and going of friars to and from the Indies, linguistic and ethnological studies of the Americas, tithes, the prestige and influence of ecclesiastics, theologians, mystics, a certain literary style, religious plays in the theater, political alliances, and enmity with England. And through all this (though not directly) there occurred the form of his radical contact with the evangelical and catholic aspiration of Spain itself.

Only secondarily does this aspiration, which in this sense can be called a program, function as an idea or have a mental existence. Then it is talked about and its reality outlined and underscored by overt attention. But at the same time opinions are expressed about that explicit aspiration, and this always involves debilitation, at the very least in the sense that it is

viewed from the outside instead of being lived from within.
"Participation" now takes on a more active character but in a
sense it is planned and becomes more a question of "taking part"
than of unthinkingly and more radically "being part." In this
programmatic phase, the existence of the collective aspiration
may take on several shades. Questions must be raised concerning
which minds are aware of it and what kind of mental image they
have, and they must cover everything from the "watchword" by
which the aspiration, conceived by a few, is transmitted to the
social body (or perhaps imposed on it), to the "enterprise" in
which people feel solidly implicated and engaged.

Because the collective aspiration is a very peculiar type
of complex vigencia, then clearly everything we have said about
the latter applies to it as well. This is especially true concerning its gradations, phases, and naturally its origin, decline,
and replacement. It is most important to remember that the collective aspiration is not simply psychological but strictly social.
It exists collectively as an invigorating aim, as a "pre-tension,"
a system of tensions operating toward the future that sets the
whole social body in motion in a certain direction, independently
of the fact that it may be thought by individual minds as well.
Even its manner of appearing as an idea has a collective air
about it, not of course in the sense that it is conceived by a
nonexistent Volksgeist, national spirit, or the like, but in the
sense that it is not the original thought of any one person.
Instead, it has the force of a vigencia with which individuals
must contend, regardless of what their personal thought about it
may be. So long as this is not the situation, there may be plans,
watchwords, decisions, declarations, and the like, but nothing
that deserves to be called a collective aspiration.

But as I pointed out earlier, this aspiration exists through
diversification. Actual participation in it occurs in the form
of fragmentation and articulation in individual life projects, by
means of which each person assumes a "role" in the common enterprise. It goes without saying that among these roles are those
of the objector, the critic, and the opponent, and intolerance
toward them is the truest symptom of the inauthenticity and lack
of faith in the enterprise. The common enterprise or aspiration
"tenses" and substantiates all the forms of the social body; it
flows into and fills them, and only in this do they diversify
into concrete and realistic personal enterprises. This is what
I call the "individual versions" of the collective enterprise.
These may be more or less schematic; they may be restricted to
a few rigid types or marked by variety and a wealth of choices.
In any case, the interesting thing is that there occurs a "jump
to another class": from "collective" to individual life. And in
the latter we find both the realization and expression of the
collective aspiration in which what we have been calling the
social structure ultimately consists.

38. The "Novels" Through which the
    Common Aspiration Is Expressed

The trajectory of human life is projected by means of the
imaginative anticipation of life. Only in this way can that
trajectory be realized. This projection is, of course, based
on the materials encountered in the circumstance, and not only
materials in the sense of things, resources, or ingredients, but
fundamentally those arranged according to certain schemata. The
verb "to live" in each society has a meaning which each individual receives and which is "injected" in him by the social context.
Regardless of the modulations that each man or woman imposes on
those schemata, the life trajectories almost without exception
conform to standards that are social and thus historical in origin.
Rarely is human life observable in its complete reality; only the
old have been able to see the entirety of other lives as their
own was being consumed. Hence the importance of the elderly and
of all kinds of "senates" in primitive societies as well as in
those which though not primitive are not overly intellectualized.
Thus the reality of life is present in the mode of imaginative
fiction cum fundamento in re.[4]
   In this sense, every man is the novelist of himself, and
he is either original or a plagiarist, as Ortega was wont to say.
Life is a "poetic task." But the novels that men have to imagine,
each one his own, are based on certain underlying assumptions.
Just as a writer finds several possible literary genres, one or
more of which he will normally have to follow (or create his own
in view of them, which is another way of taking them into consideration), so in each case man bases his life trajectory on a certain
prevailing "literary genre" of the society to which he belongs.
In principle, the "novel" that expresses each life is already
given before imagining its main character: the person who is
going to live it.
   I use the term "novel" because I am referring primarily to
the modern period, especially the nineteenth century. Taking a
larger view of things, it would be necessary to speak of "stories"
in general. But it is important to emphasize that the relationship
between the real objective of men and creative fiction is intimate
and bilateral. Fictional stories are grounded in a certain understanding of human life, on the meaning that the verb "to live" has
in the society in question. On the other hand, life projects itself,
guided by its imaginary accounts in the form of apologues, fables,
myths, parables, "ensamples" (enxemplos), stories, dramas, and
novels. These have been among the strongest forces in the realization and broadening of human life and the most powerful instruments
of paideia that man has known.
   This is why the different "types" of lives have a family air
about them. Thus, there are primitive, Greek, and Roman lives,
as there are medieval Christian or Arabic, European Romantic or
American lives of the middle of the twentieth century; all of

which are defined by a generic model proper to their type and to
which they more or less adjust in a manner that is previous to
their specific content or precise biography. Beginning with a
very vague inner impulse, the personal vocation in all its aspects—
professional, economic, amorous, diversionary, social—develops
imaginatively at first and then in fact in view of certain available models of life, a certain language, a system of values, and
a general idea of what a life trajectory or "career" can be once
it is achieved. Rather than beginning with the actual content of
a curriculum vitae, attention should first be paid to the guidelines and landmarks to be found in it. I mean that a determination ought to be made of what each society considers relevant and
thus worthy of being achieved and included in the curriculum.
When the biography of a person is summed up in a few lines, what
receives attention? Of the countless "data" that make up a life
trajectory, only certain ones are selected which differ according
to circumstances, precisely because they are the ones that compose
a "novel" in the style of those predominant at the time. And viewing things a priori before they are accomplished, the individual
tries to do and experience certain things that will impart reality
to his personal "novel," that is, to a way of life that is considered successful, harmonious, or solid. Compare the attitude toward love in the biography of a Greek of the fourth century B.C.
to that of a European of 1830. It was essential for a nobleman
of 1550 to perform deeds of personal valor, as it was for the Romantic; but it was less so in 1770, and less still in Victorian
England. The noneconomic reasons for becoming wealthy (which incredibly are almost forgotten) were very weak in 1600 in Spain,
but very strong in Germany, England, or the United States between
1850 and 1900. And what of the enormous difference between the
ambition to "be rich" and "get rich"? Indeed, the difference is
so great that whereas in some societies one of the two is extremely
desirable, in others it is looked down on, and the other alternative is favored.

The investigation of a social structure must bring light to
the characterisitics of the "novels" in which the common aspiration is prefigured, expressed, and refined. In order to do this,
it is necessary to consider a series of very precise aspects:
(1) the number of generic outlines or types of "novels"; while
some societies contain a very broad repertory of biographical
modules, in others the selection is limited to two, three, or
four possibilities; (2) the greater or lesser degree of commit-
ment to a chosen scheme; the possibilities of changing, altering,
or rectifying the life trajectory, of preferring a new "character,"
are not always the same; sometimes the social pressures are so
great that the individual hardly considers in any practical sense
the eventuality of a substantial change, while at other times it
is perfectly normal for a man to begin two or three divergent
paths and to trace a series of inconclusive life patterns (like
the literary genre which the Romantic liked to call a "fragment"

and which is quite revealing); (3) the degree of detail in the
models or patterns; such novels may either be succinct or pro-
tracted and detailed narratives, that is, they may vary from
indicating a few landmarks, which leave the personal trajectory
in an inconclusive state, to determining point by point the entire course of the biography; (4) the greater or lesser degree
of originality demanded in the generic models: it may be an
imposed norm and a statistically common occurrence for each person to try to be "unique," although all monotonously coincide
in that ambition, but it may also happen that the tacit assumption of these novels is that each person is "like everybody else,"
even though subsequently it turns out that this is impossible
and that the individual tries in vain and in an original way to
be just like all the rest; (5) and, finally, the degree of authenticity in several senses in these novels: (a) the patterns may
either be the original creation of a given society or derive
from an earlier phase, preserving its preeminence in varying
intensity; (b) for another point of view, they can be of internal
origin in the society in question or borrowed from a different
society—for example, in the seventeenth century France began to
"export" models of life trajectories that became predominant
throughout most of Europe in the eighteenth century; the same
thing had happened earlier with Spain, later occurred with England, and perhaps is beginning to happen today with the United
States, although in a less general way than with the other countries; (c) these novels may be immediate and expressed in spontaneous language, or they may appear as "rhetorical" forms taken
from a remote and alien way of life: witness the effect of Classical Greeks and Romans on European life during the time of the
French Revolution, or the Biblical impact on the English Puritans
of the seventeenth century and by extension on a part of North
American society; (d) and the variable coefficient of authenticity with which each individual experiences the collective vigencias and thus the repertory of "novels" or trajectories in a
society.

It must be said also that all this is overly sketchy. Two
more viewpoints must be added in order for it to become sufficiently
concrete and workable as a method. The first concerns age: even
though in principle any life trajectory includes all ages of life,
in fact it is rarely so in a generic biographical pattern. What
we could call the life "plot," the core around which the trajectory
is ordered and which "justifies" its contents, is centered on a
certain age bracket. There are trajectories corresponding to
"youth," others that are "senatorial," and sometimes "senile,"
though the latter indicates a socially pathological aspect. All
this gives a peculiar qualitative articulation to the life span.
In some cases long years of preparation are necessary in order to
become "somebody," whereas in other circumstances the life plot
is very short, and the continuation of life has not been foreseen
or imagined. Then the only solutions are early death or a long

122

passive decline.

The second point of view concerns sex. Heretofore we have spoken simply of "persons," not of men and women. No doubt the trajectories of both sexes have a common identical nucleus, but precisely insofar as they are imagined, insofar as they are "novels" of real people, they involve a sexual distinction. The different aspects that I have pointed out do not apply equally to both sexes. Consider the fact that until a very few years ago, the number of feminine life patterns was quite small, as were the possibilities of changing one's personal trajectory. There were two reasons why this was so: first, greater social pressure on the woman; and second, the briefness of "active" time and initiative, which was usually spent in the first pattern attempted. On the other hand, for many centuries women probably have had a broader margin of originality in certain deep levels of life, because many personal acts were not considered "relevant" and thus were not forbidden. As for authenticity, the "novels" that I have called rhetorical have no doubt had less influence on women. But of course the traditional forms, those from preceding generations, have had an enormous bearing on their lives. Regarding time, the "novels" of feminine characters have usually been articulated according to a very simple outline: youthful preeminence, with a very brief phase centered around the theme of love, and then a quick settling down to a type of life marked by lack of plot. The literary fact that many works of fiction end with a wedding only underscores this very real situation and contributes to causing it as well. It is from this dual point of view that one must interpret the present crisis of that type of fiction in order to see that the "stock" appearance it has assumed and the experimentation with new forms are indications of the need—in the "novel" and in real life—to extend the plots.

Yet another word must be added to what has been said, this time about the dénouement. What is the normal "expectation" in the "novels" of each country and each era? How should they end? It is a long way from tragedy to the "happy ending." But even assuming the happy ending, when does one find that the end is really happy? And to what degree is happiness excluded from a tragic ending? In the final analysis we see that nothing human makes sense unless we view it in the light of that theme called happiness.

39. Pleasure, Amusement, and Happiness

Few things are harder to discover than life aspiration or objective. There are many reasons why this is so: its unreal and imaginative nature that alters and changes even as it is being realized; the difficulty of any kind of formulation because of its programmatic and total contexture; its complexity by virtue of consisting of a multitude of elements connected in a way that is decisively important but hardly apparent; its "vagueness" from the rational and logical point of view, together with its extreme rigor and precision in terms of life; its intimate nature and hence the modesty in alluding to it; and the frequent insincerity, more so in certain periods, which leads men to conceal their true longings, inclinations, and hopes, even from themselves.

This is why the novel and in general all literature is a necessary instrument of such an investigation, provided there is first an understanding of the relationships between literature and life within each society. I mean that although fiction always offers information about what the real aspirations are, it does not always do so in modo recto. Instead, more often that not it must be taken in modo obliquo, with a prior determination and measurement having been made of the angle of obliquity. This is a tremendous topic of literary science, but unfortunately almost no light has been shed on it yet.

The pleasures people indulge in provide an important clue. In devoting himself to a pleasurable activity, man reveals his real aspiration (and sometimes in doing so, he discovers himself to his surprise). It could be said—and said it ought to be—that man is also insincere about pleasures, that sometimes he busies himself with things that really do not interest him. But if we look closer we find that although the activity to which he devotes himself does not offer him the pleasure he officially seeks in it, he does find another kind of pleasure. For example, it would be naïve to believe the tremendous fondness for opera in the nineteenth century necessarily meant musical flowering; but it would be erroneous to disqualify fondness for opera because of it and to assume that it was not a source of pleasure. It was, and is, a very great source of pleasure, too, although it was not only or even principally musical. For this reason pleasures must be taken concretely, that is, in the exact form in which they function. Can one believe that the pleasures of the table meant the same in a convivium of imperial Rome as in a patio restaurant in Bilbao or Pamplona? Does an Englishman derive the same pleasure from drinking whisky alone in his home from Saturday to Sunday as the patrons of a Bavarian beerhall or Andalusians drinking Manzanilla from tall glasses in a Sevillian seafood restaurant? And if we go from these elemental pleasures to those that are more complex or more linked to a personal biography, the differences are even greater.

The normal popular entertainments of a society may be quite revealing, provided that they are never taken at nominal or "face" value. More explicitly, what they tell us depends on first ascertaining whether the status of entertainment is a healthy one when considered from several different angles. In this regard, the really desirable forms of entertainment must be permitted to permitted to begin with, and the society must have enough vitality and initiative to make them available. Furthermore, the prohibitions that prevent people from entertaining themselves or that cause them to switch to substitutes must not be too strong. Conversely, there should not be a custom of excessive entertainment that would cause people to pretend an insincere degree of frivolity or even of libertinism. Above all, there should be no dearth of imagination about possible ways of entertaining oneself, nor an atrophy of the desire to do so. In short, entertainment must play a role really commensurate with the way of life.

This brings us to a delicate question. What is that role? What place do pleasure and entertainment have (the two do not exactly coincide) in the life of each society, each class, each group? What is the level of requirement below which the individual feels deficient as far as entertainment is concerned? What is the frequency of the entertaining activity? Traditionally a distinction has been made between those people who lead a life of pleasure (a distinction that goes back as far as Aristotle's bios apolaustikós) and all the rest. While pleasure and amusement appeared to be the patrimony of certain social strata, above all, of the aristocracies, and very especially during youth, they were seldom present in the lives of others, being restricted for the most part to certain festivals. Yet as entertainment becomes more frequent, does it not lose some of its zest? The expectation of entertainment, its very rarity, causes it to be charged with concentrated energy, something that daily indulgence in amusement excludes completely. It is not the same thing to receive pleasure in "massive doses," as doctors say, as to have small daily portions more or less mixed with work and habitual tasks. For example, the decline of carnival is quite significant. One cannot understand the predominant aspiration of a society, nor, therefore, its social structure, without a clear grasp of the requirements of pleasure, its dosage and its forms.

But since pleasure, entertainment, and in general what Ortega calls "felicitary occupations" affect very disparate areas of life, questions arise concerning the location and direction of these occupations in each society. That a social unit is particularly fond of hunting or parties, or that it prefers gallantry or feasting, sports or cards, are preferences that shed sudden light on who the man of that society is, that is to say, who he attempts to be.

Yet another viewpoint must be added that to me seems crucial: what we might call the "right" to pleasure. This is a complicated matter. In the first place, pleasures and entertainments are often tinged with an aura of "illicitness." The basis for this is that there are indeed obviously illicit pleasures. Beyond these appear doubtful cases in which the puritanical mind sees a more or less potential immorality. In connection with this, the sense of "danger" in pleasurable activities, even in those that are completely innocent, attracts distrust and suspicion. The fact that pleasures cost money and take time, that they represent economic loss and hours away from work, gives a "sinful" coloring to all forms of amusement in societies that place great stock in wealth and the

work ethic. Then there is the well-known hostility of many moral-
ists to any form of amusing spectacle and especially to the literature of fiction, which at best they consider a waste of time.[5]
There is a popular saying in the United States that goes: "Everything I like is either illegal, immoral, or fattening." But if
it is true that this atmosphere of illicitness makes pleasure
and entertainment more difficult, we cannot ignore the fact that
it also enhances them and gives them a particular attractiveness.
And as soon as amusement is permitted and can be indulged in normally and without problems, it begins to lose its attractiveness
and force, so that it becomes dull and its appeal to the senses
is lessened; it is desired less and it looms much less important
in the life aspiration of people. Instead, it is passively accepted and used just because it is available, the individual
imagination and true capacity to desire counting hardly at all.

When this situation becomes sufficiently established, a
curious inversion of the first occurs: from denying the propriety of pleasure to the positive assertion of the right to pleasure
and entertainment. For instance, the man of our time who seldom
goes to sports events, bullfights, movies, or the bar, feels deprived of all this. If his economic situation or lack of time
or his way of life--distribution of working hours, residence far
from urban centers, etc.--denies him access to pleasures officially
acknowledged as such, then his inner reaction is one of discontent,
and this takes the form of feeling unjustly treated, of suffering
an abridgement of his rights.

In making a tacit balance of his life, the man of a given
society draws a line and gets a result. The question is, what
result? There are epochs that are satisfied with themselves,
others that are unhappy, and still others that are irritated or
bored. Except for extreme cases, this balance sheet of life cannot be explained by objective data about what life is like for
these men. These data must be articulated with the personal
aspiration and, especially, with the collective aspiration, with
what the entire society holds as its prevailing objective. Only
in this way can real worth be ascribed to actual material circumstances. According to the country and time in which he lives,
man is more or less happy, to which must be added the fact that
his happiness or unhappiness assumes a specific form, and that
his awareness or recognition of it may vary. Naturally, happiness
is a strictly personal affair and depends on the unique biography
of each person. Yet the probability and hence the normalcy or
frequency of happiness and the ways in which it occurs depend on
the social structure. And conversely, what we could call "average
happiness" is a decisive element of each social structure.

40. The Notion of "Average Happiness" in a Period

Happiness is conditioned by the realization of our personal

aspiration. Of course, this aspiration is always unrealizable,
at least to the extent that the process of choosing that of which
our life consists always implies the preference of one possibility
and the somewhat painful renunciation of others that we also find
desirable. Man is at once the being who needs to be happy but of
course cannot be so in this world. Human life could be formally
defined by "unhappiness," provided the word is taken seriously,
meaning that it should not be taken only as a negation. Happiness
belongs to human life; life moves in the ambit or element of happiness, but always in a deficient way. In other words, life is unhappy, but this means that its mode of being is happiness, which
functions as a fundamental ingredient of each individual life
and, further, of all human life.[6]

But at few points is the transition from individual to collective life as difficult and perilous as in this area. And this
is true especially because the transition cannot be made once and
for all in a single direction. Rather, we find that it consists
of a movement back and forth that is not only difficult to explore
but open to error. When we speak of "a happy people," of a happy
or unfortunate period, when the remark is made that "happy peoples
have no history," what exactly is meant? It may be that the history of a society is assimilated into a personal biography, or
that the vicissitudes experienced by a people as a collective
unit may compare with the life trajectory of an individual. But
this presents two thorny problems: first, the "who" of the collective life is not given; whereas in the case of the individual
the subject is clear and unmistakable, in the collectivity the
most problematical point is precisely on whom happiness or misfortune fall; second, the notion of happiness has been applied
habitually to the whole of life. The Greeks became obsessive
about their conviction that while man lives one cannot say whether
he is happy or not because his fortunes can take unexpected rever-
sals (the idea of salvation presents a comparable viewpoint in
more forceful terms but with certain essential differences that
cannot be treated here); yet while the life trajectory of the
individual concludes with death, the life of a society does not
have a prescribed life span, and in principle it may linger indefinitely; thus, it is necessary to articulate historical periods
and to assign to each a factitious "biographical" trajectory, which,
as we have just seen, is anything but a certainty.

The other possible point of view concerns the happiness of
individuals as such. Naturally, it is not a question of the happiness of each and every person; to attempt such an undertaking
would lead to a form of casuistry that has no place here. Rather,
it has to do with a frequency that is not merely statistical but
structural. Elsewhere I have spoken of the "material alveolus"
of human life, in which potential personal happiness or unhappiness is located. Social structures are partially responsible
for determining the possibility, forms, and specific content of
the happy trajectories of individual lives.

127

The Structure of Society

This seems simple enough at first glance: if happiness consists of the realization of the life aspiration, then the relationship between happiness and social structure will be defined by the
ease with which the latter permits that realization, and thus by
the probability that it will occur. But the actual situation is
more complicated: what has been described is purely formal and
abstract, because it poses the question in terms of simple realization of any aspiration whatever. And this leads us to wonder.
Are all aspirations the same from the standpoint of happiness?
To what degree does the social structure intervene in the reality
of these aspirations and in their actual realization?

Aside from the approximate degree to which they are achieved,
life programs have from the outset another content, structure,
and argument that have a bearing on happiness. This does not involve the wealth and variety of the resources with which the life
program is imagined and shaped but something prior and more profound: the aspiration to happiness contained in the life aspiration. All human life begins with a certain expectation regarding
itself, with an appraisal of how far it can go. In principle,
this expectation precedes all individual diversities and arises
from a general and collective feeling of life. As such, it is
shared and encountered by all, which in no way inveighs against
a subsequent reaction to it. Few things characterize a society
or period more deeply than the expectation of what life holds.
Exaggerating the terms of the problem in order to cast light on
it, we could say that an animal is not unhappy because its expectation is minimal, whereas man is essentially unhappy because
he can be contented with nothing less than being happy. Compare
a puppy to a child: provided the conditions necessary for its
life are fulfilled—temperature, food, etc.--the puppy frolics
contentedly; as for the child, even in the best of health, he
cries and is cross with unbelievable frequency; and the basic
reason is that he becomes bored. In other words, even from the
first months of life his imaginative aspiration is much greater
than the wherewithal to achieve his aim. This begins with the
use of his own body and his immediate surroundings. A child
lying on his back in his crib soon exhausts the possibilities
offered by that situation: looking at the ceiling, kicking his
feet, or sucking his fingers. Once he has "seen" all this, the
child feels that he can go no further and that this cannot be
repeated indefinitely. Yet the panorama continues to expand in
his imagination; but since he lacks the means to continue in fact,
he experiences the primary form of unhappiness: boredom. The
need for company which the child feels so strongly is not so
much, as is thought, a desire for security and protection, fear
of being alone, or the like; above all, it is caused by boredom
and the desire to use the imaginative and physical powers of the
adult to further his rudimentary aspiration. Although they may
think otherwise, adults are the "colonies," as it were, of the
small child.

Aspiration and Happiness

In an extreme way this example demonstrates what I am trying
to say. The aspiration to happiness from which life begins may
be minimal and very easy to satisfy, or very high and hence improbable; between these two extremes appears a multiplicity of degrees
and actual forms. There are bored societies, resigned societies,
moderate societies, inflamed societies, delirious societies. How
then can what I have called "average happiness" be determined?
Can it be done by taking into account the average "aspiration"
or the average "realization" of that aim? Of course it hinges
on both things in their actual articulation. For the aspiration
places happiness at a given level, so that even its failure in
the form of "unhappiness" implies a certain degree of positive
happiness. Conversely, the realization of an excessively poor,
modest, and narrow aspiration represents a deficient form of happiness, even though the individual takes the experience to be
happiness itself.

This brings us to the conclusion that our judgment of the
happiness of a society different from our own does not coincide
with the idea that members of that society had or have about
themselves. Men who seem to us to deserve our compassion may be
quite content with their destiny. Indeed, their happiness with
their lot is all the more reason why we feel pity for them, because our impression is that happiness under such circumstances
is the ultimate unhappiness. On the other hand, we may be envious
of the lives of people who judged themselves to be hopelessly unfortunate. With this in mind, we must distinguish between what
men "judge" their happiness to be and what they "feel" about it:
in a society dominated by the idea that life is suffering and misfortune, no one will admit that he is happy; yet beneath all this
he may feel imbued with an intense and delightful happiness unknown in societies in which it is decreed that good fortune exists
on earth and is within everyone's reach.

The social structure includes among its components what I
call the specific expectation or aspiration with regard to happiness. Therefore, it determines the level at which the question
of happiness is posed and with it the degree of tension in this
area of individual lives. Furthermore, to one degree or another
that structure offers access to such happiness, that is, it makes
possible the realization of the specific aspiration. And it does
so above all in one decisive aspect: by making it possible to
attempt it. One society may protect its individual members with
a thick network of societal mechanisms offering them security,
while another may leave its members exposed and abandoned to
inclemency. If life in the first case involves a minimum of risks,
in the second it is exposed to all kinds of adversities. But the
disadvantage of the first is that the chances of seeking happiness,
especially of creating and trying to achieve it, are very small,
while in the second case, man is perhaps free to try to be happy
on his own account and at his own risk.

In speaking of the "happiness" of an era or society, we should not think in terms of statistics. Happiness is too subtle and complex a matter to tolerate them. Instead, it is a question of the average level to which man raises his aspiration to happiness and the instances (along with the frequency of their occurrence) in which that aspiration may normally and reasonably be realized. But now the social structure as such reappears and more forcefully than before. For the most important point is the latitude and freedom with which such an endeavor may be undertaken. This raises questions about the possibilities offered by each society, and behind them in the background, with a number of vague references to it earlier, looms the profile of that reality called Power.

VI
Power and Possibilities

41. Society and State

A determination of the attributes of the State naturally belongs in the study of a social structure. It is impossible to understand the social structure of a Greek city, an oriental empire, a medieval kingdom, or a modern nation, without having a clear idea of the nature of their respective states. But a direct and exclusive consideration of the various states is not enough in view of our present interests. Moreover, it could lead to error, because the "same" state, meaning an identical political structure, may affect different societies in a variety of ways, or the same society in diverse ways at different stages of its history. The independence of the Spanish American countries, for example, led to the establishment of very similar states. But because the differences between Argentina and Mexico, Uruguay and Peru are considerable despite profound similarities as well, the "same" state affects the constitution of the various social structures in different ways. The same could be said of the national European states after the Napoleonic wars much more readily than it could apply today to what are generically called "democratic states," from Sweden to Burma, from the United States to Finland, from India to West Germany. A similar confusion may arise from overlooking the transformation that sometimes occurs in the same society under the same state; for example, from the Spain of Charles II to that of Charles V, or in England from Victoria to Elizabeth II, to say nothing of the United States, where the same political system and Constitution have endured since Independence.

Of interest from our viewpoint is the relationship between society and the State. Strictly speaking, that relationship has a decisive bearing on the social structure. But things must not be overly simplified, despite the fact that an initial consideration of the phenomena induces one to do so. I refer to the fact that when we regard history from our viewpoint, we always get

131

the impression that in former times the State amounted to very
little. In the face of this impression, our reaction is to think
that the State has been developing lately at an increasing rate,
that it has been growing in importance, and finally, that its
growth has come about at the expense of society, which has been
progressively invaded, dominated, at times supplanted, at others
absorbed and annulled by the State. To a large extent all this
is certainly true. But it is not exact. For the "quantitative"
aspects involved are usually not determined. It is a well-known
fact that until the nineteenth century the State was very limited;
its attributions were minimal, and its instruments, few and rudimentary. Only a process of technical and administrative development has permitted the growing interventionalism of the State,
which has reached a state of hypertrophy that is usually called
"totalitarianism," an accurate term in a certain regard despite
its vagueness. But having said all this, which is no doubt true,
we realize that in spite of everything, the State of the <u>ancien</u>
<u>régime</u>--Elizabeth I of England, Phillip II of Spain, Louis XIV
of France, Joseph II of Austria, Frederick the Great of Prussia--
was a strong and powerful reality, so strong in fact that it was
hard to imagine resisting it. Yet such resistance began to occur
often and easily after 1789, coinciding paradoxically with the
growth of the State. In the light of this we must go back and
formulate the question with greater rigor.

In effect, it is a matter not of taking the State alone but
of considering it in connection with society. The State is an
instrument of the latter, in a sense one of its functions, and
yet at the same time one of the components of society itself (at
least of many societies). When a whole series of regulations is
charged to the society as such, the State has no reason to concern itself with them. Viewed from our present standpoint, its
"powerlessness" in many areas means only that they do not concern
it. The control exerted by the State on society is normally
limited in two ways: (1) it extends only to what is important
to it (for example, religion matters, but hygiene does not, or
vice versa); (2) it utilizes the structures and means of society
and does not duplicate them, that is, it exerts control through
them (one of the most alarming symptoms of abnormality in the
relations between society and the State is the duplication or
proliferation of functions and organizations). This means that
the State governs society by utilizing it and supporting itself
in its structure and coherence. If society is a compact, coherent,
and solid whole, then state action on various points of its structure can move and guide the entire social body. Hence the real
impression of strength given by the tenuous national State of
Europe under the <u>ancien régime</u>. As soon as European society began to feel less united, homogeneous, and secure, the State began to show obvious signs of weakness.

This could be interpreted in terms of a balance of powers,
society and State: if society is weak, the State will be strong;

whereas if the former is strong and forceful, the State will
appear weak in comparison and always subordinated to it, no
matter what its stage of development may be. However, this
view of the situation is somewhat suspect because it is based
on a highly debatable assumption: the "rivalry" or opposition
between society and the State. What really happens is this:
only a weak and sick society will tolerate the imposition of a
State, whose prepotency is but one of the signs of that social
malady. The fact that this situation is frequent in our time
should not lead us to consider it normal, much less as something
essential to the society-State relation.[1] The "docility" of a
society with regard to its state may mean two completely different things: the "surrender" of a divided, dissociated, and de-
moralized society to a coercive force that need not even be very
great, or the congruence of a healthy and energetic society and
a state that is but the guiding and executive instrument of the
authentic aspiration of that society.

If we take a close look at the way in which the state of
the ancien régime was "strong," we see that it was a question
of Power itself, that is, of authority as such. Not the slightest
doubt was admitted in regard to the royal power and its instruments.
But this did not mean that the king had great forces at his disposal, for instance, huge military or police organizations. It
means rather that inasmuch as society was in complete agreement
concerning the authority of the king, all possible disagreement
has to arise within that prior social accord. Hence it was reduced beforehand to a minimum on which the royal power, certain
of its right and the consent of the social body, could then act
with decision and ease. Nor did the ancien régime usually concern itself very much with those things that did not have to do
with authority. The problems of living together were regulated
by society through a very forceful and compact system of vigencias.
I do not know whether it has been sufficiently noted that the
first process of "intervention" by the State occurred under the
ancien régime in the eighteenth century. Decrees and ordinances
multiplied; activities that had always been spontaneous were regulated by the regime; countless were prohibited. As I see it,
this fact can be explained by a dual system: first, the State
had already begun to grow and to perfect its instruments—treasury,
bureaucracy, censuses—and it was beginning to feel the gratifica-
tion of exercising them; second, a crisis of social accord was
beginning; there was increasing doubt that the question of who
had controlling authority had been answered once and for all;
and a concerned State began to assert itself where before it had
felt no need to do so.

When the crisis of the ancien régime became evident after
1789 and put the matter of authority in doubt, when there was no
longer any clear idea about who should command, or why, or how
far, then the power of the State over society weakened, even
though in an absolute sense it was stronger than ever. And so,

whereas earlier subversion was extraordinarily rare and doomed
to immediate failure, now began an era of revolutions, rebellions,
and uprisings that were frequently successful and unlike anything
in the history of the three previous centuries, beginning with
the formation of the national monarchies around the end of the
fifteenth century and the beginning of the sixteenth. It is very
difficult to understand the European history--and especially
Spanish history--of the last years of the eighteenth century and
the first two thirds of the nineteenth if one overlooks this
change of situation. For it was during that period when the
state apparatus was perfected and its most effective instruments
developed, for instance, the army, police, administrative organization, statistics, publicity, economic resources, and education.

This consideration of the "power" of the State not as an
absolute factor but as the relationship with society and thus as
an ingredient of social structure induces us to make a distinction
between the power and the potentiality of the State. The first
consists of its firmness, solidity, and mastery of authority and
command; the second, of its actual capacity to perform specific
functions and to act in various areas of the social body. In the
past hundred and fifty years the State has been characterized by
a fabulous increase in its potentiality, in relative independence
from what has happened to its power. During part of this time--
though the years do not coincide in all countries--an imbalance
has existed between the two, and this is one of the most important
factors in the history of the period. The misunderstanding of the
two aspects of State "power" completely obscures the idea of its
reality, function, possibilities, and risks. And above all, it
beclouds the picture of the social structure that is influenced
by these very relationships. After the French Revolution (however,
I repeat that the tendency began several decades earlier) the
State became increasingly given to intervention, that is, it developed its capabilities and applied them to all strata of society. Such was precisely the purpose of "enlightened despotism,"
which in so many ways anticipated later political possibilities
that did not mature until the nineteenth century, but which were
affected during that century by the crisis of power in the concrete meaning that I give the term in this context. Perhaps it
would not be unrewarding to study the history of recent times in
terms of an effort to create a State that is both "potent" (capable) and "powerful." From this point of view, it would be an
attempt to realize its ends in any number of efficient ways,
while assuring the fullness and security of its authority. But
since this depends in turn on the very society over which the
State exercises control, since the State derives its vitality
and capabilities from society, to approach the question in terms
of society under the domination of the State is to confront the
decline and breakup of the social body and consequently to witness the decomposition of the State itself--once the momentary
effectiveness of being able to use all the social resources has

passed. This is why it has always been in vain to attempt to
ensure full state power by destroying social forces instead of
trying to achieve it by intensifying and correctly articulating
them, a process that would lead to a solid accord regarding
authority and hence power itself.

42. Public Power and Social Forces

Up to this point I have used the expression "social forces"
in a deliberately vague sense. Now it becomes necessary to pin-
point their meaning. Over and again we have seen that social
reality is never static, that it is not even composed of static
elements that are subsequently activated, but that it is formed
by tensions, pressures, and aims. It is a system of operating
forces in constant movement, and far from being separable and
different from them, its very structure consists of the form
taken by the movement of those forces. Now although in the last
analysis these forces are individual in nature, that is, even
though they are grounded in the effective reality of human lives,
they are not merely individual. Between society and individuals
intermediate realities are interposed in which individuals con-
verge. The system of these realities makes up the whole society.
One might think we are dealing with what is usually called "social
groups." The term would be acceptable if it did not involve a
risk that can be avoided by using another expression.

If by groups are meant specific groups, those that form
groupings and thus divide a society, then it must be said that
they are not what is involved here. We are not concerned, for
instance, with smaller territorial divisions such as regions,
provinces, and districts within a larger society. Nor are we
interested for the moment in social estates or classes, insofar
as they really unite different portions of the population and
isolate or segregate them from other segments; nor in the two
sexes, in societies where the patterns of life are very different
for the two and where there is no general coexistence but only
certain points of contact between men and women; nor yet in age
groups, when there is a marked and well-defined articulation between them, so that the youthful, the mature, and the elderly
live together somewhat as "groups." All these specific groups,
which are evidently of interest, are only a part, and not even
the most important, of those realities interposed between individual men and the general society.

Realizing that such groups cross and that one may belong
partially to several of them, and that no organization or division
imposed by them on the social body can be taken singly, one may
be led to the notion of an "abstract group." With his customary
insight, Simmel made a penetrating study of what he called "the
crossing of social circles." A nobleman may be an army officer,
may belong to the region of Westphalia, or be a Lutheran, a mature

135

man, a partner of a fencing club, and a member of a musical group.
His personal reality is fragmentarily ascribed to different groups,
all of which count him as one of theirs, though naturally he does
not belong completely to any of them.

But even this is not enough. If we consider only actual or
abstract groups, we overlook something quite decisive that must
be included with them: what I call social forces. These are defined by two attributes: (1) they transcend whatever is merely
individual or interindividual; and (2) they are dynamic and operative in character. I shall explain. Neither the action of one
individual nor that of several as such reaches the threshold of
what may be called "social force." In order for the later to
exist, it is necessary to have convergence of individuals at random, for instance, of persons who do not know each other, so that
their functions are impersonal and interchangeable. That convergence must be active; it is not a matter of such individuals "being
together" or coinciding in some common trait. Their association
is functional: a pressure, a wish, an opinion, an appreciation,
the organization of something, opposition to something else, a
collective entertainment, etc. This means for one thing that
social forces need not assume an institutional and permanent
character. On the contrary, in a pure state they are essentially
transitory; they are made and unmade, formed and dissolved, without leaving inert residues. A part, though not all, of "social
groups" are the precipitate, the cinders we could say, of active
social forces once their activity has been suspended or channeled
into a mechanical function. Compare a political party with what
is called a movement of opinion: when there are social forces
acting in the field of politics, spontaneous and temporary nuclei
of opinion are formed, which originate in view of a concrete situation, condense to a certain form without extraneous complications,
and vanish as soon as the occasion has passed, without the individuals who formed the movement maintaining subsequent ties with one
another. Those who agreed at a certain moment and exerted pressure
together return to mutual indifference or rivalry the next day.
Circumstantial support of a public figure is not his to keep permanently and indeed may change to opposition when his next act
arouses disgust. The same may be said of any other activity or
aspect of social life. Think of the activity that unfolds during
carnival, in societies where carnival is still alive; energies of
all kinds—economic, physiological, creative—accumulate during
this brief enterprise. Thousands of individuals work together to
organize the collective festival. There are floats, masks, dances,
and music to be planned; and it takes ingenuity, personal tension,
and efforts of all kinds to do so. Yet none of this activity is
personal but collective. The anonymous person behind the mask
expressly emphasizes this aspect. But none of this remains; there
is no permanent carnival "commission," and when one is established
carnival is already dead, because there are no social forces to
sustain it. Instead of carnival, there is something else (for

example, an official decision that there will be one). Ash
Wednesday automatically dissolves all the energy accumulated--
sometimes in enormous quantities--during the three days of festiv-
ities. The same could be said of parties when they are truly
social in nature. I mean their effect extends beyond the guest
list, as does the conversation in the salons when these are
instruments of collective opinion or esteem, or of the theater
if it is truly a public reality, or of "fame," "success," "prestige," or "discredit," insofar as they function automatically
and are not supplanted by false phenomena, similar in appearance
but arising from private or state resources through an act of
individual will.

Thus, the vitality of a society as such is manifested in
social forces. The energies of individuals in the strict sense
are something else. There may be men of great drive, endowed
with extraordinary creative powers, and yet the social forces
can be precariously weak. In contrast, a lively and supple
society may not contain exceptional individuals of any kind.
The facility, speed, and intensity with which the movements
referred to are formed and dissolved are the criteria that best
permit us to gauge the vitality and vigor of a society, that is,
the normality and health of the social body. I used the word
"dissolved" because the propensity to petrify initiatives, to
preserve them after the occasion, need, or enthusiasm has passed,
is a sure symptom of sclerosis in the collective organism, and
it can almost always be traced to a crisis of the imagination
and hence to the desiderative capability.

Social forces are the waves of society. In certain cases
they are shaped by prevailing winds that send them in a precise
direction, giving them a certain duration and a "relative" stability (for example, in the case of periodic winds). In society
as in the sea, these waves are the factor that prevents the
putrefaction of stagnant waters. But in addition, in order for
the water to be navigable, the waves must be regulated by a
pressure system formed by the mass of the water, the gravity of
the air weighing on it, and the structure of the coastlines
that lend it shape. This function in society belongs to public
power.

When this power is sufficiently strong, the motion of social
forces at once strikes a balance. A system of compensating factors
then prevents imbalance in the social body. But if this power is
weak, leaving the social forces on their own without any correc-
tive means, they become spasmodic and disturb the collective existence. At times an increase in social vitality, which in principle
would be excellent, becomes a negative factor simply because of
a lack of a power structure equal to that energy and capable of
channeling it. For this reason, the social energy ends up by
being neutralized and spent. On the other end of the scale, prepotent and unbridled public power may snuff out social vitality
by trying to apply it directly to its ends, that is, to a planned

state enterprise. Still more frequently, a state uncertain of itself and affected by an internal weakness will assert itself strongly and be suspicious of all force that is not its own, including of course social forces. It cannot tolerate their free play, and as a safety measure it suffocates, strangles, and paralyzes them. It accomplishes this, for example, through a very dense system of bureaucratic hobbles, prohibitions, red tape, and delays that kill enthusiasm and suspend the development of any and all initiative. Finally, in some cases, public power links itself to a particular social force, or, what amounts to the same thing, an institutionalized social power sets itself up as public power or identifies with it. In this case, by virtue of its "privileged" character, the social force does not freely interact with the others, but acts with a prior advantage, thereby altering the "rules of the game." We might say that the social functions are then perturbed by an unacknowledged handicap that prejudices the outcome but preserves the fiction of a game. It would be easy to place the actual situations of history in the different possibilities that I have just pointed out. And it seems evident that no understanding of a social structure can come about until there is clarity regarding the situation and function of social forces within it and the relationship they have to public power.

43. Freedom and Pressures

With this we come to the enormous topic of freedom and its relationship to pressures. But we shall touch on it instead of treating it, for my purpose here is only to refer to the points of view involved in the inquiry into a social structure. In other words, my interest here is to determine to what extent the articulation of the freedom of individuals or of social or state groups is a necessary ingredient of that form of reality called society.

As he contemplated history, the man who lived near the end of the eighteenth century, and even more during the nineteenth, had the impression that freedom had not existed before him. At best, he recognized it during some period of life in ancient Greece (almost exclusively in Athens) and perhaps in the Roman Republic. But as soon as a sense of history comes into the picture, it can be seen that such an impression is at variance with reality. Not only does it show how far removed from the truth it is to suppose that freedom was not discovered until the end of the eighteenth century, but on the contrary, it also reveals the degree to which freedom has been inseparable from European history.[2] However, so as not to use the sense of history half way, the reason for the erroneous impression of our forefathers needs to be explained also.

Freedom is not easily discernable; more obvious is the lack

138

of freedom. This elemental fact has a far-reaching consequence: the tendency to interpret freedom negatively, to see it as the absence of shackles, coercions, or pressures. Beginning with this picture, attention is then concentrated on those limitations that are most keenly felt in each case, and freedom is judged according to them. Ever since the crisis of the ancien régime, European man has had the idea that freedom may be realized as various freedoms, and he has tried to win these, more or less successfully so during the nineteenth century. Without them he felt oppressed and in bondage, and he thought that other men of other times and different societies felt similarly deprived. But the problem is whether the expression I have just written is accurate. Is it true that medieval man was "deprived" of the freedom of speech? If we use the much-repeated formula, "freedom of the press," the anachronism is obvious. Yet beneath it can we say that such deprivation existed in the Middle Ages? In order for it to exist it would have been necessary for men of that time to have had a prior desire to speak out in the modern sense. This means that the idea of freedom (or lack of it) must be functionalized and that it is to be considered not as a series of qualifications in, say, a juridical sense, but as a situation. Consequently, everything that is true of any given situation applies to it.

Above all, freedom depends on an aspiration. Not to be able to vote is a lack of freedom—if one wishes to vote. But for thousands of years no one wanted to do so. After a certain date it became frequent (though less so than is generally thought), but only for men. Then at a much later date, it occurred to a small group of women that it was illogical (as indeed it was) that only half of humanity should vote; and since these women were especially sensitive to logic, this seemed to them to be a monstrous deprivation of freedom. Bear in mind the reaction of the great majority of women: amusement or surprise. The lack of logic did not overly disturb them, because first of all they had never hankered to deposit voting forms in ballot boxes. So prevalent was this view that as feminine suffrage extended to many countries, the sincere reaction of most women was this: "What a bother, to have to vote!" In other words, the right to vote, the freedom to vote, was viewed primarily as an imposition, as a lack of freedom, specifically, the freedom to stay home and know nothing of elections. Nor can it be said that this was due only to the theoretical "obligation" represented by the vote, since such an imposition has never been effective anyway. Rather, the right itself obligated one to take a position, to vote or not to vote, with the latter being not just a matter of simply doing nothing but amounting instead to the positive and perhaps painful act of abstaining.

The history of the freedom of speech or expression and its absence would have to be traced on the basis of what has been understood by "expression" as well as on the development of the techniques of expression. During some periods, to "express oneself" meant to talk in a tavern or in a café; at other times, it

meant publishing books; in other periods, to write in the newspapers; and at still other times, it was to speak in Parliament.
Today in some countries, being deprived of the right of expression
means not having a half hour of television time. What seemed--
and was--full freedom at one time and place is slavery and oppression in another situation. Academic freedom and the right to
strike interest very diverse segments of the social body, because
the men who desire the first would not know what to do with the
second, and vice versa. It is possible to have only an abstract
interest in freedom that does not concern one's own desires, as
for example, because of solidarity or the belief that freedoms
are linked and that the suppression of one threatens the others.
But even this must be taken with some restrictions, specifically,
circumstantial restrictions. I mean that certain freedoms are
felt to be elements of a system, freedoms which because of functional relationships or historical origin--this is highly impor-
tant--really appear connected to the same way of life. For example,
it is possible for the right to strike to be upheld by those who
are really interested in freedom of worship, while the freedom of
the Press is defended by those who wish to enjoy free enterprise.
But it is highly unlikely that they demand the freedom to walk
wherever they please on the street, or the freedom not to be vac-
cinated, not to go to school, or not to report their income, freedoms limitlessly enjoyed by the same medieval man who on the other
hand was "deprived" of those mentioned earlier.

Freedom is not opposed to pressures, to all pressures, that
is. Without many of them neither social life nor freedom is possible. The latter is realized amid pressures, partly because of
them, partly also by slipping between them and tracing its pathway along the narrow margin, space or "play" which the limited
and to some extent counterposed pressures leave free. In no sense
does it arise by opposing them, by working against them, by over-
coming them at certain points, or by avoiding or modifying them.
As the most evident example, politics exists only as the interplay
of diverse pressures. Without them there is no politics; when
they are limitless and overwhelming, when they cannot be modified
and do not permit this interplay, then politics vanishes from the
historical scene and is replaced by other things. (What things?
It would be interesting to find out what appears in place of politics when it ceases to exist. I do not think this question has
ever been posed seriously and formally, but it would be worthwhile
to do so.)

But the purely quantitative criterion of whether freedom is
compatible with certain limited and moderated pressures but not
with violent and unstoppable forces is not enough. Not because
it is not true, of course, but because its truth is too elemental
and crude. In the first place, the intensity of pressures cannot
be measured absolutely; they must be gauged in proportion to the
strength of social aspirations and the vitality of social forces.
The "same" pressure may function in one way in the Rome of Scilla

and in an entirely different way in the Belgium of Leopold II.
In the second place, just as the aspiration to happiness may be
high or low, so freedom varies enormously throughout history.
The life program of the individual in each society presents a
catalog of requisites of varying breadth and content; in turn,
these requisites make demands accordingly on the surroundings in
order to be realized. Real freedom depends on what one would do.
But because these pressures, more or less precisely fixed in the
mind of individuals, either allow intentions to be realized or
smother them even as intentions, then we must consider what could
be called the level of aspiration. At times power has nothing to
suppress; it is hardly exercised at all, rarely bringing its
coercive weight to bear on individuals. Yet this does not imply
the existence of freedom; quite the contrary, the deprivation of
freedom is such that even the aspiration to it has been obliterated.
These are situations of resignation, surrender, or desperation (for
there is a difference between them). When carried to extremes,
degradation is the result. This is the only way to explain the
persistence for years upon years, perhaps for centuries, of certain
particularly oppressive ways of life. In the Dictionnaire philoso-
phique of Voltaire, Count Medroso asks Lord Boldmind: Vous croyez
donc que mon âme est aux galères? And Boldmind replies: Oui; et
je voudrais la délivrer. But Medroso insists: Mais si je me
trouve bien aux galères? And then Boldmind observes: En ce cas
vous mérites d'y être.[3] From our point of view, which is that of
freedom as an ingredient of the social structure, the important
thing, in my judgment, is the following. Life is possible as
freedom when the pressures, though energetic, do not destroy the
image that the social unit tries to grasp; and thus they normally
make possible the individual trajectories as defined by prevailing
aspirations. In other words, the absence of freedom appears as
an internal contradiction with the society that suffers from it.
Some examples will clarify what I am trying to get across. If
the predominant belief of a society is that power belongs to the
monarch, and if he so exercises it, then this does not mean a
lack of freedom, and individuals feel free in this order of things,
though subject to the authority of an absolute monarchy. On the
other hand, if the assumption of a social body is that sovreignty
rests with the people, but the people are unable to exert authority,
then this situation is a case of strict deprivation of freedom.
Although it seems platitudinous to say so, the lack of freedom of
the Press requires the existence of the Press, that is, the presence of newspapers in which opinions are expressed, in which
things are judged and criticized, and in which people are informed
about what is happening. A situation in which there are no newspapers or where they serve only to transmit information does not
involve "freedom of the Press." But if the informative function
is maintained in name only and information itself cannot be transmitted, if things are printed that seem to be opinions but are not
because nobody holds them, if it appears that things are being

discussed that cannot be discussed, then the lack of freedom is
real. When Seville and Cadiz had commercial privileges with the
West Indies, no lack of mercantile freedom was implied, just as
none is involved when only the Banco de la Nación can print
paper money, or only the State can mint coins. But if there are
external industrial and commercial structures, if businesses
exist for the purpose of producing and exchanging goods, but
they are not permitted to do in fact what they are able to do in
principle, then at that point economic freedom is being denied
them. Similarly, if the predominant belief is that each person
gets along as best he can, working or not, earning much or little,
with the standard of living he is able to achieve on his own, the
situation may be good or bad, even regrettable or atrocious, yet
it is based on freedom. Conversely, if there are labor structures
encompassing such things as unions, pay scales, contract inspection,
workers' rights, and ownership of company shares, and yet they are
not allowed to function effectively, thus running counter to the
prevailing situation, then this is precisely what destroys freedom.
Even compulsory military service is compatible with freedom; yet
despite the much smaller numbers involved, the system of conscrip-
tion is not, because it contradicts the principle that a citizen
has no reason to serve in the armed forces. One could cite other
examples.

This would be the proper vantage point from which to study
the difficult topic of intellectual freedom, about which usually
very little is clear. Whenever a real consensus exists in a society that something is undebatable, the fact that it is not discussed is not a suppression of freedom. Of course when this happens, public power need take no pains to prohibit it because it
is the social pressure as such (which is intellectual pressure
in the case of a topic of thought) that adequately prevents it.
The intervention of the temporal powers almost always occurs because that consensus does not exist in society. On the other
hand, academic freedom and the freedom to publish or speak out
publicly have not existed during most historical eras; yet it
would be incorrect to say that there has never been intellectual
freedom. From the nineteenth-century point of view, taking it
as it was understood in Western Europe at that time, this might
be true enough; but within the predominant assumptions of each
historical period freedom has existed at times but not at others,
according to whether it has in fact been possible or impossible
to perform what was recognized in principle as the normal function
of intelligence. The lack of freedom consists of maintaining all
the resources of a form of intellectual life—for example, "public"
universities, private publishing houses, journals, newspapers,
cultural associations, conventions, research centers, compensation,
etc.—but nullifying the actual conditions necessary for them to
function, that is, suppressing the inherent requirements of that
intellectual activity and by doing so denying what they are assumed
to signify. Incredible as it may seem, historical studies that

142

attempt to tell and explain any order of intellectual production of different periods of the past only rarely and somewhat by exception take this critically important aspect into consideration. Yet on it depends nothing less than the significance and with it the very reality of the science, philosophy, pedagogy, literature, and even art of a period.

In short, in order to clarify a social structure it is necessary to define in formal terms both the degree to which all the forms that go into its makeup can or cannot be realized and the interplay of pressures by which that realization occurs or is thwarted. With this, the idea of freedom stands out not as a creature of greater or lesser particular constrictions but as the degree of authenticity within a unit of collective coexistence.

44. The Margin of Individuality

So far I have referred to freedom as a condition of a society. As such it affects the lives of all the persons who belong to that collectivity, but only insofar as their lives are characterized by that common societal adherence. This means that it is a matter of a generic and somewhat abstract freedom. In other words, if what I have called "deprivation of freedom" immediately excludes freedom, the contrary situation, "life as freedom," should not necessarily be identified with the existence of actual freedom. For it offers only the possibility of freedom by establishing a context. In order for freedom to exist in fact, it is not something one has, but something one "makes." And this brings us to another area of consideration.

Actual freedom does not lie, of course, in the absence of constriction, but in the real possibility of projecting life and of realizing it once it has been projected. Its first condition is, then, imagination. The smaller the imagination, the lesser the context of freedom. The extreme case of this naturally would be the animal. Although not the least external pressure weighs on it, its minimal imagination annuls its possibilities of freedom.[4] On the human level, when the imagination is very reduced, freedom has only a very narrow margin of activity. Understand well: man is always free, he is so necessarily; but this does not mean that he is completely free. On the contrary, he may be free only to a very small degree. We must not assume that by degrees of imagination we are speaking of some abstract imaginative "faculty" or capability. Real imagination is conditioned by the materials at its disposal: memories, experiences, the dimensions of the mental horizon, and so forth. This situation, which is seldom thought of, is the first factor in what could be called the "quantification" of freedom.

Secondly, freedom requires a certain amount of collective complexity for its development. Robinson Crusoe was absolutely free in the sense that he felt no social pressure or coercion.

143

Yet the context of his real freedom was extremely small. Being alone, Robinson had no choice but to do everything himself; but that meant automatically that the minimum activity demanded for physical survival exhausted almost all his possibilities. I mean that the life Robinson could lead was already predetermined by his situation. Being the man Robinson necessitated a series of invariable acts that hardly left room for anything else. This is why the Robinson "type" is universally valid, except for personal nuances of individuality that rarely became obvious.[5] One is not free to be this or that Robinson, and once there are two men on the island, the possibility arises of two versions of men who differ from the solitary man (because now they are not so solitary): Robinson or Friday.

The third conditioning aspect of freedom is the existence of sufficient resources. To begin with, this means resources in the society, and more specifically at the disposal of each individual. This is why regardless of its other possibilities, freedom is always threatened and restricted by all forms of primitivism. The simplicity of social articulation, for example, means that very few models of life are available for the individual to choose from. The lack of technical means restricts freedom, for instance, the freedom to travel, to eat certain foods, and to have experiences of all kinds. Economic straits reduce the radius of the individual's action and eliminate from his panorama countless possibilities that are available--available in society as a whole, that is, but not really accessible to many individuals and thus not possibilities for most.

The wealth and complexity of societies thus multiply the human roles possible within them as well as the acts, behaviors, and experiences that may occur in each of them. Hence real freedom is increased to the second power by that growth. Individual human reality may appear in many more versions, and each one has a wider range of expression. The margin of individuality widens and expands, and the difference between extreme situations is incredibly great. This is why society, a situation, or within it, the biography of an individual man, cannot be understood without some attempt to "quantify" (sit venia verbo, because as is true of all human things, that quantification is inherently qualitative) the context of its possibilities and therefore the margin of individuality.

But it would be an error to let thought succumb to inertia and advance mechanically. Because after a certain point the very intensification of factors that facilitate and expand freedom and individuality threatens, diminishes, and perhaps stifles them. That point is not fixed and may be determined not in the abstract but only within a concentration or system of structural elements. If the three aspects that I have considered reach a limit that varies in each case, beyond that point they reverse themselves and act in a manner contrary to what in principle their role is. Thus an "imaginative" excess, i.e., a wealth of

144

memories, experiences, efforts, projects, and theories, restricts
freedom, for before the prospect of any fancied avenue of action,
the difficulties and reservations, the memory of failures, and
the need to consider other factors arise to produce a paralysis
of action. This is what happens in periods of accumulation and
affectation, in so-called "decadent" societies, in which by a
reverse process and usually as a reaction, situation develops
that leads to primitivism. In a similar way, when the social
body becomes highly congested, as, for example, when the population increases beyond a comfortable density, the friction is
such that the radius of action of each individual is reduced.
Whereas Robinson Crusoe could scarcely be himself because it
took all his effort to be a man, that is, to keep on living, the
person who lives in an overpopulated and structurally complicated
society can hardly do anything except continue where he is, fixed
at the point where society has him situated. Sometimes this immobility is literally physical. He must remain in the same living
quarters and job or position indefinitely. Lastly, an abundance
of resources that initially broadens the horizon of life may
come to demand the attention that formerly was directed to one's
projects, thereby causing one to disavow the latter. The poverty-
stricken man can do hardly anything, but the very wealthy man does
little more than one thing: protect his wealth. This example
will suffice to show what I mean.

In summary, it is a question of minimums and maximums. In
order for life as freedom to be realized in fact, and above all
in a way that leaves a broad margin of individuality, it is necessary to have a degree of "density" and complexity in social
forms and collective life. Yet if society becomes too thick,
the threads of the life trajectories begin to tangle and lose
their pattern. It would not be impossible, though of considerable
theoretical difficulty, to determine the optimum degree of intensification and complication in each stratum of life. In any case,
it is absolutely essential to measure that complexity and concomitantly to gauge the possibilities of the individual within each
social structure.

45. The System of Usages as Facility and Limitation

In the syllabus of a course on Man and People offered in
Buenos Aires in 1939, Ortega wrote these concise theses on the
reality and function of usages:

> Usages produce these three main kinds of effects in
> individuals: 1. They are patterns of behavior that
> allow us to foretell the conduct of individuals whom
> we do not know and who are not, therefore, specific
> persons to us. The interindividual relationship is
> possible only with people we know individually, that

is, with our fellow man, our "neighbor" (one "nigh"
or "near" us; Spanish prójimo, one who is "proximate,"
or "near"). Usages allow us a quasi-coexistence with
the stranger.

2. In imposing by pressure a certain repertory of
actions--ideas, norms, techniques--usages obligate
the individual to live at the level of the times and
they instill in him willy-nilly, the accumulated
heritage of the past. Thanks to society, man is
progress and history. Society safeguards the past.

3. By making a great portion of individual conduct
automatic and by presenting a person with a prepared
program of almost everything he must do, they allow
an individual to concentrate his life in a creative
and truly human way in certain directions that otherwise would be impossible for him. Society situates
man in a position of relative freedom with regard
to the future and allows him create that which is
new, rational, and more perfect.

An entire sociology is contained in nuce in these few lines,
and this justifies their literal repetition. But our specific
interest here is to see how a social structure includes among
its principal features the means by which usages affect the individual and his possibilities.

First of all, usages are quantitative in a dual sense:
with respect to their number, "area," or field of application;
and with regard to their intensity. Indeed, usages may be many
or few, and their effect, more or less. Each era has the impression that the number of prevailing usages has increased or de-
creased in comparison to the previous era. Probably both have
occurred, for the area of usages has been displaced and now
affects zones that formerly were exempt from regulation by
usages, whereas others that were "covered" by them are now free
or vacant. This displacement conceals the quantitative change
and makes it hard to determine. This same impression reappears
in going from one contemporary society to another. The predominant usages of Spain hardly apply to France or the United States,
and this may give rise to the idea that "anything goes" in the
latter two. Yet immediately we notice that whereas Spanish
society has nothing specific to say about certain topics, French
or American society exerts a very precise pressure in those areas.
Hence in order to understand a society it is essential to measure
the prevailing usages, not with the hope of ascertaining exact
dimensions, but with the purpose of reaching an approximate (and
of course comparative) understanding of their volume. In other
words, it is a matter of ascertaining whether a society is fundamentally or superficially determined by usages, or to put it yet
another way, whether from this point of view a society is more
or less "dense" or given to spontaneity and improvisation.

Power and Possibilities

But it is not enough simply to know the number of usages extant. These are pressures, forces that act on the individual. With what intensity do they act? There are always strong usages and weak ones, those that impel sub gravi and those that do so sub levi, as moral theologians would say with other purposes in mind. In some societies the entire system of usages is predominantly forceful, while in others it is lax. I mean that even prior to the quantification of each prevailing usage in particular the vigencia of usages itself turns out to be comparatively weak or strong. The measurement (which I repeat is always approximate and comparative) of that intensity and of the portions of the system according to which variations occur would give us a "metric map" of the usages of a society, similar to those that point out on a geographic chart the distribution of rainfall or population density. And it would not be impossible to draw a map of "isobaric lines" (taking the expression cum grano salis) that would join the points of equal social pressure. If this were done with some rigor, if within the social body one were to trace the figures of greater or lesser pressure, thus determining those more or less apt to give way and be modified, then it would allow social movements to be predicted.

This involves the need to clarify those areas of life normally most affected by usages. Yet this must not be taken to mean that some areas are regulated but not others. What varies is the principle of regulation: sometimes it is usages, at other times, law, at others, simple custom. While in certain periods dress has been legally prescribed (for example, ordinances concerning adornment, dress codes for nobles and villeins, or for married or single women, etc.), in others dress is dictated strictly by social usages in which the State takes no part, for instance, in making one's debut, wearing a tuxedo, a tie, a low-cut dress, or different colors and kinds of fabrics according to sex, age, and social standing. When usages are very weak, everything is permitted (within limits), the obligatory is reduced to a minimum, and in its place appears the criterion of frequency, which is the basis of custom. Perhaps it is the custom in some countries to breakfast on café au lait, and if someone substitutes seafood, he does not violate a usage, but simply does something unaccustomed, which does not invoke serious social reprisals as is the case with infractions of usages; for example, if someone ties his napkin to his neck or drinks champagne with a spoon. A similar infraction would occur in Spain--though not in France-- if a woman worker wore a hat, or if in France--though not in Spain--one called a lady by her Christian name.

In some cases, law and usage regulate the same areas. Whereas civilian dress is regulated by usage, uniforms and vestments are a matter of juridical ordinances of a public nature. When certain foods are forbidden by religion, or may not be eaten at certain times ("meatless days" or "dessertless days" in some countries), usages as such cease to act and are replaced by the stronger force

147

of law. The same occurs in the matter of addressing another when
it is not simply a matter of courtesy, that is, when it is not
socially imposed by a usage, but is required legally. And the
same could be said of greeting or other similar phenomena.

When usages are many and strong, life is shaped by them,
leaving only a small margin for spontaneity, improvisation, and
creativity. If on the contrary there is a general breakdown of
usages, that is, if they have ceased to be binding or barely remain so, behavior becomes unpredictable and one cannot be certain
about others or about what to do. On occasion, certain aspects of
life are asphyxiated by the pressure of excessively intrusive and
oppressive usages. Consider, for example, relationships between
men and women in many forms of society, the impossibility of intersexual friendship, the problems of having an amorous relationship,
and the impairment of marriage (for long periods of history consent
was fictitious and nonexistent from our present point of view) because of the prevailing usages, all of which result from the indis-
criminate pressure of disproportionate usages. On the other hand,
however, a crisis in the usages in this same area of life brings
about a lack of regulation of these relationships that disrupts and
annuls them to the same degree, though in another sense.

This means that although human life is creation, it cannot
begin from zero. The level from which creativity begins is nothing
less than that defined by the system of usages. Supporting himself
on them, man innovates and traces his personal course of life.
They are, then, a limitation as well as a facility.

But something should be said about a very odd class of usages:
negative usages. In a strict sense it is not proper to call them
usages, because their characteristic is precisely that they are
not used. Nor should they be called customs, because they point
to no customary activity. Yet if someone does something that in-
fringes on a "negative usage," society responds with its habitual
reprisals, and then the mechanics of usages goes into effect, revealing the larvate character of the negative usage. I would
propose the term "solences" (solencias) for this class of usages.
The negative usage does not compel anything, nor does it prohibit
anything explicit; it is simply that things are usually this way.
This or that act or gesture is usually omitted. It is not by accident, but quite significant, that the word solencia does not
exist in Spanish, or Latin, or any of the other Romance languages.
What does exist is the word "insolence" (insolencia), because the
"solence" is revealed by being denied and violated by an act that
is "unusual" (insólito). This is the primary meaning in Latin of
insolentia or insolens; not the unused or that which has stopped
being usual, but rather the inhabitual, the unaccustomed, that
which is usually not done, that which is strange or bizarre. And
for this reason, it is irritating, impertinent, challenging, insolent in the modern sense. "Insolence" is unforeseen novelty.
In Latin it was said of a very odd name that it was insolentissimun.
And since this is exasperating and appears to be a slap at the

socially acceptable, insolence is burdened with pejorative con-
notations: it is cheek, lack of respect, a desire to stand out,
shamelessness. On close examination, we see that most behavior
that seems insolent represents violations of usages that are
negative and hence rarely formulated. I say "most" because
language has an elasticity that precludes exactness; still, it
can be seen that the tendency is unmistakable.

Women in particular in nearly all societies are subject to
a set of negative usages, or "solences." I have expressed this
on other occasions by saying that woman's situation has been
that of being able to do nothing unless there was express social
agreement about the propriety of her acts. In principle, she
could do nothing; a general "solence" weighed on the distaff
side of humanity, coming to light and taking shape as women kept
on attempting behavior that was insolent, regardless of what it
concerned. This happened with the first women who tried to attend the universities; their attendance was not prohibited (not
even prohibited!) because it had not been foreseen. Yet there
was a latent negative usage that women did not go to the university. The same thing happened when a woman went swimming, or
lit a cigarette, or crossed her legs(!). The examples could run
into the hundreds. And notice that in the case of a positive
usage, its infraction is not considered specifically as insolence.
Sixty years ago the woman who painted appeared insolent, but not
the one who was unfaithful to her husband. In some countries
today the woman who wears pants seems insolent, but not the one
who appears without a hat, gloves, or party dress in circumstances
where usage dictates that they be worn.

In any social structure, therefore, it is necessary to determine the proportion in which positive usages and "solences" (or
negative usages) are distributed and located in collective life.
Only this will permit an understanding of the extent of elasticity, rigidity, or paralysis in a given society.

46. Wealth and Economic Structure

The point of view from which the economic situation of a
society must be examined does not lie within the economics itself.
Instead it is determined by the need to ascertain to what degree
and in what way the economic condition affects the social structure and more specifically the range of individual or group possibilities. This means that even though quantitative considerations are, of course, essential, they cannot be the only ones
taken into account. In fact, they are but the starting point.

Hence we must begin with an evaluation of the total wealth
of a society, though by that same measure we cannot stop there.
This evaluation is the reference point for all later determinations, and all subsequent qualifications of other kinds are made
possible through it. With many intermediate degrees, there are

more or less poor societies, as there are more or less rich ones.
But to ascertain the absolute amount of that wealth is still not
enough, for socially wealth is always comparative. A society is
rich or poor in comparison with other societies (one European
nation, for example, measuring itself by the level of others)
or with itself in other times. And it feels impoverished or
enriched, having come down or come up in the world. In the
second place, the economic awareness of a social unit does not
depend solely on its present wealth but on its potential as well:
the impression of wealth among young nations with a colonial
economy has usually been founded more on what they expected
than on what they had in fact. In other cases, dire want has
been joined to a limitless faith in the immediate economic future;
while on the other hand, many countries (in South America, for
instance) have begun to feel poor, or at least not so rich, just
when they have considerable wealth on hand. For this has coincided with the discovery of the limitation of their possibilities,
with a shrinking of their horizons.

The wealth of a society cannot be considered without including more exact particularizations in two areas. First, it is
important to know the degree to which economic units may not
coincide necessarily with social units, the first possibly
being smaller or greater than the second. For example, the
economy of different regions of a nation has had relative autonomy for a long time and has presented different levels and structures. On the other hand, while this situation persists residually,
the progressive complication of economic life has caused great portions of the world to function together as units. From this point
of view they manifest cohesiveness, yet differing societies are
included. The other area in which wealth must be considered is
that of its internal distribution. Its total amount, whether a
society is rich or poor, still does not tell much about its
structure. For wealth may be concentrated in the hands of a
few individuals or shared fairly equally, and there are countless
intermediate degrees between these two extremes. But neither is
the purely quantitative enough, and for this reason economic
statistics are not an explanation but only data essential to an
explanation. If wealth is in the hands of a few or shared by
many, the important thing to know is who controls it. It matters
whether it is the State, a noble class, religious orders, a circle
of financiers, or relatively isolated and independent individuals.
To take a Spanish example, and from the Romantic period at that,
it is evident that the deamortization of Mendizábel did not represent in principle a substantial shift of wealth, but it did
bring about decisive changes in the social structure of Spain.

Assuming that a certain amount of wealth exists and is distributed in a given way in a society, an important structural
factor is what we could call the accessibility of wealth. In
effect, economic possessions can belong to the owners in varying
degrees. "Fortune" and "earnings" are the two main manifestations

150

of wealth. And both present many variations. In some cases, wealth is invariably linked to other social conditions; it may, for instance, be restricted to a single social level, perhaps with very precise personal links. In other cases, wealth is easily accumulated and lost; it changes hands and is much less tied to social status than to work (in combination with any portion of astuteness and luck, of course). In other societies wealth appears as fortune inherently connected to a social position, for example, in the form of seigniories; and in still others, it is a matter of earning it. In these there exists the vigencia (how really exact it may be is unimportant at the moment) that wealth is the result of work, a notion that most societies have not shared. The idea that the poor man, no matter how hard he tries, stays poor, that one is either rich or poor from the start and probably forever, influences the structure of society in a way quite different from the conviction that every individual has a "chance" at wealth, and even that in principle these chances are the same for all. Concomitantly with deamortization, for nineteenth-century Spain the severance represented a drastic transformation of the economic and hence social structure. And to the degree that economic freedom is restricted, whether by state intervention or by social forces (monopolies, trusts, etc.), the chances for real access to wealth are distributed unequally according to individual relationships to those powers. This gives rise to a new form of privilege that is nearly always disguised and therefore not publicly evident and admitted.

Also related to this economic aspect are two others that contribute enormously to the articulation of societies: the proportion of security and the normality of happiness or unhappiness with the economic situation. Indeed, in the majority of human societies until less than two centuries ago, economic security was always the patrimony of a very few. Yet for two reasons it would not be accurate to say that before 1800 Europeans lived in a state of insecurity: first and formally, the experience of insecurity presupposes having lived in a previous state of security, which in general was unknown to them; and second, they had the security or certainty of the worst, and thus the direst kinds of misfortune (poor harvests, illness, disablement, orphanage) seemed "normal" to them; such eventualities were simply the nature of life and not anomalous and exceptional situations. This is why the feeling of insecurity arises in times of relative well-being and prior stability of the economic level. Clear examples of this would be Germany and Central Europe after 1918, or the United States when the Depression of 1929 befell it after years of a prosperity that was not just any prosperity--an adventure or a stroke of good fortune--but one that seemed permanent and lasting. In general terms, once an appreciable level of security has been reached, everything that threatens it appears as danger and insecurity, and the sense of

151

the latter depends on the desire for security. Spanish life of
the nineteenth century cannot be understood without the presence
of the specter of unemployment. But in turn that fear is incomprehensible without the avidness for a "secure" job, one that is
permanent and without risks, which the Spaniard refers to signifi-
cantly enough as a "placement" (colocación) or "destiny" (destino).
If, on the other hand, economic development tends to diminish the
gravest risks (for example, mass hunger), on the other, raising
the economic level and general welfare increases the changes of
insecurity. Life at the very bottom of the economic scale is
exposed to disaster and death by starvation perhaps, but not to
anything else; whereas life amid the most promising of probabil-
ities, without facing the extremes mentioned above, is nonetheless threatened by a fall that is difficult to bear without a
transformation of all the life structures and dispositions.
This is why insecurity is more a phenomenon of the upper and
middle classes than the lower; because with the latter "coming
down in the world" is less probable and less drastic. The frequency with which "safe" but poorly paid jobs are preferred in
a society over higher but tentative salaries is one of the most
revealing traits (because of its many connections with other
factors) of a social structure and thus of a collective way of
life.

Something similar happens with unhappiness, which presupposes comparison with a certain level either reached by others
or at least imagined and specifically desired by those who in
fact have not reached it (but which they could reach) or by
those who have fallen from it. To express it another way, happiness and unhappiness refer more to the situation than to the
condition. Whereas the latter is the way of being or living that
is one's lot in this world, to the point that it is almost identified with the person himself, the situation is by definition one
among several, this one and not some other; thus it is intrinsically comparative and qualitative and as a result is appraised
as more or less satisfactory. Countless men have lived on this
planet without economic unhappiness, not because they were well
off, but because their economic misfortune (which is something
else) seemed to them to be inexorably linked to their condition,
which was undoubtedly one of wretchedness, misadventure, etc.--
words that touch on zones of reality not included in the expression "unhappiness." To sum it up in a few words, unhappiness
presupposes happiness, at least in the form of an accessible
possibility, and it has sprung up as a collective phenomenon
precisely because men have begun to achieve a minimum of economic
well-being in many areas of society. Moreover, as long as man
holds to that minimum, which is defined by the most pressing
necessities, satisfying these seems to be a sufficient achieve-
ment. But as the level of demand rises to items not strictly
necessary for subsistence, it becomes difficult to fix its
boundaries. Then appears the desire for what has been imagined,

and since in principle it is now possible, it seems a deprivation if in fact it is not in one's possession. Hence the tendency to competition and rivalry that appears in all social forms
characterized by economic affluence, for example, luxury, parties,
servants, the costly summer vacations of the nineteenth century,
vehicles; or buying the latest models and the newest appliances
in the United States (what they call there "keeping up with the
Joneses"). Since all this presupposes an element of mutual presence and comparison, it leads us to other facets of the economic
structure, specifically, to the standard of living and existence
of a society in the sense of "social life."

The standard of living outlines a set of possibilities, the
scale of which is determined in large part by the economic range.
This range is first of all a function of the society itself; for
if it is poor, existing possibilities are few. Secondly, it pertains to individuals, because the possibilities in society are
not necessarily available to each person. It is not necessary
to insist on the fact that the fabulous increase of wealth in
the industrial age has expanded the horizon of generic possibilities for man to an incredible degree, and in even greater proportion the average possibilities of individuals in Europe and
America. However, the limitation and servitude implied by a
rise in the standard of living are usually overlooked. For
example, the notion of comfort makes many situations and experiences seem painful that before were felt to be normal, those that
the man accustomed to living well tends to spurn, such as uncomfortable trips, uninviting lodging, extreme temperatures, bad
food, lack of entertainment, etc. (The sporting spirit in fact
acts as an "antidote," that is, as vital compensation, to the
desire and demand for comfort, and is a case in point of how
the economy of life seeks to balance itself in apparently unconnected and illogical ways.)

Furthermore, economic amplification, which is to say a rise
in the standard or level of living, results in an increase in
the area of coexistence and so increases social or "relational"
life. The ease of traveling causes human relationships to be
much more extensive than in cases where each person is tied (or
almost so) to the place where he dwells. Even in a habitual residence the number of persons one deals with is determined in part
by the economic level. But on the other hand, this same phenomenon influences the fact that the world is progressively becoming
an intrinsically economic structure, that is, one that functions
only on the basis of money. Usually not enough attention is paid
to what this means in terms of constriction and limitation. In
societies that are very advanced economically, hardly anything is
free; in order to realize even the most modest plan of living,
the outlay of greater or lesser sums of money is required: the
distance within large cities and the means of communication this
involves; the use of all kinds of services, admission to monuments,
museums, etc.; in many places, somewhere to sit down; practically

all these activities cost money. The symbol of this world is the
automatic machine that works only when a coin is inserted in it.
For this reason poverty is harder to endure in this kind of society than in those economically more primitive (today, for example,
it is more painful in the United States than in Spain, because
in the former it is not anticipated; in Spain certain things can
still be done free, while the North American world and the indus-
trialized countries of Europe operate on the basis of economic
sources so that each detail is activated by means of payment).

All this does not exhaust the economic aspects of a social
structure. Others must be considered that have a decisive influence on the patterns that life assumes in each society. The
first of these is a fact of extraordinary significance, the effects of which are greater than its most visible manifestation.
I refer to the fact that in many societies, including of course
modern societies, especially in recent times, the form of real
existence of economic goods is that of "being for sale."[6] The
implication of this is that they function within a "market" in
the broadest meaning of the word and thus that each of them has
a "price." And by extension, that same structure is imposed on
realities that have no direct economic character but that nevertheless are lived as though they were determined by a price.
This imposes a strange quantitative aspect on nearly all the ingredients of life and establishes an abstract principle of comparison between them that other ways of life have not had. The
degree to which this may occur is an important determinant of
any collective structure. In speaking of degree, I am referring
not only to the extent to which prices apply to things but to
the full function of price. Normally price is a usage, arising
as such from the society. In certain situations, when the State
intervenes to fix prices, it ceases to function as a usage and
becomes law. But since this implies an alteration of its very
nature, it gives rise to the establishment of another kind of
price that is also inadequate and interindividual in origin:
the "black market" in any of its versions. This suspends the
very function of prices, but not their existence and universal
application, and as an example for all to see, consequently it
causes the disruption of a usage. Furthermore, insofar as this
usage exemplifies others, usage in general is thereby weakened,
unleashing all the attendant social and moral consequences.[7]
And contrariwise, consider the significance of the progressive
establishment of "fixed prices," in contrast to the agreed-on
price in each case, begun with an initial offer and demand and
reached through the delicate interindividual articulation of
"bargaining."

But two very different attitudes may be taken in regard to
economic goods: ownership and enjoyment. To what degree in
each case does the interest lie in possessing things as property,
thus holding them permanently at one's disposal, or in using and
consuming them? Each era, each country, each social class, or

154

in a certain way each individual offers a particular solution to
that balance between ownership and enjoyment of wealth. This
touches a thousand aspects of life, from the preservation or dissipation of fortunes to the commercial value of certain kinds of
goods over others, from investments to political attitudes about
property, from the greater or lesser value placed on land and
houses and the relative independence afforded by the income they
represent to the person who seeks a high salary more than a fortune; all this is transformed into the rhythm and the psychological reins with regard to getting and spending, with saving, and
with the economic stability (and not only economic to be sure)
of societies.[8]

Finally, the concept of holgura (easy circumstances, enjoyment) should be formally introduced; for without it, the economic
considerations are not rigorously applicable to the understanding
of the structure of a way of life. Within the realm of the economic and without taking human aims into account, being in "easy circumstances" usually refers simply to the amount of wealth and the
standard of living. To live in ease would mean having a surplus
of money left after paying for all necessities; and the lack of
ease, to live in uneasy circumstances, would mean some degree of
poverty. But I believe the matter is more complicated than this.
Ease (holgura) is, in fact, a certain breadth, roominess, or
margin that things leave one, giving room to play, that is, allowing freedom of movement. But this implies a peculiar--albeit
positive--lack of exactness, which in economic matters is translated as an attitude of "it's all the same." Of course this is
the contrary of good accounting and of the rigorously economic
spirit. Indeed, for the bookkeeper nothing "is all the same":
a single penny can upset the balance as surely as a million.
In societies that are economically quite evolved (usually and
not by chance the richest ones), this generous view is often
missing. People expect repayment of the smallest amounts. It
matters whether or not they pay the streetcar fare of a friend
or for a taxi they have shared. They count on being reimbursed
for a small item that another person has asked them to pick up.
They look the other way when it is time to pick up the check.
Even today a Spaniard feels uncomfortable with such pennypinching,
regardless of his wealth. He does not breathe easy without at
least some flexibility. For this reason he is more liberal with
money than other men will let themselves be, unless they move in
very high economic circles. The Spaniard feels more or less
vaguely that five cents is five cents in good business, but beyond that point life becomes sad if one insists on it. This is
why he usually gives foreigners the impression of being "generous"
("big spender" in the popular version), an impression that is not
wholly favorable, because the economic vigencias are quite strong.
Yet he arouses a kind of involuntary admiration in others. The
Spaniard thinks or feels that his economic generosity is a human-
ized form of wealth, not a result or indication of it. It is

155

"vital" wealth, and for this reason, "latitude" or "generosity" (holgura) is not restricted to the economic but has its most fitting application in reference to the totality of life structures. One can be generous with time, attention, and understanding. In short, it is the luxury of life, the actual form of its possibilities, not just its abstract or quantitative aspects.

The mention of possibilities and generosity makes it necessary to add another point, which consists of asking to whom these possibilities belong. The first impulse is to think they pertain to individuals, but the matter is not that simple or clear. It is a surprising fact that societies of other times, evidently much less affluent than ours and with incomparably less economic power, "allowed" themselves extravagances that would be impossible today, even in those countries with the greatest economic power. For example, they filled the whole of Europe with cathedrals and other splendid temples, and the proliferation of their work shows that the phenomenon was anything but exceptional. The same could be said of other expenses sustained by poor societies: monuments, palaces, the royal court, etc. One could argue that these possibilities belonged to the society as a whole, and that it (or certain powers such as the King, the State, or the Church) allowed them at the expense of individuals. But this way of approaching the question reveals how little understanding there is about a multitude of problems: about the relations between the individual and society, about the degree to which the individual enjoys these indulgences of society as a whole, about the historical change in what is of "general interest," about the function that different realities have in the lives of men. The most scandalous example of economic oppression of individual workers was the building of the Egyptian pyramids, the ultimate in uselessness. In contrast, the interest in building highways, institutions of learning, or museums seems obvious. Yet we must ask ourselves seriously how the pyramids have served Egyptians, how much satisfaction, pride, pleasure, strength, and optimism they have given them. And once a careful accounting has been made, it could be that the pyramids were an excellent investment. Coming back to our own world, we are always somewhat irritated on the surface of our morality when we see wretched towns in many areas of Spain clustered about a splendid stone church that lifts its powerful spires toward the firmament. But aside from the fact that when they were built the towns probably were not wretched and thus could afford to build them, or when one has traveled in other places and has witnessed the desolation of similar towns where the soul has no such support, because the flat, squashed skyline depresses to an infinite degree and does not tolerate the slightest upward impulse, then one can only wonder whether perhaps that proud and petulant building, which irritates us so much, is not a matter of prime necessity (I refer here to the purely human aspect, not to the religious significance of the church, for our interest in this context is independent of the character of the monument). In other words, we must wonder whether the construction of medieval churches and Renaissance palaces was not something justified by the economy of life itself, even from the individual point of view.

Naturally, the questions that the economic structure poses for a sociology worthy of the name are countless and involved. Here it was not possible—or necessary—to go into them; it was enough to refer to several decisive points where the economic structure functions as a direct component of the social structure. Hence they must be formally included in an investigation of the latter.

47. Social Classes and Their Principle

This is not the proper forum for a theory of social classes. Furthermore, I should point out that I use the term in the broadest sense, prior to distinctions between castes, estates, divisions, or classes in the strict sense. One belongs to a class from the beginning instead of joining it later. The latter is possible only in a secondary way and as a change of class. Class, then, is a partial society, not an association. It is not geographically fragmentary with respect to the whole society as is the case with regions or districts; instead, it represents a stratum within society. Notice, however, that it is a matter of secondary importance that these strata appear horizontally, with some higher than others and all subject to hierarchic and valuational factors. All this is true, but it is not the most important fact. The deciding factors are their differences and parallelism. From the outset the individual finds himself installed in one or another of these strata. By "installed" I mean a repertory of elements that form an immediate "dwelling" or "residence" in which and with which life is shaped. Class is for each person the primary and concrete expression of his social circumstance. Usages, beliefs, ideas, modes of expression, information, habits, and gestures are all primarily what constitutes a social class. For this reason, the first thing that would have to be said is that within his own class the individual is comfortable. The qualifications apply perfectly well to one's home, dwelling, or residence. Notice that this peculiar comfort does not imply satisfaction. The fact that a house may offer little comfort does not prevent its owner from being comfortable in his home, in a way that he could not be anywhere else. There is a Spanish saying: Como en casa no se está en ninguna parte (There's no place like home). But this does not mean that it may not be better elsewhere; it means that one would not feel the same: comfortable, snug, literally chez-soi, "at home." In a different social class, one is always in "another's home," regardless of how splendid it may be. The Spanish expression Estar como gallina en corral ajeno ("to be like a chicken in a strange barnyard") sums it up admirably.

157

This is why, in principle, the individual does not wish to leave his class. Strictly speaking, he cannot, because it is his, because he belongs to it, because in a certain sense he is "made" by it, by its habitual ways, forms, styles, tastes, and preferences. In a society where classes exist in a real and strong way, hostility may arise between them, each one may desire what another has—wealth, power, etc.—but always for itself, that is, from its own foundation. When this does not seem to be the case, it is because abstract social groups are mistaken for classes, groups based on theoretical criteria, or even if they are real groups, one-dimensional in nature (for example, the grouping of "salaried workers") and hence not consistent with the human reality of an actual social class. Thus the Marxist—and anti-Marxist—division of men into the bourgeoisie and the proletariat does not correspond to the real division of modern European peoples into classes but rather to an ideological mold into which it tries to fit individuals. As a matter of fact, men of different social classes belong to the bourgeoisie, as they may to the proletariat, and finally, men of the same class may be either bourgeois or proletarian.

A relationship of mutual exclusiveness (extranjería) exists between the diverse classes of a society. This relationship manifests many different degrees, but it also presupposes taking other classes into account. I mean that each class exists as such because there are others that it needs in order to be what it is. It is, then, a relative reality. But taking this statement in its full meaning leads to questions about the nature of that relation, because to say that one thing exists between two others is to say next to nothing. This makes it necessary to inquire into the principle of social classes, that is, to investigate at once the means by which individuals belong to classes and the real relationship that distinguishes and links them.

If we begin by noting that the greatest difficulty between classes arises when they assume a certain series of connections, then we realize that the peculiarity of each one affects a certain zone or dimension of life. Whereas economic cooperation among men of different classes presents no important obstacles, and the same is true of political collaboration or common participation in a military undertaking, it is much more difficult to accommodate mixed classes at a meal, a game, a party, or a wedding. In other words, it is in the area of social contact that the friction between classes is most obvious. But we must avoid the temptation of two errors that are all too easy to make. The first would be to think that it is a matter of interindividual problems, that is, that they happen when individuals as such come into contact. But this is not so, for it is precisely in the area of the interindividual that the different classes can live together, when the individual is the key, when the unique personalities of A and B eclipse the social differences of class. Two men of different social classes can become close friends; a man and a woman can fall deeply

158

in love, regardless of class differences. The difficulty arises
when actual contact is established between random individuals,
precluding the interindividual situation. Strictly speaking,
the interindividual relationship does not extend to table acquaintances or teammates, though these contacts are man to man,
each of whom keeps the "style" of his class. Similarly, I have
spoken of the difficulty of marriage (not of love) in such cases,
because whereas the latter is nourished by individual sources,
matrimony presupposes the inclusion of collective modes. The
Marquis of Santillana could fall in love with mountain maids and
cowgirls, and perhaps they with him, but if it should have occurred
to him to marry one of them, their respective worlds or styles
would have collided, for these, of course, were not in love with
each other. The second error would lie in believing that the
difficulty is due to the existence of higher and lower classes.
That this is not so, meaning that it is not the most important
thing, is shown by the fact that the discomfort or uneasiness
is reciprocal; the aristocrat feels as uncomfortable in a tavern
or in a game of mus as a farmer in a salon or at a formal dinner.
The mountain girl and the marquis would both feel the friction between the court and the common masses.

Thus, social classes correspond to certain patterns of life
that involve the whole person, and not just one activity. The
fact that classes tend to assume a professional aspect is because
in relatively unevolved societies in which the number of professions
is quite limited the potential patterns come to be identified with
them. We find proof of this in the fact that as soon as the number
of professions increases, they no longer correspond to the classes;
instead we see that each class encompasses many professionals, so
that at best each is identified with a "type of profession." But
even this is overstated, because on closer examination we see
clearly that the contrary is true: the fact that certain professions are usually followed by people of the same class suggests
an analogy among them although inherently they have little connection with one another, as for example, between a doctor and a
writer, a miner and the ticket agent of a trolley, a telephone
operator and a seamstress.

But this means that there must be few classes. The question
is, how many? It is not possible to give a fixed number, yet beyond a certain point of increase, the classes begin to break up
and become something else, for instance, professions or economic
levels. The articulation of a society into classes depends on a
principle that acts cohesively within them and diversifyingly
within society. But we must hasten to add that this principle
is only a principle. I mean that although the formation of classes
begins by means of it, the classes themselves cannot be reduced to
it. The different patterns of life possible in each case are centered on and organized around a guiding principle, but they also
extend beyond it in many directions. And the nucleus or principle
is usually that dimension of life that is relevant at a certain

moment (and I say "at a certain moment" and not at each moment
because inasmuch as society is always something that comes from
the past, probably the creative principle of the present class
is no longer the most relevant dimension of life, but instead
it used to be so and now its consequences are prolonged by the
collective inertia). That principle may be religious (castes,
patricians, and plebeians in Rome), racial, ancestral, economic,
or the like. The different modes of confronting those aspects
of life create the plurality of classes or patterns of life,
and synchronism with one of these modes produces the bond of
individuals to each of the classes. The other aspects then con-
verge on this original point. Just as the molecules in glass
arrange themselves around a nucleus of crystallization and along
certain "system" lines, so the life patterns condense about the
generative principle of classes.

But the final justification of classes, the reason they
consolidate and endure, is that each one represents a member of
the social structure, with a specific function within society.
For this reason the classes are irreplaceable, and this is the
vital and historical compensation for their hierarchical order.
This ordering is inevitable, not because it is a matter of the
mere "privilege" of one class with respect to others, but because
order and hierarchy are essential to any functional complex.
Hence it is true of a structure of collective life, regardless
of the nature of that structure and the assumptions on which it
rests. Of course this hierarchical order does not authorize
scorning any of its elements, much less considering any of them
expendable. On the contrary, that order excludes those possibilities. In a disorganized and amorphous aggregate, an element can
be eliminated--part of a given amount of water perhaps, or a
scrap from a piece of fabric--but not a part from a machine, and
much less a member of a living organism.

Therefore, the concrete study of a social structure makes
it imperative to have a clear understanding of social classes.
This involves determining how many; which ones; what their generative principle is; whether it is current or a holdover from
another time; to what degree or depth the division of classes
affects individuals; what the relationships between classes are;
what the connections of movement are within each one and with
respect to one another, that is, how much rigidity, stability,
or lability they show; and finally, in connection with this, how
each class feels about itself.

48. The Lability of Classes

The force of classes is variable, and the differences can
be enormous from one society to another or from one time to
another. Among other factors, this is due to the modification
brought about in those "patterns of life" by different ingredients

of social life. The predominance of any one of these can result
in the blurring of class changes; these undergo both a transformation and a displacement. Not only do they take on a different
contexture, but also men are redistributed within them along different lines. The periods during which this occurs appear as times
of crisis for the social classes. Their appearance changes, and
they seem in the process of disappearing. But actually what happens is that new forms are being prepared. Sometimes it is simply
an optical error; when there is no exact notion of what classes
are, efforts are made to understand them according to what is
assumed to be their principle. Then, upon discovering that social
reality does not conform to that scheme, it is thought that the
classes have either broken down or disintegrated entirely. The
truth is that they are based on a different principle and are
present, but not in the place where they are being sought.

This means that in many cases the supposed attenuation of
classes is more apparent than real. Yet the question remains
whether disintegration can actually occur, and if so, whether it
can be total, that is, whether it is possible to move forward, or
perhaps achieve, a "classless society." Perhaps the only factor
that can really weaken classes is their multiplication. It is
essential that classes be few. When they conform to this rule,
they stand out in sharp relief and assume precise functions in
the general society. But if the classes are more numerous, their
differences are necessarily smaller, their internal justification
less clear, and their social functions poorly defined. Then their
lability increases, as much in the sense that one pattern may be
displaced by others, as in the ease with which an individual can
go from his original class to a different one.

Each man is born within a social class; he is installed in
it and partially shaped by its style. In the strictest sense,
it is impossible to switch from one class to another, if by this
we mean that an individual stops belonging to the first and starts
belonging to the second. Rather, we could speak of "access" or
"ingress": a man of class A enters class B, is included in it,
acts within it, but retains traits of his native class while doing
so. When the class principle is strictly intrasocial, even this
is impossible. This is true under a caste system. One belongs
to one of them once and for always without appeal. In a society
of estates where lineage is the generative principle, it is likewise meaningless to speak of transition. One simply belongs to
the lineage into which one has been born, and one is only born
once. But the rigidity of this pattern is moderated by two factors: first, the awareness that the principle of lineage is not
absolute, meaning that although it is not a social condition in
the literal sense, it was so originally. In a Christian society,
for example, the awareness of a common origin moderates the rigorous notion of lineage. The noble is noble a nativitate, yet he
knows that both he and the lowliest plebeian are descended from
Adam and Eve. In other words, what holds for a member of a lineage

161

does not hold for lineage itself. The latter is not noble a radice but as a result of an ennobling act, as a result of a sociohistorical occurrence. The second factor of attenuation is this: as long as the consciousness of noble lineage is viable, so is the power of ennoblement. For example, royalty still has the power to ennoble. Therefore transition from one class to another is possible, not spontaneously, but through the generative class principle. We might say that instead of going directly from one class to another, one goes from a class to the power than can engender them and thence through it to the second class.

The great change that has occurred in classes has been to base them on an economic principle and order them according to wealth. It might be argued that this has always been the case. But it has not. There have always been differences of economic levels, always the rich and the poor, and classes have more or less coincided with these levels of fortune. Yet this was not the class principle. One was not noble because one was rich; on the contrary, because one was noble and thus situated in a particular set of social circumstances, one had wealth. In Guzmán de Alfarache, Mateo Alemán complains that honor (honra) and social hierarchy are being replaced by money:

> It is the sonne of Nothing; the Child that knowes neither father, nor mother; the Earth's off-spring, beeing raised out of the dust thereof; it is a fraile Vessell, full of cracks, of flawes, and of holes, uncapable of containing any thing in it, that is of any moment or worth. Favour hath indevoured to mend this broken Bucket, and to stop the Leaks thereof with clouts and with rags; and putting thereunto the rope of private interest, now they draw up water with it, and it seemeth to bee very beneficiall and profitable unto them. It is one of Peter the Taylors sonnes, whose father, howsoever he got it, were it well, or were it ill, made a shift to leave him something to live upon. Or like unto that other, who by stealing from others, got wherewithall to give, and wherewith to bribe, and suborne. These are the men that are honoured now a daies, they speake high language, and utter arrogant words, and presse into all your great assemblies, and principall meetings, as if they were the only men, and none but they. These now take the upper hand, sit downe first, and take place of all men, whome heretofore you might have ranked amongst your Muletters, or scarce so good men as they.
>
> Behold, how many good men have with-drawne themselves from the Court, and live a private and retyred life at home? How many habits of St. Jago, Calatrana, and Alcantara, sowne with white threed? How many of the ancient Nobilitie of Zayn Calvo, and Nunno Rasura,

trodden under feet?

Tell me I pray, who is that that gives honour unto some, and takes it from other some? Marry, it is more or lesse wealth.[9]

Yet at the same time he is affirming the old principle, for having "more or lesse wealth" is not itself honor, rather it gives honor, that is, it lifts one into the realm of nobility: "These are the men that are honoured now a daies," now they are admitted to a social circle that is not economic, and then, as if they belonged to it, "they speake high language," that is, with authority, and "presse into all your great assemblies," thus entering into the ambit or abode of the other class, to which, because of wealth, they have been given access.

It is a different matter, as I pointed out earlier, when wealth is the principle of class articulation. For money belongs to what mathematicians call "continuous scalar magnitudes" and admits of every possible degree. One is not simply rich or poor; it is possible to be very rich or very poor, more or less rich, or more or less poor, with innumerable degrees of each. And since these degrees are not fixed, so that wealth may be acquired and lost and acquired again, then economic classes would be practically indefinite, and one could go from one to another according to the vicissitudes of fortune. This means that if classes really were based on economics, there would soon be none, because their extreme lability would dissolve them.

It is something altogether different to say that classes have a powerful economic dimension. What is not economic about them, but social, is precisely what segments economic continuity and thus defines the differentiated strata that are nothing less than social classes themselves. If by classes we understand economic levels, then it is possible to imagine a classless society (by which I mean to say that it is no more than imaginable). But such assimilation is purely arbitrary, so much so in fact that the dissolution of the so-called "economic classes" may occur as easily through unification of the levels as by the introduction of unfettered mobility. In a society where everyone has the same, there are no "economic classes"; but neither are there in societies where all have access to wealth according to personal capabilities. In this case they acquire it in all possible amounts, and, further, instead of remaining at a fixed level, they spend their lives going from one to another. Then, regardless of the names used to describe the process, men implant or install themselves in patterns or styles of life that are determined by wealth only in part, and society is functionally articulated in view of those styles. Or what amounts to the same thing, there arises a new structure of classes as members of the social body.

49. The Profile of Each of the Social Classes
     and the Degree of Their Internal Adherence

Having defined classes as the modes of installation in
society and therefore as patterns or styles of life, we must
now turn our search for a concrete understanding of a social
structure to the equally concrete determination of its classes.
It is not enough merely to enumerate them; instead, we fall
short if we say that in a society there are such and such
classes, for example, that in the Athens of Solon there were
pentakosiomdîmnoi, hippeîs, zeugîtai, and thêtes; nor have we
gone far enough if we add the quantitative factor of possessions,
which was the principle of classification. It is necessary to
consider other facets, specifically, those concerning the different types of installation. This is what I call the profile of
social classes.

In stabilized societies, those unaffected by sharp crises,
the classes exist according to long-established patterns. These
consist of a gamut of modalities and are composed of elements of
different origins and functions: vigencias, usages, "solences,"
customs, preferences, tastes, values, information, common knowledge, forms of expression, linguistic nuances--at times quite
pronounced--amusements, and a scale of internal hierarchies.
Each individual fashions his life with all this, and the verb
"to live" has a very precise meaning for him, conditioned as it
is by that class pattern. The life of other classes is "another
kind of living" to him, better or worse than his, but in any
case not his, in other words, a kind of life subject to forms
he cannot live by. Thus, within the framework of his social
class, each individual imagines the personal life he wants to
live, and he judges his success or failure, his unhappiness, by
its norms. Formally speaking, he would have nothing to do with
the forms of another class. In fact, they do not represent authentic reality for him. This explains the enigmatic historical
phenomenon in certain periods of people "playing" at belonging
to another class. It is one of the factors that explain the
pastoral novel of the Renaissance, and even more the roles of
shepherds and shepherdesses played by eighteenth-century aristocracies. To imagine oneself being a shepherd is to take an unreal
vacation from one's own condition, to wit, that of a gentleman or
lady of Versailles. The proof that it is a delightful game of
pretense and not something else lies in the fact that the de-
light--along with the wish to play--ends as soon as things are
less remote: after the fall of the ancien régime, shepherds are
alarmingly near, and it never occurred for a moment to the courtiers of Louis Philippe to play at being Lyonnais weavers.

Each class represents a plot-like scheme of life, a "type"
of aspiration, within which are contained its full and deficient
forms, its happiness and misfortune, its perfection and awkward-
ness, its attractiveness and unsightliness. An investigation of

a specific society must uncover and trace these schemata, pur-
suing the generic aspiration that impels them and ascertaining
the requisites within each that measure success or failure. To
put it another way, the profile of the classes must be drawn in
keeping with what they really are, not by contrasting them to
an extraneous scheme, for instance, comparing them to what
classes are--or are thought to be--today. Even in the case
that a justifiable connection exists between present classes
and those of the past, that bond must be both functional and
historical; in other words, the actual derivation of classes
must be taken into account, meaning that present classes must
really be shown to have arisen from previous ones. Likewise,
the "homologous" situation of certain classes with respect to
others must be considered. Specifically, this has to do with
the fact that classes may have functionally analogous roles
such as guidance, leadership, defense, economic maintenance,
etc. Ideologies have tended to take a scheme--generally one-
dimensional and abstract--and project it boldly over the whole
of history. This is what happens, for instance, when some try
to define all societies in terms of a bourgeoisie-proletariat
framework, which at best is useful in interpreting one aspect
of European social classes since the nineteenth century.

Naturally, when we say that the profile of the classes
must be drawn in keeping with what they really are, this does
not mean solely from within. For as I pointed out earlier,
it is essential that classes exist as part of a plurality and
that they take form as classes in relation to others. Thus
each class has an external outline, the appearance that it presents to others. For this reason also, a feature of classes
is the complex of their relationships to others: relative
proximity or remoteness, mutual awareness, greater or lesser
accuracy of the image that each has of the others, hostility
or affection, admiration or disdain, imitation, interindividual
contacts among class members, mutual trust or fear, impression
of "importance," the experience of each as an "ascending" or
"descending" class, and so on.

As we come to the binding link of individuals to their
class, we must touch on a final and very delicate point: the
degree of adherence of each class to itself. It is not a
question of satisfaction, for this concerns the situation of
each class, "how things are going for it." Adherence, on the
other hand, depends on the more or less profound sense of
belonging and on its affirmation. An aristocrat may be
totally pessimistic about his future and yet feel himself to
be radically and irrevocably an aristocrat, to the point of
being aware, perhaps with anguish, that he cannot be anything
else. And it may also be said (for this does not necessarily
follow from what was said above) that he forcefully affirms
his aristocracy maintains the aspiration to be an aristocrat,
and does not wish he had been something else.

When this happens, individuals feel "installed" in their class, at home in it, comfortable in a peculiar way that, to repeat, has nothing to do with whether things go well or badly for them. Even in the extreme cases of an oppressed class, people experience the painfulness of that oppression, they wish to overcome it, but they do so from within their class. During their Babylonian captivity the Israelites felt oppressed and unhappy, but they also felt themselves to be Israelites and were determined to remain so till the end. A similar situation may develop when classes coexist.

When the principle of classes is uncertain, installation is much more difficult. What has been called "class conscious-ness" is usually the deliberate affirmation of belonging to an ideologically defined group, and as such it compensates for the deficiency of installation. The "proletarian" must have "class consciousness" precisely because he does not spontaneously and effectively feel proletarian, but rather something else, perhaps one of the populace or people, or perhaps he feels nothing of the sort to any sufficient degree of clarity. Be-cause the concept of proletarianism is abstract and based on a single dimension of life, it does not imply a life style because it does not encompass those ingredients that make a pattern of life possible. Nobody can be proletarian, i.e., live proletarianly, because a certain economic condition is not the equivalent of a total way of life. The same is true of being "bourgeois." Both terms are defined emptily and negatively in reference to each other. To be proletarian means not being bourgeois; and to be bourgeois means not being proletarian. But since no one can live life on the basis of not being, since nobody can settle into the negation of a way of life, which in turn is the negation of the other, this scheme (and of course all analogous ones, for this is only one particularly widespread example) is the formula for un-happiness.

Elsewhere I have used the term "proletarization" to mean the loss of social form and with it the impossibility of "in-stallation." Inevitably this phenomenon leads to unhappiness and in this sense it is possible to speak of the "proletariza-tion" of all social classes, including the aristocracy. And more than just being possible, it actually happens in many societies. Consider, for example, how often proletarization (in this sense) occurs in the army or the clergy, or for that matter among intellectuals. In these cases it does not concern their salaried condition or low standard of living and the doubts they have with regard to its meaning and justification. Analogous phenomena occur among minority groups, either racial, religious, or political, when for some reason they cease to be nestled or "installed" in their particular alveolus.

In summary, then, a social structure remains unintelligi-ble without a sufficiently clear idea of the degree to which each class adheres to itself and remains installed within its own context. For only within the latter does society assume its real form, that form in which individual lives actually function, in which there appear the connections among individuals as such, and in which, finally, lie the modes of realization of those lives. In more succinct terms, I refer to human relationships.

VII
Human Relations

50. Persons, Men and Women

The human individuals who compose a society are divided
into two approximately equal halves: men and women. This fundamental fact represents one of the constitutive factors of the
collective coexistence. But because it is constant and common
to all societies, it appears that once acknowledged it can then
be ignored, and indeed this is often done. But the truth is
that things do not happen in so simple a manner. What, specifically, is constant in this situation? Only abstract elements:
half of the "persons" are "men" and half, "women." Yet do these
three words always mean the same things? And secondly, are they
always in the same relationship, or better, in the same relationships?

The most profound, though apparently subtle, difference concerns whether men and women are persons secondarily, or whether
persons in a secondary sense are men and women. In other words,
is the primary emphasis of the collectivity on the common, personal, or if you prefer, human dimension, or rather on the sexuate
disjunction of man and woman?[1] The state of that balance is decisive in every society, and in each emphasis will clearly be on
one side or the other, or will fluctuate between them.

From the strictly social point of view, meaning that which
refers to the forms of collective life, the main difference lies
in the fact that when the distinction between man and woman is
primary, then the strongest vigencias are partial and group-oriented;
whereas when the emphasis is on individuals as persons, then the
general vigencias predominate. What happens most often, however,
is that the general vigencias, with few exceptions, coincide
almost completely with the masculine, while partial or group vigencias are mostly feminine. This has immediate consequences. The
first is that the world (in the sense of social reality) is primarily masculine, that is, the world is "a man's world," in which,
naturally, there are as many women as men. (Although from our

168

contemporary point of view we tend to consider this regretful
and almost monstrous, we cannot ignore the sense in which woman
builds "her world" within that of man. Someone ought to assume
the urgent task of carefully measuring the inventions of humanity,
the fine and delicate creations that are due do woman's age-old
adaptation to the same structure that now seems abusive to us,
especially because our era is one of the few that have noticed
it.) Elsewhere I have used the expression "the feminine half of
the United States" to designate the women of that country, and
as I did so I had to point out that I used it deliberately to
emphasize the fact that women are not simply half of the "population" of the United States, half of the American individuals,
but half of the society, at least.[2]

The second consequence is that inasmuch as the generic usages
are predominantly masculine, woman, except for a small group of
specifically feminine usages derived from her biological condition or from its immediate personal or social repercussions, is
subject to a vague and indeterminate panorama of negative usages,
which I earlier referred to as "solences." The pressure exerted
habitually on woman is negative; it does not compel her to do
this or that, but not to do it, unless there is express social
agreement that each action or manner of behaving is socially per-
missable. There is hardly any need to underscore what this means
in terms of limitation, paralysis, and impoverishment. Yet it
would be an error to look only at the negative side. With it we
should consider what it implies in the way of selectiveness and
resignation. For thousands of years woman could not do just anything, which of course amounts to a frightful restriction, yet
this exempted her from triviality, degradation, and vulgarity
that come from being able to do anything one likes. This necessity of selecting imposed on woman by society, this rigorous obligation to "elect" which had nothing to do with her personal
decision, has produced in her that peculiar elegance woman has
in comparison to man, above and beyond all individual differences
and qualifications.

Because generic usages are more or less identical with the
masculine, the third consequence is that woman stands somewhat
"apart"; she is different and in addition to being elegant,
"distinguished," that is, differentiated, and this causes her
to attract attention. At first glance one might think that
being subjected to a tight network of negative usages, woman
would be unprepossessing, whereas in situations where she is
free she would unveil her potential, gaining strength and standing out as she did so. This is true in the case of outstanding
individuals. The woman with initiative and creative ability will
appear more real and her personality more striking if she has
freedom and independence. But considering women as a whole, the
situation is reversed, for those who are not especially qualified
(who naturally make up the majority) and who are unable to create
fade like dim and abandoned silhouettes whenever they cease to be

molded and sustained by restrictive usages. And, in fact, those societies in which woman is subject to the pressures of strong negative usages are the very ones in which she attracts the keenest attention and hence statistically—allowing for exceptional individuals—has the most influence on collective life.

Of course throughout most of known history, especially in modern times up to our century, priority has been given in the West to the sexuate dimension, that is, the bisexual aspect, with emphasis on the personal or human. Yet within this generic situation, the differences between one society and another and between one period and another have been considerable. Therefore alterations in the balance of such a delicate matter and of such absolute scope affect the very foundation of the social body, and regardless of the degree, such modifications turn out to be decisive. One of the first tasks presented by a study of social structure is that of determining the prevailing situation in this regard, by comparing its previous conditions and, above all, by ascertaining the direction in which the balance is being displaced.

51. Models

What I have called the "novels" in which the common aspiration is expressed (V, 38) have, in addition to the features already studied, another quite different characteristic that is of interest to us now from the viewpoint of human relationships. In fact, in addition to the novelesque content of biographical "novels," we must consider an ingredient in them that is not, properly speaking, imaginary. I refer to their sources of real inspiration, or to put it another way, to the fact that they are conditioned by the actual lives that each of us encounters in the social surroundings.

This exemplarity is the function of models. Each person steers himself along in his life project by starting with the patterns realized in the lives of others. Naturally, since no one can be another person, another life can represent only a pattern in view of which the individual creates or imagines his own circumstantial biography. The forms of exemplarity are quite diverse and require conditions that must be briefly enumerated. In the first place, there is the presence of the models in question. This may or may not be direct; in most societies before and even into the nineteenth century, their immediate presence was the rule. Consequently the field of action was restricted, but at the same time their influence was complete, rich, and vital. Normally, exemplarity was exerted within a class: the most perfect and brilliant models represented a level toward which other individuals tended; however, such projection was not easy from one class to another, because circumstances prevented one from being like the model, and one could not even imagine

oneself really achieving what it represented. But while total
realization might be impossible, this did not prevent a partial
or fragmentary approximation. Indeed, this aspect of exemplarity between classes was very important: certain aristocratic
patterns could be realized by the middle class; some intellectual facts might be included in the life of aristocrats; and
these might find that they could enrich their lives with traits
borrowed from plebeian forms. To cite two far-reaching examples,
snobism and plebeianism have been decisive factors in the organization of various European societies.

Direct presence presupposes some type of a stage. Examples
would be the so-called "social life" (salons, theaters), popular
festivals, the streets, and, above all, that splendid reality
called the "Main Square" (Plaza Mayor), which has been the basic
stage on which the drama of collective European life has been
acted out from the time Greece until now. The degree to which
urban forms facilitate or hinder the collective presence of
different social classes is another question that we shall consider later (VII, 54). Whenever the forms of coexistence are
complicated, as is the case in our time, immediate presence becomes more difficult, but on the other hand, the dimension of
indirect presence expands enormously. Yet we must not assume
that in societies without technical informational media the process of exemplarity was reduced to the area of physical presence
and thus restricted to a given society. For certain individuals,
belonging to privileged social groups, would leave their own
society in order to have direct contacts with others; and upon
their return, they brought back to their world the influence and
attraction of foreign models. Throughout the Modern Age (and to
a lesser extent and with slower rhythm during the Middle Ages
also) certain European communities have influenced others in this
manner. Ambassadors, nobles, artists, humanists, monks, students,
and the military, who went from Salamanca or Burgos or Madrid to
France or Italy, those who went from Paris to London, or from
London to Holland, or from Berlin to Paris or Rome, served as
models to others and returned enriched by those that they encountered in their travels. No doubt the scope and tempo of
this exemplarity were not up to those made possible by present
means of communication, but neither can there be any doubt that
in this way the models were effectively present, directly so in
the case of the minorities who came into direct contact, and
indirectly so but interpreted and activated in the majority,
who had access to exotic models through the privileged minorities.

In the second place, the exemplarity of models has to be
facilitated by a prior interpretation, that is, by its appearance
in a precise type of foreshortening in which they function exem-
plarily. For this reason, a system of prevailing values is necessary by which the models may be assessed. However, the system
of concrete human preferences is so intimate and fundamental within each society that it is almost impossible to translate the

names that designate it, and even within the same language trans-
position from one epoch to another is somewhat problematical.
While "qualities" or "virtues" are relatively abstract and can
be transferred from one situation to another, concrete human
images correspond to an all but incommunicable secret aspiration
of each social unit. The difficulties of translating the Greek
or Latin names of vices and virtues are well known. These problems begin even with areté, which is different from virtus,
which in turn is quite different from "virtue" (virtud); but the
difficulty grows when we come to the key Greek word kalón, which
designates everything that is humanly worthy, and when this notion functions concretely, as in the term kalokagathós, which is
nothing less than the "model" or "exemplary" man, then the word
is simply untranslatable. The same thing happens with such terms
as bien nacido, hidalgo, honnête homme, "gentleman," and galantuomo;
for they represent historical human models, circumstantial manifestations of exemplarity. In many societies the names of the models
are borrowed and inauthentic. Strictly speaking, if one wishes
to understand the mechanism and context of exemplarity in them it
is necessary to appeal to the names themselves. In each social
unit which names incite, spur, enthrall, move, and arouse a desire
to be like that man or woman? Without this information, there is
no way of knowing what to make of one of the deepest and most ef-
ficacious sources of a way of life.

In the third place, one must consider the dimensions in which
exemplarity appears. In societies with a very simple structure
and a minimal diversification of human types, the models may function as a short registry of the complete versions of mankind:
warrior, cleric, scholar, magnate, matron, etc. But when the
society is more complex, the models exert their attractiveness
along independent lines that are not always the same. Some eras
have been especially sensitive to physical exemplarity: so it
was during a great portion of Greek history and again during the
modern Western history; many others, for example, the European
Middle Ages, have lacked this appreciation or have possessed it
only to a minimal degree and as an exception to the rule. Models
may attract because of their competency and not because of piety,
or vice versa; perhaps it is their learning or personal valor
that most sincerely moves the men of a community. Thus, it is
necessary to inquire into the the living human dimensions in this
regard, to raise questions about the hierarchy, and to ascertain
the exemplary contents of each.

Finally, it is essential that the visibility of models be
considered. First of all, there is a difference between the
direct and indirect view of living models. Is it the same for a
girl of today to see the image of Ingrid Bergman or Ava Gardner
on the screen, as for a girl of the Romantic period to see the
Duchess of Frías in her salon or in the loge at the Opera, or for
a French girl of 1860 to follow the comings and goings of Empress
Eugenia and her court? Can seeing Napoleon enter on horseback

after a victory compare with reading the memoirs of Eisenhower
or Rommel? Is it the same thing for an intellectual to see and
hear Valera or Castelar in the Ateneo as to read the books of one
of our contemporary authors, or perhaps read an interview with
him in the newspaper? Bear in mind what happens with religious
models. Aside from the permanent exemplarity of Christ--which
is of a higher and much more delicate order--Christian life has
been nourished throughout its history by the exemplary contempla-
tion of saints as models of human religious perfection (placing
equal emphasis on both adjectives). Very well, for a long time,
a certain "intemporality" toward which all forms of culture have
tended has permitted figures of remote times to function as
vaguely current models. In some cases, their brilliance is such
that they are not eclipsed; but most of them are not translatable
to our situation. They have nothing to say to us; they may be
revered, but they are not usable models. For it is necessary to
have models capable of being relived from our own situation, so
that they are in a sense current. In this regard, the images we
are offered of contemporary saints (I say their "images," not
their actual reality as it appeared to others) are usually not
compelling and normally do not move us to admiration and thus to
emulation. One reason for it is that almost without exception
it is a question of men and women directly devoted to religious
life, such as priests, friars, monks, or founders of religious
institutes, in other words, "professionals" of religion (taking
the term in its true meaning--in order for it to be clear--it
would be enough to say "professed religious people"). To state
it in other terms, it is a matter of people being in circumstances
not comparable to those of the great majority of the faithful,
and, therefore, their examples do not affect our sensitivities
in those points where they would be effective. Actually, the
man or woman who may aspire to the saintliness of contemporary
saints cannot hope to duplicate the actual conditions of that
saintliness, because it is not accessible and imitable. They do
not find in it a human life similar to theirs, based on the same
world, with the same problems, joys, pains, desires, and values,
yet endowed with religious perfection. They do not encounter a
close model, one immediately intelligible and effective in our
time, which is defined by historical awareness and, beneath its
serious sins, opposed to inauthenticity.

These models mold life. Beneath their attraction and prestige, all human forms are organized along the lines of their
gentle dominion. The woman combs her hair, dresses, and moves,
glancing out of the corner of her eye at some other woman of
exemplary attractiveness; the boy makes the same gestures as the
actor, the athlete, the writer, or the politician whom he admires.
Gestures mold actions: the way one extends his hand or takes off
his hat foretells his manner of loving; the cadence of speech
bears in it the germ of a form of poetry or a style of thought; by
extending the manner of dress or the way one selects a gift, we

173

sense a certain economic, moral, or perhaps political sensitivity. The enjoyment or displeasure evoked by an image, a prayer, a religious vocabulary, or a liturgical form to an incredible degree reveal an entire religious trajectory.

The clarification of a form of collective life requires a thematic investigation of its models, including the dimensions in which they act, their contents, their degree of vivacity, the means by which their presence is manifested, and last but not least, their deficiencies, including not only those aspects in which models simply do not exist, but also those in which the models proposed (and in every case one must ask: proposed by whom and to whom?) and perhaps imposed do not function as models, because they lack exemplarity.

52. Love

In addition both to the formal conditions in which individuals meet and their installation in social groups, and especially in classes, real human relations are also defined by their contents. An adequate enumeration of these contents and an analysis of their respective realities would be a task for anthropology or sociology. Since here—lest we forget—we are attempting to point out the methods that will permit a social structure to be effectively investigated, it is sufficient to consider certain human relationships only insofar as they intrinsically condition the structure of each society.

The two halves of humanity are divided and also linked by their sexuate condition. Sex difference is neither specific nor a simple adventitious quality. It belongs to what I have called the "empirical structure of human life,"[3] and so without being a necessary requisite of life, it is a constituent of what we call man.[4] The sexuate condition—not to be confused with the strictly sexual dimension, which is but a particular and limited activity within the total structure of life—is the radical mode of installation of each person. Thus, it is more profound than that of class, because it affects deeper strata of the person, and from them impregnates and penetrates all other aspects of life. Therefore, "human life" in its empirical form is realized through a disjunctive duality: man or woman. But as I stated at the beginning, it is as much a matter of connection as of division. Sex is not a mere "difference," but also a relation, more precisely a polarity; each of the sexes co-implicates or "complicates" the other. Each is included in the other precisely in the form of polar reference. Hence, the sexuate condition does not consist of the terms of the disjunction, but in the disjunction itself as seen alternatively from each of its terms. For this reason, human life is projected from one sex toward the other. Far from being a "separation" between the two halves of humanity, the sexuate division causes life to consist of each fraction being

174

involved with the other, creating a kind of "magnetic field" in
society and causing coexistence to have a certain configuration
and dynamic structure and to function basically as an "enterprise."
Installed in their respective sexes, man and woman live all real-
ity--not just its human dimensions--from it, and collective life
appears divaricated into two radically different forms: within
one's sex and with the opposite sex. All this of course is prior
to specifically sexual occupations, relations, or activities,
which are consecutive to that much broader and of course permanent dynamic installation. It is, in so many words, the ambit
in which all sexual behavior originates, and for that matter, it
includes even "asexual" activity (which can never be "asexuate").

All amorous relations are based on this condition; that is,
the foregoing determinations are at the level of the empirical
structure, and this is an area where historical variation may
occur. In other words, the different social forms are variants
of this structure, which is realized in each case according to
circumstantial peculiarities. For that reference of each sex to
the other does not always happen in the same way. Take the factor of presence, for instance. It is incorrect to say that men
always coexist with women. The fact is that this is somewhat the
exception: depending on the society, there is a greater or lesser
"distance" between man and woman. Breaking out of their respective
isolation, they have sporadic meetings. These may occur relatively
frequently and easily, but hardly ever have such encounters de-
served to be called "living together" in the sense of habitual
coexistence. Our age is an exception, and the consequences--good
and bad--that this is going to have are still not clearly fore-
seeable. The social "distance" between the sexes is the first
factor that must be determined, and with it the forms, places,
and frequency of the "meetings." Seeing someone furtively in
church or in a passing automobile is not the same experience as
contemplating that person at length in the theater, dancing with
her, being alone with her, working face to face together in an
office, sitting side by side in a university classroom, a bar,
or a car, or walking together in the street. This involves not
only quantitative differences but also the ways of addressing
oneself to the other person, depending on whether the encounter
takes place in solitude or in the presence of others, whether
these are acquaintances or the anonymous public, whether such
relationships are marked by normality or clandestineness, whether
they occur in an atmosphere of calmness or tension, whether they
are easy or hard to arrange, and, finally, whether the initiative
in arranging them can be ascertained.

All this influences the forms of sensitivity that men and
women have toward each other. The configuration imposed by sex
on collective life gives rise to perceptive modalities that are
not sufficiently understood. Yet the sexuate "orientation" of
the perceptual field and the resulting "perception of beauty"
are surprising phenomena. In a room full of people, in a crowded

subway car, in a photograph taken of many people grouped together,
the eye is suddenly drawn to the beautiful woman before knowing
anything about the other people present. Sometimes in a rapidly
moving car, a woman will pass by whom we really have not ever
seen: we do not know what she is like, nor could we give the
sketchiest description of her or recognize her if we met her a
few minutes later. We only know she is pretty. In reading the
novelists or dramatic authors of the sixteenth or seventeenth
century, we are surprised by their accounts of love at first
sight: a gentleman enters a garden in pursuit of a falcon; un-
expectedly he meets a girl, looks at her, and from that moment
is madly in love. His name is Calisto; hers, Melibea.[5] At other
times love springs into being upon seeing the lady behind her veils,
praying devoutly in church. Perhaps he has seen her eyes for a
fraction of a second as she is offered holy water; or it may be
that he has seen only her white hand between the curtains of
the litter, and from that moment he can never forget that hand.
Or, finally, the maiden is smitten and throws herself into a
thousand amorous follies because from her window she has seen a
cloaked figure and the gallant quivering of a feather on a hat
tipped in greeting. One might say that all this is the stuff
of novels and plays, yet, leaving aside all the elements of
literary exaggeration, a foundation of reality remains, without
which such literary stylizations would not have been socially
tolerated, as they would not be today. Recall what we are told
about the orgiastic sensitivity of the Arabs in regard to physical
beauty and consider whether such feelings are invariable or not
and whether they can be treated as "constants." A review of a
treatise on moral theology will quickly reveal that often things
with the same names mean something quite different from what we
understand by them.

The way woman is regarded and treated depends in large part
on the frequency and proximity of her presence. When her presence
has been something more or less "unusual," man has looked on her
as something literally "lovely," and he has felt obligated--to
her and to himself--to make an amorous gesture, at least in the
form of a tendency and an effort to do so. This is the significance
of gallantry. In an age like ours, when any man sees dozens of
women every day for several hours, the traditional attitude is
impossible for quantitative reasons; not only of course because
of the attention and effort it would require, but also because
the "amorous" gesture, repeated hundreds of times, loses all
verisimilitude, which is precisely what justified it and gave
it meaning, not a literal truth that it neither had nor did
anyone expect it to have. (One of the most delicate problems
of the relationships between men and women in our time is that
of finding the proper substitute or "vicarious" replacement for
such gallantry; for the latter is impossible; but because it
performed a very important function, when it disappeared certain
delicate mechanisms of life stopped working; and they must needs

be set in motion again, even though by other means.)   In this
regard it is necessary to ascertain the state of these relationships in each society.

But there are more serious things. The very content of
actual love is historically variable. People do not love in
the same manner in all times and in all societies, albeit a
functional nucleus and certain natural elements may reappear
in all situations. People love on the basis of certain underlying assumptions, and first of all, in view of certain types
of men and women that are nothing less than models in the most
vigorous sense of the word. Second, they love according to a
repertory of gestures, emotions, and values that characterize
each form of collective life. Third, there are "quantitative"
factors, that is, a given intensity of love (at times it has
one temperature and others at other times), a certain prevalence
(on some occasions the thing to do is fall in love, while at
other times love is not the "in" thing, and in every case it is
a matter of a given type of love), and a statistical frequency.

Let us not forget that what is called "love" is an interpretation of certain life realities (I use the plural because
they are many and quite diverse), an interpretation that the
individual who experiences them originally finds to be predominant in his surroundings. More exactly, first he finds the interpretation and then he discovers—or seeks—in himself the corresponding reality. The youth knows that "love exists," that men
and women fall in love with each other, and this is presented to
him with varying attributes of necessity, beauty, interest, mystery, fear, and cynicism. He reads stories about love or he
witnesses it in its imaginary representations, and he understands
it before really having experienced it.[6] And when something
really does happen to him that has to do with all these things,
he interprets it as love. The process consists of referring the
new personal reality to those inherited notions, making it conform to the mold, forcing it (within certain limits) to be love.
This means that real love is conditioned by the prevailing forms.
Only on that general and collective attitude can the authentically
personal nuances of individual love exist.

By that same token, love is inseparable from a "language,"
a rhetoric and a poetics, a way of speaking to the beloved and
of expressing oneself in the love relationship. And it must be
understood that all these things belong to love intrinsically,
that they form a part of its content. But on the other hand, it
also must be made clear that love is never exactly what "is said,"
for it also has an arcane dimension. In addition to the public
forms of love predominant in a society, it also has real forms.
For example, it is necessary to determine how much of lyricism
and sensuality is merely amorous rhetoric and how much is real,
just as one should ascertain the proportion in which men and
women share the amorous initiative. Likewise, it is essential
to consider the margin of freedom of expression and behavior

177

enjoyed by each, the esteem or disdain they feel for each other, the normal fleetingness or permanence of the love relationship, the greater or lesser claim to exclusiveness and its fulfillment, and the importance or triviality of the phenomenon of love. This may be a purely superficial matter, relatively unconnected to others and hardly affecting the deeper levels of the person; or it may be a radical advent that involves the man or woman or both to the very core of their being, decisively marking their lives. In societies where love is "easy," it normally loses temperature, gravity, and hence declines in interest. Correpondingly, there is a drop in its power, violence, and delight. In societies where there is great freedom in love, those that are dominated by what we could call "diffuse sensuality," the specific acts of love, of any kind, decline in value, intensity, and the ability to move people. Allowing as much as you like for rhetoric, in a climate of "inflation" the value of a Romantic kiss is, nevertheless, incomprehensible. Witness Victor Hugo when he says: "Enfant, si j'étais roi, je donnerais l'empire" ("Child, if I were king, I would give the Empire"); or Zorrilla in an Oriental (Dueña de la negra toca ["Lady of the Black Toque"]); or in a story of Azorín in which the kiss of Doña Inés and the poet Diego de Garcillán, in Segovia of 1840, spreads in concentric waves that agitate the entire city, shaking it with a passionate storm of eroticism, gossip, envy, jealousy, admiration, remorse, and sacrifice. Until there is a clear idea of all this, we cannot know the meaning of the word "love" in a specific setting and thus cannot understand what the reality of that form of collective life actually is.

53. Marriage and Family

It goes without saying that the forms of marriage and the family constitute important elements of any social structure, so important indeed that societies are often classified from this point of view: monogamous and polygamous. This is so obvious that an understanding of it does not even figure in what deserves to be called the method of investigation of social structures. Here we are interested in finer historical variations, those that occur within a general "type" of matrimonial and family organization, for example, within modern Western societies. And taking another type, whether it be the polygamous Moslem family, the Tibetan, or any primitive organization, it would be necessary, once the investigator had gotten into the study, to make analogous determinations, though with other contents. Thus, we shall confine ourselves to the extant forms of our modern Western world.

First, a distinction should be made between marriage and the family. The elemental fact that marriage usually produces a family and that both things are therefore closely linked often

178

leads to considering them from the same point of view and even
to equating them. Yet whereas marriage is an interindividual
relationship entered into by two preexisting individuals who
function as such, the family must be viewed primarily from bottom to top. I mean that we are not to seek it in its genesis in
the conjugal couple but rather in the children. The family is
principally parents, brothers, and sisters (and in more extended
forms, grandparents, uncles, aunts, and cousins); only secondarily is it the wife and children. "One finds oneself" in the family
without having selected it, unlike matrimony, which is based on
choice, does not precede the individual, and is rigorously personal in nature. The merging of marriage and the family into a
single consideration is simply a form of confusion surrounding
them and a way of hindering the understanding of both. The
theoretical consequences are serious, and from them derive many
others that affect things themselves in their reality. This is
why years ago I pointed out that among the causes of the crisis
of the family must be included some of its defenders who have
arisen in recent times.

Of the many aspects of marriage, only a few intervene directly
in the makeup of a concrete social structure. No doubt the others
can have repercussions in it, but to study them in detail would
be an endless task. For this reason, I shall restrict myself to
a concise indication of the points where the forms of matrimony
coincide immediately with those of society.

Let us begin with the statistical frequency of marriage.
Countless men and women are always marrying, but not with the
same degree of "normality." Whereas in some societies the bachelor is absolutely exceptional, in others there is a considerable
number of people who, without precise reasons, in fact do not
marry. Usually this is closely related to the average age at
marriage. The tendency is to early marriages in the first kind
of societies. When it is delayed for economic or other reasons,
when there is no normal age for marrying, then exceptions become
frequent and ultimately end up not being exceptions at all.

On the other hand, when we speak of age, are we referring
to the man, the woman, or both? For long periods of European
history, men have customarily married much younger women. In
other times their ages are fairly even, with only slight differences or none at all. The consequences of this are many, for
example: the evenness or unevenness of generations, economy,
the degree of independence for the woman, fertility, and so on.
One of these consequences seems especially important to me:
whether or not the marriage is a relationship based on equal
personal and historical levels. When the husband and wife are
more or less the same age, subordinative factors in the relationship tend to disappear, and friendship is more probable. Too,
the repertory of memories, values, experiences, etc. is approximately the same for both, whereas when there is an age gap many
things have personal meaning for the husband but not for the wife

(and the reverse is true but in different ratios).

In turn, this has a decisive influence on the amount of freedom of choice in regard to the marriage partner in each case. We tend to forget today that in many other societies marriage has had little to do with the preferences of the contracting couples--especially on the part of the woman--and indeed it would be possible to inquire with some degree of seriousness about the frequency or infrequency of actual consent. For long periods of history marriages have been arranged by families without consulting the interested parties, especially the girl, with the determining factors being such things as lineage or social class, wealth, politics, endogamous preferences, and sometimes race and religion. Naturally, in such cases love has little to do with marriage. It is a long way from these extreme forms to the free and spontaneous mutual selection by two individuals with minimal family or social intervention. In every society the matter is determined in a certain way somewhere between these two extremes, and it is important to know just where and how.

And insofar as marriage is alien to love and personal preference, what happens to them? Do they find an independent channel in relationships outside marriage? Or are they foresworn entirely, becoming only occasional exceptions? Or does the first hold true for the man and the second for the woman? The same questions need to be asked regarding amorous relationships before marriage, above all when marriage comes late. In some societies "freedom" is reserved for the male, while in most cases the woman is restricted to marital or premarital love. In other forms of collective life, the difference between the two sexes is less, and in some a situation of equality prevails. This has an evident connection with the existence and importance of prostitution and other analogous social forms.

In any case, marriage has a different significance for each of the partners joined in it. It may be that both (or perhaps only the woman) are absorbed by the higher union and have no autonomous life. At the other extreme, the spouses continue more or less "on their own," prolonging his or her life pattern, which is merely "associated" with that of the other person. In other words, marriage sometimes represents the nullification of the woman; or on the contrary, it may mean that she begins to circulate socially--in societies where the single woman "does not count" and only the married woman has access to "society"; or it may bring about a new dual enterprise and reciprocal personal enhancement; or finally, it may amount to very little, a relatively superficial association with a certain probability of being a passing one as well.

This brings us to the crucial question of the stability of marriage. From the standpoint of social structures, this does not exactly coincide with its indissolubility, for there are societies in which, though short of divorce, marriage is still unstable; whereas in others where legal separation is possible, marriage

remains statistically stable because either divorce seldom occurs
or does so in view of a new situation that in principle will endure. Naturally, stability is greatest when in addition to certain social conditions that make for stabilization, it is reinforced by religious and legal sanctions against dissolution. For
its part, the latter restrains and slows--although it does not
prevent--instability arising from strictly social causes.

Finally, another factor must be taken into account: the
"duration" of marriage, which has nothing to do with what I have
just said. I refer now to the fact that the specifically matrimonial relationship as a form of coexistence of man and woman
admits of many possibilities. Often it is regarded as a simple
process for starting a family (this view dominates the theories
of the so-called conjugal society, which are nearly always blind
to marriage itself). In other words, the life of a marriage may
have a "plot" or "argument" and hence a capability for durability
as something that, although it gives rise to a family and exists
within it, is not reducible to the family. Of course the study
of social structure requires that a series of samplings be taken,
for societies are not homogeneous, and the condtions of marriage
are hardly ever the same in all social classes or groups, in the
big cities and small communities; indeed, they may differ at the
same time for couples belonging to different generations.

As for the family, I emphasize that from the standpoint of
the individual who "finds himself within it" (hence primarily
from the standpoint of children), it is a partial society and
more precisely the mode of normal insertion in society in the
strict sense. The fact that the origin of this partial society
is an "association" (of the spouses) is no sign that the family
itself should be understood as an association, because marriage is
not yet a family. And the husband and wife belong to, and form
part of, the family only when a secondary condition affects them,
which results from the appearance of children in the family (or
in some cases, their incorporation into the family made up of
preceding generations, to which the other spouse already belongs
as an offspring).

Thus, the family sensu stricto is a social reality, but a
most peculiar one, because its actual functioning is determined
by interindividual relationships. From birth the child finds himself in and with a family that he has not selected or sought, a
family that is defined by a set of collective usages and vigencias.
To a certain extent, the same could be said of parents regarding
their children: they also find themselves with the latter; and
the same thing happens to brothers and sisters concerning each
other. But on the other hand, the enormous closeness of the
family relationship means that the actual manner of existing is
personal, that is, that in this relationship, along with the
"functions" or "roles" of father, mother, son or daughter, brother
or sister (in principle assimilable to the social relationships
of teacher, disciple, companion, judge, accused, elector, deputy,

etc.) there appears the individual and human reality of each person assuming those functions.

This dual aspect or penchant of the family is common to all its forms, but one or the other feature predominates according to their alignment. The size of the family is particularly important. When the family is regarded in terms of lineage, it may include three or four generations (in the genealogical sense): grandparents, parents, children, grandchildren, with all collateral branches and probably servants, too. In this situation, its "social" dimension is the most important, i.e., its properties as a collective institution. Through a series of intermediate stages we have the other extreme: the family who gathers in the dining room or kitchen: parents, children, brothers, and sisters. Because here the closeness is maximal, the substance of this form is above all individual and personal. We could say that in these circumstances it is a function of the marriage and depends fundamentally on it.

But these are not the only aspects that must be considered. Within the family there are diverse relationships that vary with each society. These include the economic—entailment, primogeniture, frequency with which each spouse possesses private capital or the preponderance of income and thus of jointly owned property, relative duration of child support, and so on; matters of authority—that of the father over the children, and all the possible degrees in each case; continuity—normality of residing in the same city, of continuing in the father's profession; social class—parents and children belonging to the same class or the frequent ascent of the children, for example, in countries of heavy immigration or with a colonial economy; the amount and nature of the normal variance between parents and children; the keen or attenuated awareness of lineage and name; and so forth.

All these elements allow a precise determination of the degree to which the family in a given society performs its primary function of being the elemental facility with which individuals find themselves from birth. But there is still another question: from birth, yes, but until when? Until what age does the family accompany and sustain the individual? At what point does it leave him either alone or almost so, abandoned to his own devices? Or on the other hand, are the terms reversed, with the family being the first serious problem the individual must confront? Since the family is the elementary form, not of society, but rather of the articulation of the individual in society, its organization and state of being becomes a decisive factor of all social structure.

54. Friendship

Friendship is of course an interindividual relationship. But like all relationships, it is conditioned by collective usages

and vigencias. In turn, in its complete reality friendship
functions as an element or component of the forms of collective
life. And, above all, together with friendship in the formal
sense occur its "socialized" forms, interacting with its more
authentic modes and forming a direct ingredient of society.

In the formal sense friendship occurs in the very precise
area of life called "intimacy." It is an intimate phenomenon
(and in this it resembles love), but on the other hand, it is
based on respect. I believe these two traits are essential to
the phenomenon of friendship. Understand that in speaking of
respect, it means respect for intimacy. Love also respects
the beloved person, but not his intimacy; rather it invades and
penetrates it with an intrinsic violence, as sweet as you like,
but still essential to it. Love's way of treating a person consists of invading the intimacy of the beloved person and of de-
manding to be invaded in like manner. This does not happen in
friendship; it feeds on reserve; elsewhere I have observed that
it is always a tacit nonaggression pact. This means that friends
are given room (this is inseparable from friendship, and where
it is missing there is something seriously wrong in the relationship), but not abandoned. There is always a restraint between
friends, and indeed the delightfulness of friendship lies in large
part in its freely imposed limitation, in the gesture of gripping
and checking the rein deftly so as to maintain the inner effusion
in its proper proportions. Whereas it is a mark of love to be
immeasurable, friendship is always measured, it must be composed
of measure and adjustment. We could say that it is an exact
feeling.

Do not think that on this basis authentic friendship is
something cold or at best lukewarm. On the contrary, in order
for friendship to reach its full, plenary form, it must overflow
from an impulse that, precisely because it is overflowing, can
divert a part of its thrust into checking and limiting itself to
friendship. One could say that friendship is a feeling that includes its own boundary or dike; the point where it ends is a
part of its substance and is what causes it to be precisely
friendship, not something more or less. Clearly, here lie the
difficulty of friendship and the reason for its comparative
rarity. Most friendships are more or less than what they aim to
be. That is to say, under the name of friendship—as in the
name of love—lie hidden its various approximations or deficient
versions. As a matter of fact, most so-called friends are often
companions, comrades, simple acquaintances, or also past and
residual friends.

In the strictest sense, all this belongs to individual life,
yet the modes of friendship (all of them and not just true
friendship) occur by virtue of certain social conditions. Let
us consider first a few quantitative aspects. There are enormous
individual differences in every society, but underneath them there
is a normality in regard to the number of friends a person usually

has. Some societies live in "friendship"; others, on the contrary, are characterized by the unusualness of friendship. The degree of social "proximity," whether people tend to live apart or in mutual presence (in part because of the structure of cities, about which I shall later say a word), determines the probability and thus the frequency of the relationship. In attempting to understand a form of collective life, it is necessary to determine the circle of friends that it is normal to have within it; and having ascertained these facts, it is essential also to trace their map, i.e., mark out precisely their hierarchies and distances.

Secondly, it is necessary to consider the origin of friendships. Some come from childhood, and according to a commonplace, the oldest friends are the best friends. Sometimes it is said: Somos amigos desde niños; amigos íntimos ("We have been friends from childhood; really close friends"). Very likely this is not so, for childish friendships develop before the birth of intimacy in individuals; that is, if the childhood friendship is nothing more than that, then probably it is not close at all but trivial, inert, or family-based. In order for childhood friendship to be close and authentic, it must be renewed and revalidated later on. The natural time for friendships to be formed is during adolescence and young adulthood, the years of study and apprenticeship. By then the person is "formed" but still fresh, porous, and without crust or caution. Since at that age one still does not amount to much and has no memories or past, he cannot live from his own inner resources and so he lives with others in spontaneous and easy company. (The frequent phenomenon of the diffident, "withdrawn," and solitary adolescent does not alter the situation, because it is his way of living with regard to others, and nearly always he shows an exacerbated sensitivity for friendship and especially for close friendship.) As a person begins his personal trajectory, it normally interfaces with others and is realized in a collective environment. This does not mean that later very deep friendships may not be started. But now they take on a marked individual and concrete character and for this reason are few and unlikely. After youth, friendship is always an unexpected gift, something that cannot be counted on to happen, and it depends on the occasions, that is, on the configuration of life. I mean that it has conditions that are fulfilled in varying degrees and manners: enough time (the gravest threat to friendship today), a minimum of economic sufficiency, trust (collective distrust and suspicion are a social sickness that makes the creation of new friendships almost impossible and corrodes those already established), and, above all, concord, for when a society is deeply divided, when one wonders first of all what the next person thinks, what his political and religious ideology is, friendship is automatically vitiated and adulterated. It might be

thought that it would be easier and stronger within one's own
group, but it is not, because a relationship based on one measure
or another of partisanship is not properly friendship for the
very reason that it feeds on external and public coincidences
and not on small, private, and heartfelt affinities, in a word,
on intimacy. But notice that the word "concord" does not mean
uniformity. The most varied differences in opinions, likes,
and tastes do not prevent friendship, but instead stimulate it,
provided that they do not affect the fundamental personal strata
and that they leave a deep zone untouched and free for intimacy.
Religious differences or political opposition to not thwart
friendship. On the other hand, politicization and fanaticism
drive it from its strongholds. In passing, let it be said that
they inherently contradict friendship insofar as they are thema-
tically based on a lack of respect.

But until now I have not touched on a delicate point: sex.
And it must be said that friendship has nearly always been understood as a relationship within one's own sex. Furthermore, the
opinion is very widespread (and above all, has been until now)
that intersexual friendship is impossible, that it is less than
friendship and therefore of little moment or that it is simply
love. Indeed, in the immense majority of known societies, friendship between man and woman has been extraordinarily rare.[7] But
I believe that far from being impossible, intersexual friendship
is the culmination of the phenomenon, its purest and most intense
form; that for us men our best friends are almost always women;
and that if anyone can understand a man or woman a little, it
will be some person of the other sex. But it should be added
that the normal beginning of friendship between a man and woman
requires improbable social conditions that rarely occur (such as
have occurred in the past thirty or forty years, for example, due
to which there has been a flowering of friendship between men and
women that is one of the creations or re-creations of the half
century that has just passed). It is well to recall the difficulties encountered in establishing friendship with persons of the
other sex by those who have the talent for it: how they found
no collective patterns through which to express such friendships;
how they saw their feelings distorted by the pressure of vigencias
and by the interpretation which they themselves, impelled by those
vigencias, gave to their own feelings. Nothing sheds more light
on certain fine nuances of the social structure than the story
of some of those friendships and of their almost certain vitiation
and failure.

All this obliges us to attempt to clarify the mechanisms of
the constant interaction between the individual and collective
life, which is the substance of social reality. Stated in other
terms, we must inquire into the forms of collective living, that
is, the immediate actuality of social life.

55. Social Life

Each individual sees a certain number of people. Many of them he simply <u>sees</u>: strangers he meets on the street, at church, at shows, or in the café. Others are people he sees and, for example, greets: they are acquaintances, neighbors, merchants, or clients whom he occasionally "runs into" because their respective life pathways cross. A third group is made up of persons with whom he deals, that is, people to whom he directs specific social acts in an individual manner. This group includes very diverse subgroups, and these should be arranged in order of frequency and closeness of the relationship. There are people whom one sees only once a year; others, every two months; others, every week; some, every day; and relatively independent of the frequency, these meetings are marked by different degrees of intimacy.

The first task in determining the conditions regulating collective interaction in a society is to make an approximate evaluation of the weight of each of these groups in each of the social strata. If we compare several units, we will find enormous quantitative differences with a structural significance; for example, from the standpoint of the "vital balance" and hence of happiness. When the conditions of life in different countries and eras are compared, rarely is there any consideration (in conjunction with the economic level) of the security, technical progress, and the significance of the extent and intensity of collective life. The economic conditions of many Latin peoples would be intolerable within the forms of "social life" and conversation of some Nordic peoples. And at times there is an effort at material improvement without realizing that it involves disturbing a collective style, with consequences that are hard to predict, especially since usually no mental effort is made to imagine them. What are the results—good and bad—of replacing the apartment house with its common patio and continuous corridors with a subdivision of small proletarian houses? What is the connection of climate to collective life? What effect on the actual way of life does the fact have that the women of a village or city stop going to the fountain with their pitchers because water is available from faucets in their homes? What is the significance of the partial substitution of movies for theaters, or bars for cafés? Is it the same thing to spend the evening playing forfeits as to spend it listening to the radio or watching television?

Second, it would be necessary to determine the articulation of "social distance." An informal society is not the same as one full of etiquette involving such things as introductions, the use of the formal <u>usted</u> or its equivalents, the reserve among neighbors, the normal inaccessibility of other homes, the absence of women in extrafamiliar social life, and the isolation of classes. And in this regard, how many persons are "close" in each case, and what is meant by "close"?

A third determination that must be made refers to the

dimensions in which social interaction occurs. To what degree
are there "whole" relationships involving the entire person?
Or is it more normal to find "airtight compartments" that do not
communicate and in which social life occurs disjunctively? There
is also job companionship which does not extend to family life;
people may work together in a shop or office but not attend a
show together or know each other's families. There are players
who will sit facing each other for three hours every day and
not know anything about each other. There are "men only" meetings that begin and end around a table in a café or club without
affecting any other sphere of life.

Without a doubt the most important aspect is the mixing or
separation of the two sexes in social life. The differences between societies, periods, classes, and cities on this point are
extreme and absolutely decisive. The Andalusian "cities of woman-
less streets," of which Antonio Machado sang, and the cities of
the United States are worlds apart. The distance is still considerable between Madrid and the small Spanish provincial cities of
today.

Each society articulates its forms of social life, many of
which cannot be understood unless we bear in mind that they are
expedients to cover the lack or failure of other forms. The
"visits" of the nineteenth century and the first part of the
twentieth, the entractes at a performance, carnival, religious
outings, fairs, the all but public toilette of ladies in the
eighteenth century, and the tapadas[8] of the seventeenth century
are all forms that cannot be explained directly by their "face
value"; instead they must be reinstated in a total situation,
within which they have meaning and from which they are understandable and full of significance, perhaps as conditions for certain
portions or shades of happiness.

The systematic connection between the possibilities and modes
of social life is materialized, so to speak, in the form assumed
by cities, and it acquires vitality and movement (and therefore
full intelligibility) in the use of them, that is, in the utilization and distribution of time and in the articulation of daily
life. Let us take a closer look.

56. Cities

As Ortega pointed out some time ago, one of the most sugges-
tive themes of all is the morphology of cities. In few things is
collective life revealed better than in them. And the reason is
clear: in a certain way the city is "utilitarian"; it is designed
to fulfill life functions, from the most elementary to the most
complex. Therefore, it corresponds to what people actually do:
in other words, it reflects the real content of their lives.
Furthermore, because it is a collective creation, it does not
depend on personal whim or even on inspiration. Thirdly, since

a long time is required to build a city, it does not reflect a
passing tendency, mere improvisation, or the consequences of an
act of individual will (save for a few exceptions, which in turn
are revealing because they betray collective structures that have
made them possible). But on the other hand, the city is also
artistic (and for this reason it may be beautiful or ugly, but
inevitably one or the other, or both in some proportion), that is,
expressive, and what it expresses is a style, a soul structure,
an aspiration that transcends the merely functional and utilitarian. When a city can be equated with these functional traits, it
means that they and nothing else are the imaginative aspiration
of that society. To put it another way, the fact that something
is intended to be utilitarian is not in itself utilitarian, but
rather goes beyond that category and reveals profound dimensions
of men who are so.

Because of all this, a city is the text in which the contexture of a soul may be read. But an important note must be added:
just as it takes a long time to build a city--this is why it is
not a capricious creation--so it lasts a long time. Except for
its founding phase when it is still not a city, it is always old.
Normally the individual lives in a city created neither by him
nor his contemporaries, but by his ancestors. Certainly he transforms and modifies it, and above all, he uses it in his own way,
revealing his particular vocation in so doing. But first and
foremost, the city is inherited and historical, something handed
down from earlier men. It is nothing less than society itself.
This is why it is hard to understand, and this is why, too, it
is profound and profoundly revealing.

The first thing to be said in studying the structure of a
society from the standpoint of cities is that there may be none.
For there are forms of social life that are not cities (normally,
though, they coexist with these). This is what is called ruralism,
and nothing is more urgent than determining the proportion of
ruralism in a given society and its function within it. Of
course this function includes the dynamic state of such ruralism,
whether it is in a stationary situation, a residue in the process
of disappearing, or, on the contrary, whether the society is
becoming ruralized.

Naturally the opposition between city and country is not
absolute; ruralism in cities (and I would add that it is manifested
in cities, and properly speaking, it is an attribute or inclination
they reveal); for if there were none, it would be difficult to
speak of a society. The country as a human "world" does not exclude the existence of towns (poblaciones), nor does it even require that they be small. Hence, while a ranch, an Andalusian
cortijo, or grange, or a Basque, Galician, or Asturian village
may be small, the Castilian town (pueblo) is not, much less the
Andalusian, to say nothing of some African towns. Yet all are
strictly manifestations of rural life. The latter is characterized by being located in the country in three senses: First,

location in a given area, either where one was born or has become
established (for example, through colonization); second, a livelihood as a peasant, plowman, farmer, or cattleman; and third, ownership of land. Obviously it is a relatively secondary matter whether
the farmer lives in the country or "goes" to the country (as is
frequently the case in Castile, Andalusia, and much of France) from
the rural town. Under these circumstances the way people live
together is based on a series of common usages, especially agricul-
tural usages, what is referred to in each region as the "way of a
good farmer," but also on traditions, games, songs and dances,
dress, customs, and food. Finally, it is characteristic of the
rural world to be made up of "few" people who are personally known
to one another and who call one another by name. This being so,
the "outsider" is readily apparent. It is, then, a closed, finite,
defined world, familiar to all who live in it.

Furthermore, this minimal world articulates with others
similar to it with which it establishes infrequent and exceptional
communication in the form of festivals or economic transactions,
or both at the same time with a fair. There are other rural units,
other towns or villages that lie beyond the unit in question but
with which it has an essential affinity, and this is the principle
of a district or a region, as the case may be. And confronting
them is the outer world, the alien and--in principle--opposing
world of the city. Although it may be geographically near, the
city is existentially very distant because it is defined by another
way of life and, consequently, by another human type. This is why
it is not an easy task for the rural person to "install" himself
in it; he is full of misgivings about the city, he feels like "a
lost chicken," and he regards the urban man with suspicion and
hostility, thinking that he is going to dupe and mock him. For
his part, the city dweller usually feels disdain for the "bumpkin,"
"hayseed," "yokel," "rube" (the names are significant) and tends to
see him as a comic figure, awkward and dull, who moves in the city
like a duck on land. This situation has nothing to do with the
rivalries and hostilities between villagers, for these differences
are based on nothing less than common assumptions within which the
parties understand one another very well. Hence the abstract
error of considering workers and peasants to be a single class,
the proletarian; for the social distance between them is enormous,
much greater than between the farm worker and the landlord, or
between the different groups of city dwellers.[9]

To a greater or lesser extent, all cities are rural. The
reciprocal function of the urban and the rural elements in them
is a delicate theme of great importance in understanding them.
Some cities have turned their backs on the country; others are
open to it; and in some districts there are gradations all the
way from the rural to the purely urban, which ignores the country,
denies it, and at best relates to it through "excursions" and
the like.

Then there are the cities themselves. The reason why cities

are decisive in any society, even in those heavily weighted toward
the rural, is that they are the instruments of "sociality," or if
you like, of sociability. A society is a society thanks to its
cities. And the forms of these marvelously reflect the social
structure. I am not going to attempt a morphology or typology
of cities. Here I shall only refer to several procedural points
of view that lead toward it, or in a more restricted sense, toward the interpretation of what cities mean within a social unit.

The first point of view to consider is the size of cities,
about which the Greeks were so concerned, especially the authors
of political treatises or politeîai. Under a certain size a city
is not possible, because it does not reach the development or
have the diversification of types, professions, and services required by urban life. On the other hand, if it surpasses a certain magnitude, unity becomes problematical. Naturally, it is
not a question of constants. The limitation of the ancient city,
in which people traveled on foot, or at most on horseback, in
litters, or in coaches, does not coincide with that of the modern
city with its means of frequent and rapid transportation. Nevertheless, these means are in fact quite limited, because their
proliferation tends to complicate and obstruct things. The large
cities of today tend to break up into boroughs, within which life
goes on with only sporadic visits to other areas. Within countries
the echelon of city sizes is important (in Germany, Italy, the
United States), as is the discontinuity where the pattern goes
from small or medium cities to those enormously larger (Paris
in France, which is far larger than the others; Vienna, Buenos
Aires, Rio and São Paulo in Brazil, and even Madrid and Barcelona
in Spain).

The social criterion for distinguishing between large and
small cities is whether or not the inhabitants know each other
personally, whether the street is a place of strangers. Even in
relatively large cities certain groups still maintain mutual
acquaintanceship: the aristocracy, intellectuals and artists,
the high middle class, and the common people of an entire district.
But beyond a certain size relationships become anonymous, even
among minorities unless they are exceptional and outstandingly
gifted.

A second point of view is that of the seclusion of cities.
The extreme case is the walled city. But even without walls,
a city can be closed and isolated, either because it is "wrapped
up" in itself, as Ortega described the Madrid of Philip IV, or
as it was depicted in La Verbena de la Paloma; or because the
surrounding countryside is inhospitable and unattractive. Even
the great cities of the United States are more open than those
of Europe or South America. At the other extreme from the walled
city stands the small North American city, for instance, in New
England, which properly speaking is "in the country," where
vegetation grows everywhere, and which can be interpreted either
as a city full of connecting gardens or as a park or field with

190

houses inside it. Without sharp delineations it extends with
fewer and fewer houses along the highways until it connects so
imperceptibly with other cities that it must be indicated by a
roadsign: "Welcome to X" or "You are entering Z."

Thirdly, cities present diverse internal structures. The
Classic Mediterranean cities, and to a lesser extent, those of
Medieval Europe as well, have been characterized and defined by
a center, almost always a square--agora, forum, zoco, main plaza.
They are "cephalic" cities, as it were, with a head where life is
concentrated and where, above all, the entire city comes out to
see and meet itself. When a city is very large there are usually
several of these centers, and then it beomes "polycephalic," con-
taining two, three, or four plazas around which life is organized.
Sometimes such centers serve only parts of the city and reveal
only a topographical diversity; in other cases, they imply a
differentiation of function: there may be a center of mundane
life, an economic center, perhaps a popular center, and possibly
a political one. Finally, we find "acephalic" cities, in which
social life has no center and is simply inorganic. These cities
have less unity and especially less of a "public" character.
They lack a "Main Square" and are generally minimally political.
Most cities in the United States are like this. Sometimes the
city is not organized around squares, but linearly, along central
streets. This is the "Main Street" of American cities; it is the
mark of cities without a head but with a spinal column and verte-
brae, and perhaps with secondary plazas that serve as subordinate
centers, for instance, at the end of the main street (like Soria
in Spain).

A fourth aspect is the social organization of the cities,
i.e., the urban distribution of the social classes. There are
cities with sharply defined quarters, such as those of the Middle
Ages or the Renaissance; they had their noble district, their
guild districts or streets (embroiderers, brassworkers, tanners,
ironworkers, weavers, brothels), and their Jewish quarter or
ghetto. These relatively isolated and independent groups met at
certain points: cathedral, market, plaza, and only on such occasions did they see each other and have social contact. But there
are (and more especially have been) other kinds of cities in which,
even with the persisting difference between quarters of different
social level, the various social classes live together in the
same areas. In the nineteenth century stratification of several
groups in horizontal planes on the different floors of the same
building was a frequent occurrence. Thus a doctor would live on
the mezzanine in consideration of patients for whom it was painful to climb stairs, an aristocrat would occupy the main floor,
a notary the second, an officeworker the third, a seamstress the
sotabanco, or "garret," and a shoemaker and an errand boy or
waterboy in the inner wings. Recently, there has been a return
to a division by districts, and the different social classes now
see one another only occasionally; they no longer have the minimal

contact and greeting on the stairway or at the door of the building. The social and political effects of this are especially serious. (In recent years when the difficulty of finding housing has caused people to live wherever they can find a place regardless of taste or convenience, a mixing of social classes has again come about, but it is an unstructured and random mixing.) And as far as the most recent times are concerned, we should consider those cities in which people do not reside, but which are designed for other collective functions. Thus we find industrial or financial centers, public and private offices, shows, and commerce juxtaposed to residential areas or cities. These are devoted exclusively to private and family life (for instance, the suburbs of North American cities), which causes a cleavage between the urban groupings and a constant flow of traffic between the two parts. Witness the commuters of the United States who go to the big city in the morning and return in the afternoon after work to a frame house with a lawn and trees in a suburb as many as ten, twenty, or fifty miles away. In Spain, insofar as anything similar happens, it is exactly the reverse: the official who offers his service in a small city lives in Madrid or Barcelona and commutes to the location of his position. This is what was originally called "Guadalajarism," and as travel facilities have improved, it has grown to include Soria, Zaragoza, Oviedo, Murcia, and Granada.

In cities where services of all kinds are centralized, this forces the different urban segments to interact. This is what happened with the cathedrals of the Middle Ages and a good portion of modern times. Such has been the normal effect of trade, which was concentrated in a few streets where buying and selling occurred. The same is true of shows, which are concentrated in adjacent locales; of banks (until a few years ago all the banks of Madrid were on Alcalá Street); and of cafés, located in certain areas of the city. But in other urban structures (and this is a growing trend) all these services are scattered. Churches multiply, and instead of attending the same one, the faithful quickly go to the nearest one. Nearly everything can be purchased on one's own street or those adjacent. People go to their neighborhood cinema, which shows the same film as ten others. People frequent the café within walking distance, and they use the services of one of the nearest branch banks that have sprung up all over the city.

Finally, beginning with the industrial age, it is necessary to consider the cities with a proletarian periphery, which in some cases is simply synonymous with the working class, while in others it represents regression and social degeneration, and in still others it is composed of "marginal" groups not assimilated into the general society of the urban complex: Jews, Negroes, Indians, newly arrived immigrants, and those who are dissenters or who have been defeated. These are the different forms of urban outskirts, suburb, and in the recent Spanish meaning, "slum," banlieue.

57. Time and Daily Life

The amount of time that each person has is gradually invested
in the tasks of daily life. A form of collective life, among
other things, a particular way of spending one's alloted time.
And the amount of this time and its use reveal the aspiration of
each person in society. How much time one may ask. Is it not
fixed at exactly twenty-four hours per day? Few examples show
more clearly that with man nothing is natural, by which I mean
that nothing is merely natural; instead everything human always
requires the free and imaginative intervention of the individual which transcends physical data and transforms them into
ingredients of a personal life.

Men are in the habit of complaining (at least in our time)
about the lack of time. In contrast, we know of others who have
felt the painful need to "kill time," which to them was evidently
bothersome and excessive. Apparently twenty-four hours is not
always the same amount of time. To begin with, it is not a matter
of indifference whether or not time is treated "quantitatively"
in the formal meaning of the term. In primitive ways of life
time is divided into two parts: day and night, and night hardly
counts except for rest. The first, daytime, is divided and articulated in turn by the position of the sun over the horizon, but it
is a very vague division. Among ancient and medieval peoples,
and even today among country people, the time of day is only
approximate and imposes only a fluid "configuration" to the day
and does not amount to a strict quantification. This appears
only with exact timepieces, and then every hour opens and like a
grenade hurls its awesome content at us: sixty minutes, each of
which (and this is simply frightful) contains sixty seconds. From
this moment, instead of flowing by more or less rapidly, or immers-
ing us as it eddies around some delight, or becoming hard and re-
sistant in waiting, time is transformed into a measurable and
exact quantity that arrives, passes, ends, rephases, and causes
us to live on the alert and uneasily.

The "set time," the interference with the series of actions,
the need of sumultaneousness, is the most serious matter; that I
have to time my arrival at the station with the steam pressure
in the pistons in the locomotive; that my arrival at the office
must coincide with the vertical minute hand of the clock; or that
the applause in the theater must precede the passing of the last
bus that will take me home. I believe that railroads brought
about the first quantification of human time. The consequences
have been--and will continue to be--tremendous.

Moreover, of the time at his disposal (which is more or less
measured), man divides it into two parts: that which he considers
his own and that which belongs to others. This division coincides
approximately with Ortega's separation of occupations into "felicitary" and "laboral" classifications. The time that each person
"sells" in order to earn a living is not "his"; it is alienated

time that he feels he has lost. His own time is the free remainder that he can use as he likes. What is the ratio of each type in each society, in each way of life, in each class? Except for excessively oppressive types of work (such as the forced labor of slaves, galley oarsmen, prisoners, or extraordinarily burdensome economic conditions), there is always some "free" time. But the judgment as to whether time is free or not depends on the way it lived subjectively, i.e., on the life aspiration. This is the great problem of "leisure" (the Spanish word ocio is barely adequate to convey the meaning, and the fundamental question would be: why?) or French loisir, or the Latin otium (as opposed to negotium), or Greek skholé (from which derives not the idea of vacation but school). To the common man many tasks that are not his work seem like leisure--especially those that do not involve muscular effort--and of course this includes the activities of the aristocracy, which he interprets as the "leisure class," even though an aristocrat may consider his tasks to be burdensome, a corvée, and which in fact do require great effort. In contrast, the writer, the artist, or the researcher does not regard his time as alienated time, even though he may feel fatigued and have to force himself to finish his work. He complains about not having enough time precisely for his work.

In our day, between one's own time and that sold utilitarianly in order to live, it is necessary to consider also a third portion that we might call "no man's time." This absorbs a considerable part of our life, mutilating, slicing, and reducing it. This is the time lost in several ways: to begin with, in getting from one place to another (not traveling or going for a drive, which are two ways of "investing" time); or the hours and hours spent daily on streetcars, buses, subways, suburban trains, or what is worse, in waiting for them; or in the hours spent in line before the ticket window; or in the countless minutes that vanish before the red light at intersections; or the endless hours lost in bureaucratic red tape, the latest form of human sacrifice in which the victim is time itself, the substance of biographical life. And this is the reason why after the workday has been reduced everywhere, after going from a workday that lasted ten or twelve hours from sunup to sundown to the almost mythical eight-hour day or even less, we hear unceasing complaints that there is not enough time.

The distribution of the workday is one of the factors that most subtly and deeply affect a way of life. To get up early or stay up late, to eat at certain hours, to work during the first part of the day, leaving the free time for the day's end, or perhaps to have it extended with breaks and less haste from morning to night--all this reveals an average predominant aspiration in a society, a series of desires, and an idea of what a happy life is. The man who rises at dawn, rushes to work, interrupts his work for half an hour or an hour at the most for a brief lunch, and tries to finish by five in the afternoon so as to have

194

a part of the day exclusively for himself has an idea of the
happy life that is quite different from that of the person who
prefers to stay in bed until the day is well begun, to go home
and have a hearty, slow lunch with conversation afterward, perhaps to take a siesta later, and to return to work until dark,
leaving no time to start any other activity except to take a
stroll, have an aperitif with friends, or take in a show.

How much free time does the average man of each group have
in a given society? How does he use it? What is his idea of
"wasting time" and, in contrast, of using it to advantage?
These are questions that must be answered in each case. And it
is also necessary to ascertain whether in each period the prevailing articulation of daily life responds to the authentic
desires of individuals, or whether they regard them as a collective imposition, as something that persists inertially and that
they would like to change. What is the sentimental place of
official "amusements," of strolling, of conversation, of doing
nothing except, perhaps, sunning oneself? How many hours alone
does the man have? How many the woman? What do play, reading,
sport, and gallantry represent? What is the place of boredom in
a society, and where does it lead? Does it lead perhaps to pur-
suing science, to making money, or to conspiring, or possibly to
considering it as the very substance of life itself? If we are
sincere, we must admit that so far sociology and history do not
allow us to answer these questions satisfactorily for any society,
not even for our own; and without an answer we do not know what
"living" has meant for those men, much less the meaning of
"being happy."

58. Ages and the Life Trajectory

It is not only everyday time, the time of daily life, that
may be ordered in a variety of ways; the sum total of man's
earthly life is ordered in different manners, and this temporal
disposition affects the deepest notes of life's melody. First
of all, the life trajectory may be more or less long. Perhaps
this is not factual or certain for every individual, but it is
so when viewed statistically and as a result of the empirical
structure of life. Although death is certain and the hour uncertain, vaguely and unsurely but with tenacity people count on an
approximate duration of their stay in this world. Generally men
live so many years; they may die sooner, but if they do, then it
is felt that they have died "ahead of time," that such deaths
were premature. They may die later, but then it is thought that
the extra years are a stroke of luck or an unexpected gift that
was not due and not to be counted on. The economy of life ad-
justs to a probable horizon and operates according to it and--I
repeat--to its uncertainty.

Earlier (Chapter II, 11) I referred to the repercussions

that the contemporary fact of average human longevity is beginning to have on generations. It affects each individual life
and interindividual relationship in a similar manner. The horizon of life, which until recently was closed off at about sixty,
is expanded today at least fifteen or twenty years more. And
since the life trajectory is longer, it is "stretched" farther,
that is, it has a different curvature and figure, and its articulations in the form of ages vary in absolute duration and function
in the total span.

In every society there is an age for considering oneself to
be an adult, and it is usually different for the two sexes.
Childhood may be very brief or quite long, as may youth also.
But a simple chronological determination of its duration would
not be sufficient; rather, it would be necessary to set forth
its delineation through a series of relatively independent aspects.
For example, in some societies sexual initiation is precocious,
at least more precocious than in the preceding era or in the
neighboring society, but it may be that economic dependence on
the parents lasts longer. Thus, if on the one hand it seems that
childhood is shortened, on the other, it is lengthened. Perhaps
the young soon feel that they are ready to assume important positions yet feel excused for years and years from doing intellectual,
literary, or artistic work that is important, mature, or adult.
This may be the situation of recent years. It may happen also
that a youth has to face the dangers of war from a very early age,
while a system of senatorial authority excludes his participation
in public life until very late.

Youth is sometimes fleeting, sometimes decades long, and the
latter condition may indicate vitality, flexibility, innovative
capability, or the fear of maturity, resistance to settling down
with a set attitude or way of life, or insecurity and a desire
for endless provisionality. It is necessary to determine what is
involved in each case. Something similar happens with maturity;
man dwells in it for long years, as though it were an age marked
by permanence and stability, or it may seem to be the harbinger
of approaching and inevitable decrepitude. Finally, old age
sometimes functions as an empty wait for death, while in other
societies it is an age of positive attributes, sure of itself,
perhaps even proud and hopeful.

The pattern of ages affects woman even more profoundly. From
the biological point of view, it must be admitted that woman is
more precocious than man and that she ages more quickly. But
even though this may be so, it seems unlikely that it is a question of a rhythm that is solely biological. Instead, it seems to
involve a life structure outlined by a specific social situation
doubtless based on biological conditions. As a matter of fact,
childhood has increased: girls of fourteen, who in other times
were often married, with some exceptions today seem like children

to us. On the other hand, youth, which ended shortly after child-hood a century ago, now lasts incredibly longer. Although the expression is too odd to ring true, today we hear people speak quite naturally of "a girl of forty," and although the ear may not protest, the intuition does when people speak of "an old man of sixty." Today woman has acquired what she has rarely had: a long mature age, similar to that of the man, into which she can enter with the prospect of fulfillment and not imminent decline. Finally, woman outlives man an average or three or four years.

All this has profoundly changed the "argument," or plot, of feminine life, something that was necessary in order to sustain the new trajectory. In many societies woman lived in absolute subordination and dependence until a time came when she began to function as a woman. In that type of situation her period of apogee as a woman was very short, in theory eight or ten years, in fact much less. Early marriage (almost always to a much older man) and immediate motherhood, repeated at close intervals, combined to force a quick social "retirement," marked in most cases by the surrender of the specifically feminine claim to being a woman and by physical decadence.[10] Often this period was reduced to a flash of three or four years, from her appearance in society until some months after marriage. We might add that throughout long ages, especially in some societies, motherhood has decimated women, or at the very least has exposed them to illnesses and ailments at an age that we would consider juvenile today.

All this affects the synchronization of collective life. Only the extension of youth and full maturity of woman can offer a real and sufficient basis for the normal functioning of monog-amous marriage, between persons of approximately the same age and level. In societies where the woman is soon spent, the most fre-quent solution is a great age difference between husband and wife. But this has the following consequences: the impossibility of early marriage for the man and therefore a long time spent lead-ing a "bachelor's life"; the marked subordination of the woman to a much older and more experienced husband; the lack of a common historical level by virtue of belonging to different generations; less probability of the "friendship" inherent in marriage, not only because of the age difference, but even more because of the lack of independent maturity of the woman when she goes from childhood to marriage with hardly a transition.

Our era is marked by an extreme "duration" of the woman and by an age parallel between the sexes. But it would be an error to believe that all earlier societies have followed the same pattern. Their differences are great, and only a fine measuring in each of the ages and of their mutual articulation will allow us to reconstruct the actual outline of the life trajectory.

197

59. Death and the Value of Life

Although death might appear to be a constant and invariable
element because it is the inevitable end of all human life, the
contrary is true. It is hard to find any reality about which
interpretations vary so deeply, or one that has more influence
on the perspective in which all others appear. There are several
reasons why death is pre-lived in different ways. One of them is
its frequency of occurrence, the way it constantly appears around
us; all men die, and death happens once for everybody, but inasmuch
as the average life span in Europe around 1500 has been calculated
at twenty-two years, and in the United States in 1953 at sixty-nine,
this means that death struck two or three times more often than now.
If instead of European conditions, we compare this to the situation
in India or China, which in nearly every period of history have
been marked by enormous mortality rates, it is clear that the experience of death in the world in which we live can vary greatly.
And this leads to a modification in the awareness of the certainty
of death. In some ways of life it is always imminent; it is regarded as something that can happen at any second, striking us or
those dear to us down when we least expect it. In contrast, in
other situations death seems more remote. We might describe it as
certain in each case but improbable at any given time—certain and
inevitable but unlikely. Ascertaining the degree of probability of
death with which people live their lives in each society is indispensable for understanding that way of life and for a whole series
of human behavior.

High infant mortality, the disappearance of thousands of people
due to starvation, epidemics, floods, and all kinds of disasters,
and the many unexplained deaths due to vague, undiagnosed illnesses
are all factors that lead to a prompt collective acceptance of
death as something belonging to the very nature of life, as something within its daily scheme of things and not as a curtain in
the background that limits life in the future. In other ways of
life, however, death is more or less situated and contained within
certain boundaries. The great calamities appear averted, and people
are assured that there will be no hunger, pestilence, earthquakes,
or—in some phases of history—war. Death is rationalized and reduced in size; insurance companies foresee and calculate it statistically, estimating its probability even for an individual: on
the basis of his age and a medical examination, they fix the cost
of the policy, which is to say, they decide on the likelihood of
death. Each death is explained, and the reason why each person
has died is known (or at least sought). It is a long way from the
vague "pain in the side" that ended so many lives five centuries
ago, and even as late as two hundred years ago, to the accuracy
of modern medical diagnosis. Every life is defended incredibly
more; men struggle against death as though in principle it were
possible to conquer it. Where before death's scythe mowed unchecked,
now extraordinary remedies are tried: operations, transfusions,

organ transplants; doctors go by airplane to visit patients, and
these go from continent to continent in search of famous hospitals.
Iron lungs work hastily, racing against the pace of death. As a
result death seems more and more to be something violent and accidental instead of inevitable and natural. We still cannot measure
the transformation that this will bring about in human sensitivity,
in the way people feel about being installed in life. We who live
today, at least those of us who are already adults, do not feel
overly affected because we are subject to earlier vigencias, just
as the certainty of flying is subjectively undermined by the memories of a time still quite recent when flying was simply preparing
oneself to fall. Unless other factors change the situation, within
a few decades the enormous transformation will be completed. And
I add this reservation because the threat of war, especially atomic
warfare, is introducing into people's minds the notion of the
possibility of death with a force unknown for centuries in the
West. Perhaps it is a necessary compensation for a balanced
economy of life.

But it is not only a question of the frequency and likelihood
of death. Once it occurs, or insofar as it threatens to occur,
what does man do with it? Throughout history human concern for
death has varied in intensity and content. Yet this is not to be
considered as any sort of "preparation for death," but first as
a concern for more trivial things. Consider, for example, the
type of Spanish woman, so often encountered during the past century
and well into this one, who could be called a "pre-widow," who
spent her life anticipating, foreseeing, and considering certain
the death of her husband. Think also about the reaction to the
death of someone not close: whispered conferences about when it
will happen, the tolling of church bells when it does, the wake,
the burial as a collective ceremony, funeral rites, and a long
gloomy period of mourning with the suspension of social life and
very nearly of private life, too. Compare these customs with the
reduction of the presence and rites of death to a minimum. In
some societies it is almost disregarded (such is the dominant
tendency in the United States); hardly any emphasis is placed on
it, and details are held to a minimum. Mourning is restricted to
wearing an appropriate suit to the funeral and does not extend
subsequently into daily life, and the situation tends to "normal-
ize" as soon as death has occurred (at least in external relationships and social life). From the Hindu wife, for whom the death
of her husband meant the end of her own life in the pyre, to the
situation where the person passes away almost "on tiptoe," unnoticed
and without disturbing anyone, the distance is so colossal that it
could occur only in human things, i.e., in historical things.

This suffices for my present interest, which is to show that
a social structure is partially defined by the reality assumed by
death within it and to point out the various points of view from
which it must be considered in order to determine its concrete
function. A careful study along these lines would reveal that the

differences between societies, which may otherwise be quite close
together, may be great and, above all, that change is sometimes
very rapid within the same society, perhaps perceptible from one
generation to another.

In connection with this a word needs to be said about a
closely related topic, although it should be considered independently and not as a strict parallel. This concerns the value of
human life within each society and for that reason the resistance
provoked by violent acts, especially those of an individual nature
such as crime. Nor should consideration be restricted to fortui-
tous and unpremeditated examples, but broadened to include deliberate and willful instances, such as the death penalty. During
long periods of Western history (in order not to look too far
afield for examples) the death penalty was not important. If it
was applied rather liberally, it was done with perfect natural-
ness, as something proper about which there was no reason to be
greatly disturbed. But lest we think only of cruelty and hardness
of heart, the important thing is that this same spirit was shared
to a certain extent by the victims themselves. To be hanged or
decapitated was certainly something lamentable which ought if possible to be avoided. It was a serious mishap, a bitter pill, a
stroke of evil fortune, but with occasional exceptions it was
nothing more. Recall the Memoirs of Captain Alonso de Contreras,
the methods of the Santa Hermandad in the times of the Catholic
Kings, or the humorous references by writers to executions in the
sixteenth and seventeenth centuries, in reality (Jesuit letters,
Barrionuevo, Lettres of Madame de Sévigné) and in fictional accounts (Cervantes, Quevedo). Whereas the executioner Alonso
Ramplón in an atrocious burlesque letter to his nephew Pablos
tells how he has just hanged and then quartered the latter's
father and of the fine way he bore up, Victor Hugo writes Le
Dernier Jour d'un condamné à mort ("The Last Day of a Man Condemned to Death"), Larra and Espronceda portray El reo de muerte
("The Criminal Condemned to Death"), and Dickens arouses English
opinion against executions. In Notre Dame de Paris consider the
pathos, lyricism, and rhetoric that for several chapters mark the
sorrowful anticipation and description of the little gypsy
Esmeralda's death on the gallows; and compare it to the following
passage from the end of Salas Barbadillo's novel La hija de
Celestina ("Celestina's Daughter") describing the execution of
the protagonists: "Perico's luck turned sour; for within two
days, they made him a gem for the gallows by hanging him from
them, to the satisfaction of the whole Capital. Elena did not
accompany him, because that afternoon they took her out--arousing
pity and painful sorrow in the hardest hearts--to the Manzanares
River, where, first garroting her, according to the law, they
put her into a cask and lowered her into the water."[11]

What is the value placed on life in each society? How much
imagination or how much mechanical automatism accompanies thoughts
about death? This is quite probably a deciding factor, not just

a question of "cruelty" or tenderness." All of which leads us
to the more serious question of how death figures in the horizon
of life, what its place is, its importance in the view of the
finalities of life, and for this reason how it is organized in
the total outline of life.

60. The Perspective of Finalities

The words that I have just written might cause one to think
that when death is referred to without imaginative expansion, it
ceases to be an awesome reality, whereas a consideration that
effectively brings imagination into play regarding it gives death
a fearful and direful aspect. Normally no doubt this is true,
but if we analyze things with rigor, they are quite a bit more
complicated. For what really happens is that lack of imagination
skeletonizes death and reduces it to its consequences (or better,
to some of its consequences) and, above all, places it at a re-
move from us by converting it into the death of anybody, or nobody in particular, and by that same measure trivializing it.

This is good and bad in the sense that it removes both the
horror and attractiveness of death. For we must not forget that
death may exercise--indeed, often has exercised--a singular fas-
cination over men. Here of course we cannot go into individual
attitudes; they do not count as components of a social structure.
Our interest is in the vigencias of this dimension of life, those
which the individual encounters and which exert their pressure
on him regardless of his personal position. For this touches on
the predominant attitude in which each member of the society
participates as a member, although he may react against it in
disagreement.

Imagine a society defined by a collective forgetfulness of
death. Naturally, all the people within it know they must die,
and reality takes it on itself to remind them of it at every
step. Nevertheless, the contents of life omit death, and it remains external to them, unconnected and extrinsic, like an end
to life that lies "outside it." In this situation the person
who is most intimately occupied and preoccupied with death finds
no collective grasp to which to connect his personal attitude;
and insofar as he moves among social structures and activates
common resources--beliefs, usages, values, modes of expression--
his life is estranged from death, and only by virtue of a violent
inner effort can he regain for himself a fastness in which death
exists. This implies, however, that even for him that existence
will be somewhat exceptional. On the other hand, the individual
who is the least inclined to orient his life in the direction of
death, whose beliefs instill in him a maximum of indifference
about the topic, will have no alternative but to deal with it
at every step if he finds himself in a society that makes death
its central interest, and, therefore, even though his own vocation

would lead him away from it, his life will be fashioned to an appreciable degree by a variety of activities concerning death.

But death functions in two quite different meanings, each of which in turn divides into two different possibilities. Although it would be oversimplification, we could point out four perspectives of death. No doubt there are many more, and this outline is insufficient, but since here we are not dealing with individual life but with the function of death as a component of different social structures, our interest is precisely in the outline that turns out to be collectively operable.

Death is a boundary and accordingly has two sides: on this side lies the end of life; on the other, a mystery that can be interpreted in many ways: annihilation, reincarnation, different degrees and forms of immortality, and doubt. The two slopes, the two sides of the boundary are inseparable, but attention is often centered preferentially on one or the other, at times almost exclusively so. In certain societies what counts is the finiteness of life; one day sooner or later life will end, and we call it the day of our death. At other times, having accepted this, we think and feel that "life" is more than "this life," which is a provisional and fleeting trajectory that bears us through the doorway of death to the other life. The next life is like a suction on this one, drawing it and causing death to appear not as a wall or barrier but as a passageway—a more or less narrow doorway—or like a black hole leading us to nothingness if annihilation is what we expect beyond the pale. It is hardly necessary to stress the importance to a collective way of life of the predominance in a society of one or the other of these beliefs. The outlook on each and every element that we have studied in this book changes according to this final all-important _vigencia_ that affects everything else and gives it a precise meaning.

Furthermore, these two interpretations of death, the _cismun-dane_ and the _transmundane_, each leave the way open for two possibilities: those based on the connection of death to life. I shall explain.

Let us begin with the cismundane attitude. Life is finite, a person's days are numbered, and one of them will be the last. Regardless of what he does, man will finally die: he will become incurably ill, or suffer an accident, or be killed. In any case, man will live day by day, and one of them will have no tomorrow. This attitude is based on the belief in the extraordinary nature of death, which makes it inevitable and independent of life. This is what I call unconnected cismundane death. Properly speaking, it has nothing to do with life, which is lived in its own way until it ends. It is possible, of course, for it to be more or less exposed to death, more or less perilous; a life that abstains from excesses and avoids risks and adventures is less vulnerable and makes death less probable at each moment. But that is all. Consequently, life appears indifferent from the viewpoint of death,

and the latter appears as something "inorganic" in the sense
that it does not articulate with life or confer articulation on
it.

Within this cismundane attitude, however, things may take
a different slant. In order for this to be so, it is enough
that death is felt as something that forms a part of life. If
one believes that life ends positively in death, then death
gives unity and coherence; then the whole of life is oriented
toward death, each life act anticipates a certain mode of death,
and each postulates and demands it through an internal logic and
does not accept just any kind of death. Conversely, death reacts
on the life that has been lived, structuring, "explaining," and
interpreting it; in other words, it gives the true significance
to life acts, which are incomplete, inconclusive, and imperfect
until death gives them the final touch and the fullness of their
reality. Life is oriented toward death, not in the sense of
seeking it, but in that of choosing it. Life becomes a search
for a worthy death, and, I repeat, in the cismundane sense. For
this reason death appears as a good chance or opportunity that
should be taken. No one expressed this feeling better than
Quevedo who nostalgically idealizes the attitude of Spaniards
before his time:

> And with her (virtue) lies illustrious Liberty
> who, when she knew where death and honor were,
> used never to seek longer life.
>
> Once, the strong nation, prodigal of soul,
> was used to think growing old in fortune's arms
> was an affront the passing years contrived.
>
> To wile away the time in idleness
> and torpor—that was something alien
> to Spaniards, in the past.
>
> No one would count the years, but how he lived them,
> and not an hour went by that was not marked
> by eager striving after valiant deeds.[12]

Instead of wishing to prolong life, growing old in an inert way
and suffering "the affronts of age" that mar the harmonious sil-
houette of a life well ended, one should take the opportunity for
an honorable death when it is offered. And over against the
number of years, one should consider the form, the figure, and
the manner in which one lives them. Only this allows an understanding of Spanish life in the Golden Age and in a certain way
in any other age, because when we Spaniards have lived otherwise
we have felt diminished and deprived of our authentic mode of
being. The same duality may occur in the transmundane attitude

toward death. The view of the other side of the mortal bourn
may be positive or negative according to whether or not one has
hope. But in either case, we find the possibilities of disjunction or connection with earthly life. He who thinks that at the
last he will be annihilated, regardless of what he does and notwithstanding his anguish over it, severs death from the pattern
of life, leaving both mutually indifferent to each other. In
contrast, the distrustful position of Sénancour, which moved
Unamuno so much, is radically contrary: L'homme est périssable;
it se peut; mais périssons en résistant, et si le néant nous est
réservé, ne faisons pas que ce soit une justice ("It may be that
man perishes; but let us resist as we perish, and if nothingness
awaits us, let us not act as though it were justice").[13]

And the same may be said of the hopeful attitude, including
the firm belief in immortality. When this faith becomes mechanical (and this happens in many societies) the "other life" seems
assured by meeting certain conditions in a somewhat abstract way,
that is, in a way that is unconnected with the total and complete
pattern of earthly life. If certain requirements are fulfilled
(morality, rites, sacraments, etc., according to the case) then
one shall gain an extraterrestrial life in one form or another
according to the diverse beliefs. And this happens in a way
that is relatively independent of life in the world where one
has lived. I say "relatively" because the link between this life
and the next is reduced to the points of contact necessary to fulfill the requirements. Hence it is all the same whether one has
lived in one human way or another. It matters not whether life
in this world has shown pattern, beauty, plenitude, intensity,
and authenticity, provided the door to the everlasting has been
opened. This is what I call disconnected death, for there is no
link between the two lives except a certain conditioning, and in
no case is the future life presented as a maturation or perfection, as a coherent culmination of this existence.

Nevertheless, over against this attitude there is another
that affirms those connections. Although in the Dances of Death
all the human types of the time are paraded before our eyes
(the Pope, the Emperor, the Constable, the Doctor, the Priest,
the Plowman, the Maid, etc.) and mention is made of their respective offices or means of livelihood, the gist is equalitarian and
in this sense, abstract. All end the same, all die equally, the
only difference being their reward or punishment according to
whether they have done "good" or "evil." Except for this, at the
hour of death everything else is a matter of indifference, and it
matters not whether one has been a pontiff or a girl, a knight
or a plowman, this person or that person. This is not the assumption that enriches the Coplas of Jorge Manrique, even though he
also points out that everything passes away, that death destroys
all, that it hides and removes everything. In the first place,
the memory of all that vanished world is full of its color, savor,
and aroma. Everything is individualized and personally lived; it

204

is irreplaceable and irreparable, even though perishable and
destined to pass away. Hence the joy and melancholy that fill
the couplets:

What of the dames of birth and station,
    Their head-attire, their sweeping trains,
        Their vesture scented?
What of that gallant conflagration
    They made of lovers' hearts whose pains
        Were uncontented?

And what of him, that troubador
    Whose melting lutany and rime
        Was all their pleasure?
Ah, what of her who danced demure,
    And trailed her robes of olden times
        So fair a measure?

And when Jorge Manrique begins to narrate the death of his father,
Grand Master Don Rodrigo, he is very careful to sketch his life,
to explain who he was, and to present the death that befalls him
as the fulfillment and the supreme culmination of his earthly
life, his biography. To this end he includes not only the earthly
life but also honor and fame; and these are not scorned or discounted beside eternal life, but held in lesser esteem (worthy,
though less so in comparison). Thus the future life is intimately
linked to the one the Grand Master is ending historically and cir-
cumstantially in his villa in Ocaña:

Then having risked his life, maintaining
    The cause of justice in the fight
        For law appointed,
With years in harness spent sustaining
    The royal crown of him by right
        His lord anointed,

With feats so mighty that Hispania
    Can never make account of all
        In number mortal,--
Unto his township of Ocaña
    Came Death at last to strike and call
        Against his portal:

Death encourages him, relying on its persuasion, on its invitation to undertake the long voyage, and on what Don Rodrigo has
been, what he has wanted to be, what he has preferred and prized:

For you, are only half its terrors
    And half the battles and the pains
        Your heart perceiveth;

The Structure of Society

Since here a life devoid of errors
   And glorious for noble pains
      To-day it leaveth;

A life for such as bravely bear it
   And make its fleeting breath sublime
      In right pursuing,
Untainted, as is theirs who share it
   And put their pleasure in the grime
      Of their undoing;

The life that is the Everlasting
   Was never yet aught attained
      Save meed eternal;
And ne'er through soft indulgence casting
   The shadow of its solace stained
      With guilt infernal;

But in the cloister holy brothers
   Beseige it with unceasing prayer
      And hard denial;
And faithful paladins are others
   Who 'gainst the Moors to win it bear
      With wound and trial.

And since, O noble and undaunted,
   Your hands the paynim's blood have shed
      In war and tourney,--
Make ready now to take the vaunted
   High guerdon you have merited
      For this great journey!

Upon this holy trust confiding,
   And in the faith entire and pure
      You e'er commended,
Away, --unto your new abiding,
   Take up the Life that shall endure
      When this is ended![14]

And with still more concision and heart-rending attachment,
Quevedo expresses this connection of death to life in his love
sonnets:

From the white day to take, the ultimate
Shade will be able to close my eyes:
And this soul of mine from its raging
Ardor then will be pleasingly parted;

But it will not leave on the farther shore
The memory of where it burned;

206

Human Relations

My flame to swim the frigid water has learned,
And to lose respect for the rigor of the law.

Soul to whom all love a prison has been,
Veins which have given fuel to so much fire,
Marrow consumed in such a glorious blaze,

Will leave their body, but not their care:
Ashes will be, but ashes aware,
Dust, but enamored dust.[15]

And perhaps in a more explicit way, with full awareness of
the finiteness of life but without using it as a pretext to deny
life or to refuse to bear its responsibilities:

It does not grieve me to die: I have not refused
To end this life; nor have I tried to
Stay this death, which was born
At once with life and care.

I regret having to leave abandoned
A body that a loving spirit has girded;
Empty a heart, forever inflamed,
Where all Love sheltered reigned.[16]

One may wonder why this study ends with the testimony of
poets. I am interested in showing that it is not a matter of
mere possibilities, but instead that these four ways in which
death functions have in fact occurred in different historical
circumstances, and that the different perspectives were not
simply imagined. And for this reason it was necessary to bring
in the voice of poets, not men of theory, for theirs is a voice
modulated by human circumstance, the expression of a sensitivity
that is not only individual but the key to discovering the hidden
heartbeat of time.
     But we must be mindful that individual attitudes are many
and varied and that none of them is enough to characterize a
society. Beyond what each of us may think, feel, and believe,
there is the generic attitude about time which we all encounter
and with which we must make our life. What position does our
world (not we) take in regard to death, annihilation, immortality?
In what measure is it disinterested, anguished, doubtful, or con-
fident concerning everlasting life? With profound insight, Unamuno
titled his book Del sentimiento trágico de la vida en los hombres
y en los pueblos (On the Tragic Sense of Life in Men and Peoples);
for a people may possess that sense despite the fact that many of
its men do not, or some men may feel it, like foreigners in the
midst of a people that does not even suspect it. The status,

vitality, and authenticity of the <u>vigencias</u> in this regard must be investigated with even more care and rigor than in other points. For here is the keystone, and only if clarity penetrates this far can one seriously inquire into the nature of a social structure.

Notes

Notes to Chapter I

1. Translator's note: In his Man and People Ortega introduces the concept of the interindividual that Marías picks up in this work. The interindividual encompasses such relationships as love, family life, and friendship and refers to those acts in which we do not cease to act as acquainted individuals or lose sight of the prime source of an act or feeling.

2. Introducción a la Filosofía (Reason and Life), Obras, II, p. 320.

3. Translator's note: To my knowledge no adequate English equivalent of vigencia exists, since it may include law, custom, usage, belief, and prevailing modes of all kinds. "Vigence" would be an alternative to vigencia did it not suggest an etymology that is without basis in English language and history. For this reason I have decided to retain the original term with its formal definition.

4. One may consult two concrete studies of regional societies in my books Nuestra Andalucía (Díaz-Casariego, Editor; Madrid, 1966) and Consideración de Cataluña (Ayma; Barcelona, 1966); also found in Obras, VIII. (Neither of these works has been translated into English--trans.)

5. Arnold J. Toynbee, A Study of History, vol. I (New York and London: Oxford University Press, 1946).

6. The Decline of the West, in which the problem of "cultures" is presented at length.

7. Especially in The Crisis of European Conscience (1680-1715). In European Thought in the Eighteenth Century, he begins with the results of the first book.

8. España en su historia. The theoretical points of view are emphasized more in El enfoque histórico y la no hispanidad de los visigodos and in Ensayo de historiología, in which he introduces the term vividura, and in the new edition of the first book under the title La realidad histórica de España.

9. In my Introducción a la Filosofía (Reason and Life) I
have repeatedly treated the problem of situation. See especially
Subchapters 9, 20, 21, 35, 68, and 79. In the present work I
have restricted myself to considering the peculiarities of historical situation, keeping to a minimum references to the prior problem
of "vital" situation, that is, the situation in which the individual finds himself; although, of course, this vital situation is
always historical also.

10. Cf. my work "La vida humana y su estructura empírica"
(in Actas del Congreso Internacional de Filosofía, Brussels, 1953,
included in Ensayos de teoría (Barcelona, 1954); Obras, IV).

11. Considerable--though not complete--information in this
regard is given in the book by J. H. Van der Pot, De Periodisering
der Gechiedenis (een Overzicht der Theorieen), The Hague, 1951.

12. See my book Generations: A Historical Method (University
of Alabama Press, 1970); in Spanish, El método histórico de las
generaciones (Madrid, 1949), included in Obras, VI.

13. K. Joël, Der Säkulare Rhythmus der Geschichte (Jahrbuch
für Soziologie, 1925), also Wandlungen der Weltanschauung (Tübingen,
1928).

Notes to Chapter II

1. See my Generations, Chapter V.
2. En torno al casticismo, I: "La tradición eterna."
3. See my Los Estados Unidos en escorzo (Obras, III [Pub-
lished in English as America in the Fifties and Sixties (Pennsylvania State University Press, 1972)--trans.]).
4. See my study "Los géneros literarios en filosofía" (in
Ensayos de teoría, Obras, IV [Published in English as Philosophy
as Dramatic Theory (Pennsylvania State University Press, 1971),
Chapter I--trans.]).

Notes to Chapter III

1. See my Biografía de la Filosofía (Obras, II), Chapters
II and III, "The Meaning of Aristotelian Philosophy" and "Stoic
Philosphy"; see also "Marco Aurelio o la exageración," San Anselmo
y el insensato (Obras, IV). (Biografía de la Filosofía has been
published in English under the title A Biography of Philosophy,
University of Alabama Press, 1984--trans.)
2. A central theme of Ortegan metaphysics: cf. Historia
como sistema. See also my Reason and Life, especially Chapter
VI, "The Structure of Human Life."
3. In Spanish forastero and extranjero mean, respectively,
"stranger" and "foreigner."--trans.
4. This would not apply to English in the same way because
the use of diminutives is less common than in Spanish.--trans.

5. Two interesting theatrical examples are The Women by Clare Booth Luce and La casa de Bernarda Alba by Federico García Lorca.

6. Usía is a corruption of vuestra senoría, "your Lordship," a reference to eighteenth and perhaps early nineteenth century aristocrats; majo refers to the colorful lower classes of the same era.--trans.

7. Mester de clerecía was the verse form of educated poets in medieval Spain. It consisted of Alexandrines (14 syllables) and consonantal rhyme in stanzas of four lines each. Mester de juglaría, its popular counterpart, consisted--usually--of half-lines of eight syllables and rhyme in assonance.--trans.

8. Del Imperio Romano, Obras completas, VI, 71-75.

9. Politics, III, 16, 1287 B 5-8: "Again, customary laws have more weight, and relate to more important matters, than written laws, and a man may be a safer ruler than the written law, but not safer than the customary law." (English version from The Basic Works of Aristotle. Ed. Richard McKeon [New York, 1941]--trans.)

10. Now the latter are beginning to be. (Author's note of 1960.)

11. Traditionally tú has been the form of address for children and those very close to one; usted is the more formal form to convey respect.--trans.

12. In the sense in which I have defined it rigorously as "the apprehension of reality in its connectedness." See my Reason and Life, especially Chapter I. Of course, this is the idea that underlies all of Ortegan sociology and theory of collective life based on a prior theory of real human life, that is, individual life, but to which society inexorably happens. His is a theory that is possible only through use of vital reason, which in its concrete form is historical reason.

13. See my study "La novela como método de conocimiento" in La Escuela de Madrid (Obras, V).

14. Ortega y Gasset, Ideas y creencias (Obras completas, V, p. 375 ff.)

Notes to Chapter IV

1. Both Marías and Ortega use the word "radical" in its fundamental Latin meaning of "root." Thus they describe Life as the "radical reality," i.e., that reality in which every other reality that is not life is "rooted," that is, in which it appears in some form. This is the keystone of Marías's metaphysics.--trans.

2. Ortega, Ideas y creencias; see also my Reason and Life, especially subchapters 4, 27, 29, 30, and 43.

3. Cf. Reason and Life, V, 42.

4. A reference to the Latin etymology of the word (from credere, to believe, trust; hence "credit," "creed," "credo,"

"credential"; Spanish creencia, "belief").--trans.

5. Cf. my Idea de la metafísica, Chapter VII ff. (Obras, II).

6. See, for example, the famous book by Gilberto Freyre, Casa-Grande e Senzala (translated into English as Masters and Slaves.--trans.).

7. See especially the prologue to Historia de la filosofía by Bréhier (Obras completas, V).

8. See my Reason and Life, Chapter II, "The Vital Function of Truth." (Marías invariably uses the word vital in the sense of "life" [Latin vita, "life"], and in those cases where it is used in this translation, it retains that basic meaning.--trans.)

9. See my Reason and Life, Chapter I.

10. See especially my study "La novela como método de conocimiento," in La Escuela de Madrid (Obras, V).

Notes to Chapter V

1. Cf. my Reason and Life, especially Chapters VI and IX; see also my book La imagen de la vida humana (Obras, V).

2. Cf. Reason and Life, Subchapter 76, "Lo personal y lo histórico en la vocacion."

3. Throughout this chapter Marías uses the word pretensión to indicate aim, objective, that which one strives to be and to achieve. For obvious reasons, the cognate "pretension" is inadequate, unless it is taken in its etymological context rather than its vernacular usage.--trans.

4. See La imagen de la vida humana; also "La novela como método de conocimiento."

5. In my book La imagen de la vida humana I have shown that what one gains with fiction is precisely condensed and accumulated time.

6. For the problem of individual happiness, see my study "La felicidad humana: mundo y paraíso," Ensayos de teoría (Obras, IV).

Notes to Chapter VI

1. An extraordinarily penetrating view of this problem is found in Ortega's Del Imperio Romano.

2. Again I refer to Ortega, Del Imperio Romano.

3. Count Medroso: "So you believe that my soul belongs to the galleys?"
   Boldmind: "Yes, and I should like to free it."
   Count Medroso: "But what if I like it there?"
   Boldmind: "In that case you deserve to be there."

4. Of course, it is not only a question of fantasy; but the absence of any is sufficient to exclude the presence of freedom.

Nor is fantasy enough to bring about freedom. But given other conditions (that lie beyond the present context), the realization of freedom is a function of fantasy. Moreover, insofar as the animal is capable of imagination or fantasy, it has a "quasi-freedom," that is, something "homologous" to human freedom. At the other extreme, if the expression "freedom" has any meaning applied to God, it is because we attribute it to Him, via eminentiae, something that is also homologous to our imagination.

    5. Elsewhere I have alluded to the differences (subtle but significant) between the Robinson Crusoe of Daniel Defoe and the Spanish "Robinson," Pedro Serrano, who lived a century and a half before the Englishman and whose story is told by the Inca Garcilaso de la Vega in the Comentarios reales. See El oficio del pensamiento (Obras, VI).

    6. Cf. my Reason and Life, Chapter I.

    7. See my article: "Un aspecto social de los precios" (1948), included in Aquí y ahora (Obras, III).

    8. See Reason and Life, I.

    9. "El hijo de nadie, que se levantó del polvo de la tierra, siendo vasija quebradiza, llena de agujeros, rota, sin capacidad que en ella cupiera cosa de algún momento, la remendó con trapos el favor y con la soga del interés ya sacan agua con ella y parece de provecho. El otro hijo de Pedro Sastre, que porque su padre, como pudo y supo, mal o bien, le dejó qué gastar, y el otro que, robando, tuvo qué dar y con qué cohechar, ya son honrados, hablan de bóveda y se meten en corro. Ya les dan lado y silla, quien antes no les estimara para acemileros. Mira cuántos buenos están arrinconados, cuántos hábitos de Santiago, Calatrava y Alcántara, cosidos con hilo blanco y otros muchos de la envejecida nobleza de Laín Calvo y Nuño Rasura atropellados. Dime: ¿Quién le da la honra a los unos, que a los otros quita? El más o menos tener" (Guzmán de Alfarache, Part I, Book II, Chapter IV). English version taken from James Mabbe's The Rogue, Vol. II (New York, 1923), based on the edition of 1623.

Notes to Chapter VII

    1. Cf. Reason and Life, I.

    2. See Los Estados Unidos en escorzo (Obras, III).

    3. See my study, "La vida humana y su estructura empírica" (Ensayos de teoría, Obras, IV). A more recent and complete work is his Metaphysical Anthropology (Pennsylvania State University Press, 1971); the Spanish original: Antropología metafísica: la estructura empírica de la vida humana (Revista de Occidente, 1970)—trans.

    4. See my Idea de la metafísica, Chapter X (Obras, II).

    5. The tragic lovers in Fernando de Rojas' La Celestina—trans.

    6. See La imagen de la vida humana.

7. See "Una amistad delicadamente cincelada," Ensayos de convivencia (Obras, III).

8. A reference to ladies who hid their faces behind their mantillas or veils.

9. See my article, "El campesino y su mundo," Aquí y ahora (Obras, III).

10. Read what Gilberto Freyre has to say about colonial Brazil and the first half of the nineteenth century in his Casa-Grande e Senzala (Masters and the Slaves), published by Knopf in 1946.

11. "Amargóle la gracia a Perico; porque, dentro de dos días, le hicieron joyel de la horca, colgándole della, con satisfacción de toda la Corte. No le acompañó Elena, porque a la tarde la sacaron--causando en los pechos más duros lástima y sentimiento doloroso--al río Manzanares, donde dándola un garrote, conforme a la ley, la encubaron."

12. Y aquella libertad esclarecida,
     que en donde supo hallar honrada muerte,
     nunca quiso tener más larga vida.

     Y pródiga del alma, nación fuerte,
     contaba por afrentas de los años
     envejecer en brazos de la suerte.

     Del tiempo el ocio fuerte, y los engaños
     del paso de las horas y del día,
     reputaban los nuestros por extraños.

     Nadie contaba cuánta edad vivía,
     sino de qué manera; ni aun un hora
     lograba sin afán su valentía.

     (Epístola satírica y censoria
     contra las costumbres presentes
     de los castellanos, V, 34-35).
     (English version by Denise
     Levertov--trans.)

13. Sénancour, Oberman, Lettre XC.

14. English version of the Coplas by Thomas Walsh in Hispanic Anthology (New York, 1920); the Spanish original:

     ¿Qué se fizieron las damas,
     sus tocados, sus vestidos,
         sus olores?
     ¿Qué se fizieron las llamas
     de los fuegos encendidos
         de amadores?

     ¿Qué se fizo aquel trovar,
     Las músicas acordadas

que tañían?
¿Qué se fizo aquel danzar,
aquellas ropas chapadas
que traían?

Después de puesta la vida
tantas veces por su ley
al tablero,
después de tan bien servida
la corona de su rey
verdadero,

después de tanta hazaña
a que no puede bastar
cuenta cierta,
en la su villa de Ocaña
vino la Muerte a llamar
a su puerta. . .

. . . .

No se os faga tan amarga
la batalla temerosa
que esperáis,
pues otra vida más larga
de fama tan gloriosa
acá dexáis.

Aunque esta vida de honor
tampoco no es eternal
ni verdadera,
mas con todo es muy mejor
que la otra temporal
perescedera.

El vivir que es perdurable
no se gana con estados
mundanales,
ni con vida deleitable,
en que moran los pecados
infernales;

mas los buenos religiosos
gánanlo con oraciones
y con lloros,
los caballeros famosos
con trabajos y aflicciones
contra moros.

Y pues vos, claro varón,

215

tanta sangre derramastes
de paganos,
esperad el galardón
que en este mundo ganastes
por las manos;

y con esta confianza,
y con la fe tan entera
que tenéis,
partid con buena esperanza,
que estotra vida tercera
ganaréis.

15. English version by Kate Flores in An Anthology of Spanish
Poetry (New York, 1961). The Spanish original:

Cerrar podrá mis ojos la postrera
sombra, que me llevare el blanco día;
y podrá desatar esta alma mía
hora a su afán ansioso lisonjera;

Mas no de esotra parte en la ribera
dejará la memoria, en donde ardía:
nadar sabe mi llama la agua fría,
y perder el respeto a ley severa.

Alma a quien todo un Dios prisión ha sido,
venas que humor a tanto fuergo han dado,
médulas que han gloriosamente ardido,

su cuerpo dejarán, no su cuidado:
serán ceniza, mas tendrá sentido;
polvo serán, mas polvo enamorado.

16. English version by translator; the Spanish original:

No me aflige morir: no he rehusado
acabar de vivir; ni he pretendido
alargar esta muerte, que ha nacido
a un tiempo con la vida y el cuidado.

Siento haber de dejar deshabitado
cuerpo que amante espíritu ha ceñido;
desierto un corazón, siempre encendido,
donde todo el Amor reinó hospedado.

Index

Abel (Biblical), 97
Abelard, 88
Adam (Biblical), 85, 86, 161
Adenaur, Konrad, 111
Alcantara, 162
Alemán, Mateo, 162
Alembert, Jean le Rond d', 109
Alfonso XI (of Spain), 118
Algarotti, Francesco, 109
Alexander the Great, 97
Andalusia, 189
Aquinas, Saint Thomas 108
Arabs, 176
Aragon, 21, 117
Argentina, 19, 104, 131
Aristotle, 15, 38, 49, 63, 125
Assumption, the (as dogma), 91
Ateneo (of Madrid), 173
Athens, 138, 164
Athenian democracy, 38
Austria, 132
Azorín (José Martínez Ruiz), 178

Babylonians, 97
Balthazar, 97
Barcelona, 104, 190, 192
Baroque, the (as art form), 22
Barrionuevo, Gaspar, 200
Bayle, Pierre, 107
Belgium, 141
Bergman, Ingrid, 172
Berkeley (California), 104
Berlin, 104, 105, 171
Bilbao (Spain), 124